CITY OF MYTHS, RIVER OF DREAMS

THE ROAD TO TIMBUKTU

JAMES MARR

latitude14.com

COPYRIGHT

Published by Latitude14 Publishing
www.latitude14.com
First published in 2013 by Matador

The CIP catalogue record for this book is available at the British Library.
ISBN e-book 978-1-7384756-3-6
ISBN paperback 978-1-7384756-4-3

OTHER BOOKS BY THE AUTHOR

Fiction

KILL AT FIRST LIGHT

Non-fiction

SHORT STORIES FROM A LONG CONTINENT

The Americas Overland

CITY OF MYTHS, RIVER OF DREAMS

The Road to Timbuktu

WHY DO GOATS CLIMB TREES?

An Overland Traveller's Tales in Africa

AUTHOR'S NOTE

City of Myths, River of Dreams, the story of a road trip from the Barbary Coast to the Gulf of Guinea, was first published in 2013. During the intervening years, a lot has changed in this corner of the African continent. By 2023, much of the Sahel region was suffering an Islamist insurgency, stability further disrupted by a wave of military coups. This republished version contains the original story of our 2009 journey, overlaid with some of the major events to have occurred since the book was first written.

FOREWORD

ALL GREAT JOURNEYS BEGIN WITH A HANGOVER

BORNHOLM – April 2008

A Baltic storm lashed the island. Inside the restaurant, four bodies huddled round a table. Rain splattered the windows; thunder split the night sky. A thin bottle containing a fiery liquid made the rounds. We were determined in our quest; an adventure was in the offing. Glasses clashed together.

'To Timbuktu!' we declared.

Timbuktu has long held a curious allure. From the late eighteenth century, this mythical city provoked a succession of outwardly sane men to abandon their families and the relative comforts of Europe, board a sailing boat armed with a musket, a compass and a loud frock-coat, step ashore on the disease-ridden shores of West Africa and, in the company of an interpreter and a couple of asses, vanish into a menacing land. They were called explorers, adventurers, or geographical missionaries, and they were feted as heroes, dead or alive. When the illusive Saharan city was eventually discovered, they found the gates hanging off their hinges, sand piling up in the alleyways, the buildings crumbling to dust, and the promised gold long gone. That was the cruel irony of their quest. And yet it bore legends.

Thankfully, our travels through West Africa were not burdened by the responsibilities weighing those explorers of old. We were not searching for the route of a mighty river, or trying to locate a lost City of Gold. Neither were we to fill in the blank spaces on maps that were the imaginings of medieval geographers for in these days of internet, accessible travel and mobile telephones, the very idea of discovering and recording little-known kingdoms is laughable. In truth, the overland journey we were embarking on, with our modern Toyota Hilux 4X4, was a breeze.

Nevertheless, what might we be up against on the road to Timbuktu? African law and order itself can be considered the definitive portrayal of the hold-up, and incidents of banditry and kidnappings were on the rise. What would we do? Rather than a boxed pair of engraved flintlock pistols, fine amber, shiny beads and a bale or two of embroidered cloth, we'd barter our lives with a bundle of tatty clothes, a couple of defunct mobile telephones, five deflated footballs, one pump and, in my case, a British passport which declared: 'Her Britannic Majesty's Secretary of State requests and requires in the Name of Her Majesty all those whom it may concern to allow the bearer to pass freely without let or hindrance, and to afford the bearer such assistance as may be necessary.' A quick flash of such a splendid document would surely repel the most determined of plunderers.

Our journey, from the bustling Tangier of Morocco's north coast to Tema, a major seaport in southern Ghana, was a very different prospect from the hazards faced by those explorers. We had no sponsors to satisfy and no duties to perform. On the contrary, a touch of debauchery behind a distant dune held a certain appeal. And if we didn't find a nugget of gold...well...it really didn't matter. We were seeking treasure of an alternative type; adventure, companionship, the pleasure of the open road, unfamiliar cultures, and the magic of participating in arguably one of the world's most unusual music festivals: the Festival in the Desert.

Essakane is sixty kilometres to the west of Timbuktu and has become synonymous with the annually staged Festival in the Desert, an event originally organised by the Tuareg in January 2001. With these semi-nomadic herders and traders spread over no fewer than five African countries, the first of these events was a traditional gathering, a celebration of Tuareg culture, dance and music, and an opportunity to discuss the challenges they faced. Since the festival's inception some of West Africa's leading music artists, and many musicians from around the world, have come to play at Essakane. In addition to the music the festival promotes the values of hospitality and tolerance, and is a celebration of peace, even though peace in the Sahel is something of a paradox.

Over the previous one hundred years the Tuareg themselves have staged a number of rebellions in their quest for autonomy and an independent state they call Azawad. The rebellious rumblings we experienced during our trip were to erupt into full-scale conflict in 2012, the situation made worse by Islamist insurgents determined to strengthen their grip on the region. All too soon the music in Timbuktu was silenced and the tourists fled. Initially, French military intervention dispersed the Tuareg rebels and pushed back the Islamist groups. Stability of a sort returned to Mali for a short period of time. By 2023 though, Mali and its neighbours, Burkina Faso, Guinea, Chad and Niger, were all under military rule following a spate of coups, the region as a whole menaced by the escalating Islamist factions, and the Western military aid replaced by opportunistic Russian mercenaries. Currently, the Sahel faces increasing instability, a growing humanitarian crisis and a volatile future.

The eighteenth-century explorers have been described as the first overlanders in West Africa. Today the term overland has been adapted to encompass long-distance, vehicle-based travel and applies equally to the lone cyclist, the individual traveller with their own vehicle, or companies offering multi-itinerary group tours using specially adapted trucks. Starting with the hippy trail in the 1960's, a global business has developed in its wake. Unquestionably, therefore, an overlander must be a person who participates in such a journey. Or so I imagined. But are they? If I was to adopt such a role for the foreseeable future, I felt I should at least acquaint myself with its definition. I reached for the *Oxford English Reference Dictionary* (second edition, revised), and this is what I found:

overlander: 1. a person who drives livestock overland (orig. one who drove stock from New South Wales to the colony of South Australia).

2. (*slang*) a tramp, a sundowner.

If the first definition held little relevance to what we were about to undertake, the second one seemed full of promise. A tramp, a sundowner: in other words, a wanderer who likes a stiff drink at the end of the day. The definition fitted the bill perfectly. I felt I could happily embrace this life of an overlander.

So, to all those itinerant romantics out there – CHEERS!

Weaving our way from the cosy Bornholm restaurant in April 2008, our “Declaration” suitably anointed, we ventured into the wet and thunderous night, our minds awash not only with an abundance of euphoria and Danish schnapps but a catalogue of hugely important tasks, given we could remember any of them by the morning.

A journey to the interior of Africa is to be planned most carefully, we pronounced, laughing when the puddles of rainwater sloshed up our legs. A profusion of lists would be called for. I rubbed my hands gleefully. I love a list. I like the orderliness a list confers. If one is to travel in Africa, one must prepare a suitable list. Then, beyond the shadow of a doubt, all will be well.

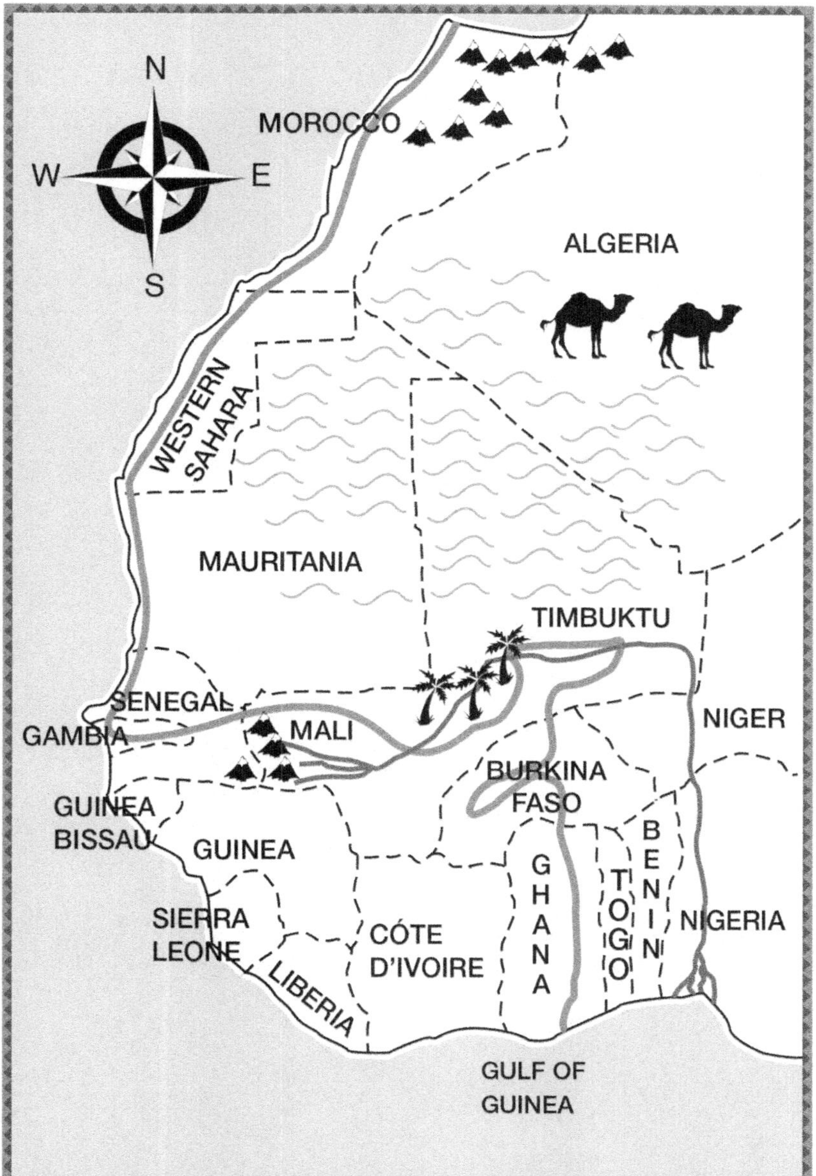
N
W
E
S
MOROCCO
ALGERIA
WESTERN SAHARA
MAURITANIA
TIMBUKTU
SENEGAL
GAMBIA
MALI
NIGER
BURKINA FASO
GUINEA BISSAU
GUINEA
SIERRA LEONE
CÔTE D'IVOIRE
LIBERIA
GHANA
TOGO
BENIN
NIGERIA
GULF OF GUINEA

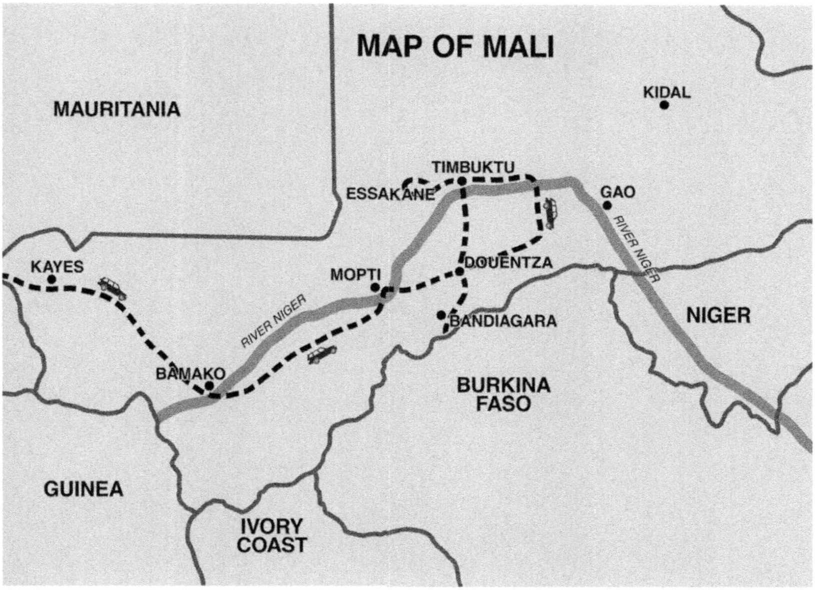
MAP OF MALI
MAURITANIA
KIDAL
TIMBUKTU
ESSAKANE
GAO
RIVER NIGER
KAYES
MOPTI
DOUENTZA
RIVER NIGER
BANDIAGARA
NIGER
BAMAKO
BURKINA FASO
GUINEA
IVORY COAST

1

SPAIN

BEYOND THE PILLARS OF HERCULES

This is how the story goes. Driven insane by the cruelty of his stepmother, Hera, Hercules slaughtered his wife and children. As penance for his crime, he was handed the task of completing twelve labours by King Eurystheus. By accomplishing them, not only could he earn forgiveness, he would attain immortality. It was no mean settlement, until you read what he had to do. Number ten of those twelve labours involved capturing all the cattle belonging to Geryon, a savage, three-bodied monster terrorising the western extremities of the known world, and herding the beasts safely back to Eurystheus.

The extremity of the western world, at least in the time of Greek mythology, existed in the region of the Rock of Gibraltar and various legends abound concerning the

Pillars of Hercules, the promontories flanking the entrance to the Straits of Gibraltar. Diodorus Siculus, a Greek historian of the first Century BC, held that Hercules used his massive strength to narrow an already existing strait separating Spain and Africa, in order to prevent ferocious Atlantic sea-monsters from entering the Mediterranean and wreaking havoc. Others tell of him smashing through a mountain range that had once linked the continents of Europe and Africa. Whichever of the legends one chooses, the ocean beyond the Pillars of Hercules was truly feared. A large sign affixed to the Rock bore a message for all approaching sailors: '*Non plus ultra*' – nothing further beyond. At which point, anybody in their right mind made a brisk about-turn.

Arriving at the southern Spanish port of Algeciras, across the bay from Gibraltar, Christine and I could have readily made a brisk about-turn ourselves. The foul autumn weather accompanying us the length of Europe steadfastly refused to budge. Snow had dogged us until Madrid. Along the Costa del Sol a cloudburst slashed the temperature to six degrees centigrade. Today, had those sailors of old wished to heed the ancient message pinned on the Rock, they wouldn't even have been able to read it. Even gazing southwards provided us with no relief. The Straits of Gibraltar were the equivalent of a bar-room brawl. A true white-knuckled scrap between the Mediterranean Sea and the Atlantic Ocean was in full swing.

I've always considered this sea passage, leaving modern Europe for the exotic Maghreb, to be a milestone in previous journeys. The occasion should be savoured out on deck, enjoying the warm, saline breeze, watching Gib slowly shrink beyond the ferry's wake, the Jebel Musa, supposedly the southern Pillar of Hercules, emerging steadily from out of the sea. But it was not to be. It seemed even Helios was in no mood to illuminate our departure from the shores of Europe; it was without question the washday of the gods. And if the unfolding drama at this port was any indication of things to come, then the lack of sight-seeing opportunities would be the least of our concerns.

We slowed to take it all in. Perhaps a clue lay in the raised voices, forlorn looks and abandoned luggage. Having already witnessed the white-tipped troughs out to sea, we feared the worst. Even the ticket touts were absent. Their forest of arms sprouting bewildering wads of paper had hitherto been the soft introduction to Morocco's quayside mayhem. By contrast, nobody gave us a sideways glance when we stopped by the barrier opposite the terminal's glass doors.

Alarmed, I leapt from the Hilux, hurrying towards an identically dressed Englishman dodging the luggage and the agitated crowd, an overlander twitching with nervous energy, intent on paying the ferryman and getting his African adventure underway. Seconds before we clashed, the automatic doors swished apart, dispelling my reflection. Inside, the ticketing hall was ominously still. And nothing of what unfolded featured in my painstakingly constructed list. Item number 510: Ferry to Tangier.

I marched to the line of ticket booths, working my way from one to the other, receiving nothing more than a chorus of '*Mañana!*' and doubtful expressions. At each booth came the same reply: 'The sea is too rough, *señor*. Today, sailing to Africa is not possible.'

'Nonsense!' I scoffed. One of them must have a boat going to Africa.

At the very last booth I came to, the fellow gave me a measured look. 'You have one option,' he divulged, his bushy right eyebrow arching. 'The Tarifa to Tangier ferry sails in one hour. I can make you a ticket for this boat.'

'Tarifa?' I exclaimed.

Bushy eyebrows pushed up his glasses, confident of capitalising on the crazy glint in the eyes of this *hombre loco*. 'Tarifa,' he repeated.

I snatched a look at my watch. 'I haven't time to get there.'

'Yes! Yes!' he jabbered, bullying his keyboard with a rigid finger. 'If you go quickly...you can make it...no problem.'

We were due to meet our friends, Jean-Pierre and Susie, at Agadir in six days. Not only did we need that time to traverse the Atlas Mountains, but I had a schedule designed to maintain order amongst the African chaos – and we hadn't even left Europe.

I plucked a fold of Euros from my shirt pocket.

'Go quickly!' Bushy eyebrows urged, replacing my crisp money with a flaccid ticket.

I bolted from the terminal, still infused with that European folly of immediacy, expectation, intolerance. But who was to say if the ferries would be operating the next day, or the day after that? How quickly would they clear this backlog of passengers and vehicles?

'We could be stuck here for days,' I reasoned back in the car, tapping the ticket on the steering wheel. Nevertheless, neither of us relished a ferry crossing in this stormy weather.

'We should go for it,' Christine said.

'We have to.'

I drove to Tarifa as rapidly as the regular squalls and the slick, hilly road permitted. It was going to be tight. On reaching the summit of the hill, the *Mirador del Estrecho*, we passed a field of wind turbines, their enormous white propellers thrashing the air for as far as the eye could see. Their frenetic movement added urgency to our flight. It was a perfect day for creating electricity, I reflected, not so great for catching a ferry.

We began our descent to the coast, the Atlantic Ocean an undulating patchwork of greens and greys and blacks, slashed with streaks of white. From one side of the windscreen to the other not a ship could be seen. My stomach churned.

At the bottom of the hill, with five minutes to go before the ferry's departure, we took a wrong turn in the town, losing ourselves in a maze of alleys suitable only for a horse and cart.

On account of the constant winds blowing off the Atlantic the people of Tarifa are known to tolerate a level of insanity amongst their community. From October to May, when regular Atlantic storms ensure the swell is at its best, half the population of Tarifa are said to be migratory surf-dudes. Winter, then, is presumably when visitors are allowed the greatest degree of latitude where madness is concerned, which was good, considering we were trying to force our pickup down a series of right angles not much broader than a gutter. Between attempts at keeping our bull bar from unhooking wooden shutters, ripping off door handles, crushing potted plants and flattening downpipes, we caught glimpses of the November rollers thundering toward the coast, topped with crouching surfers skimming the emerald sea. On a day like today, unquestionably these guys are the maddest of the mad.

Eventually popping free from the backstreets of old Tarifa, we tore through the entrance to the port, a damp, flapping ticket thrust in the direction of the girl bending to the wind.

'*Adelante!*' she screeched, jabbing the air with an outstretched finger.

Beyond the mesh fence the ferry breathed gently on its mooring ropes, the rise and fall of the yellow light flooding from its cargo deck like a siren's call in the gloom. We zigzagged round the kilometres of fencing, chased over the tarmac, bounced up the ramp and slid to a halt in front of a seaman frantically flapping his arms. The ramp slammed closed immediately behind us. Crewmen shouted, ropes were hauled, chains rattled, engines roared and propeller blades bit the water. We were off.

I sat back, allowing myself a tight grin. A small victory achieved.

'Made it!' I declared, looking at Christine. 'We're on our way to Timbuktu.'

Before we'd even left the harbour, the ferry made a gut-wrenching heave. We shared an anxious look between us as we made our way to the staircase and the upper deck. I checked myself on the way – if we're going to Africa, we must be determined, resolute, tough. There was no way my hero explorers, Daniel Houghton, Mungo Park or Richard Lander would have sat this out at the local inn.

Three-quarters of the way up the stairway, in the time it took to grip the handrail, progress was held in check, our bodies weightless at the zenith of the ferryboat's rise. Then gravity returned, falling...falling... My foot went down on the step with a thud, followed by a bang as the ship's bow thumped the sea. The hull shuddered, the vibration passing through the deck, the rail, to my hands, to my shoulders, round my head.

I swore silently and rushed the last few steps to the top. 'We'll be on the other side in a jiffy,' I mumbled to no one in particular.

2

MOROCCO

THE DEVIL'S HASTE

Ahead, through the ferry's sea-splattered windows, the sheets of rain briefly parted and an outline of land revealed itself. My pulse beat that bit faster as Africa loomed from the tumbling waves. Before long the ferry ceased its rolling and pitching. Warehouses and cranes replaced sky and sea. The passengers smiled, unfurled their limbs and turned up the volume; the weight of our plight lightened; cheeriness was in the air. We had survived the voyage.

On the docks in Tangier, for a fee, a man with a laminated identity tag hanging from his neck will process your paperwork.

'How much do you charge?' Christine asked the fellow hovering by her window.

Tugging at a woollen jumper savaged by moths, he looked momentarily perplexed by the question. He had on his head a cap that in former times might have belonged to a British Rail stationmaster. He fingered the peak with his left hand as he said, 'It's up to you.'

We filled out the forms the man gave us and handed them back.

'I need your passports,' he said.

Our brains whirred and clicked at this latest request. We gazed at the immigration office. Then back to this man loitering beside our open window.

'I'll come with you,' Christine said.

I locked the car and walked in the opposite direction. At a small window in the side of a very large building an official took the proffered car papers. 'Where are you going?' he asked, glancing at the documents.

'To Mauritania.'

'Mauritania,' the man repeated, sucking his teeth. He made a note in a book with a pencil. 'And you are not coming back?'

It was the manner in which the question was phrased that immediately set me on my guard. Was it indeed a question at all? Did nobody ever return from Mauritania?

'I'm not coming back,' I stated with assurance and the man regarded me with narrowed eyes.

After changing money at a Bureau de Change, it was rush hour by the time we hit the streets of Tangier. Daylight was already fading and the rain had forced everyone into a car, causing vast queues and a melody of blaring horns. Finally reaching the southern outskirts of Tangier, beyond the windscreen the green neon sign of an Ibis hotel sparkled like an emerald on the blisters of rain. It was a welcome sight. We squeezed into the car park and retired for the night.

THE MOTORWAY between Tangier and Casablanca is a toll road and as good as any we'd left behind in Europe. It was all but deserted. Despite the rain bouncing as high as the bonnet, we were soon abreast of the old pirate republics of Salé and Rabat. The latter, having by and large shed its eye patches, wooden stumps and shoulder parrots, is now the capital city of Morocco.

Over the years Salé has featured frequently on travellers' itineraries. The Romans named Salé "Sala Colonia", including it as part of their province of Mauritania Tingitane. Pliny the Elder described it as a desert town infested with elephants. Even Daniel Defoe's Robinson Crusoe was incarcerated by pirates in Salé.

Ever since the days of the pirates, it's said that Salé and Rabat have lived in a state of animosity. They continue to face each other down, like a couple of dishevelled gunslingers eyeing each other from opposite sides of the Bou-Regreg River.

BY THE EARLY seventeenth century Algiers, Tunis and Tripoli, on the southern Mediterranean coast, and Salé, on the Atlantic coast, had come to be known as the Barbary Coast states. While Algiers, Tunis and Tripoli were all protectorates of the Ottoman Empire, Salé declared independence, calling itself the Republic of Bou Regreg.

Salé was divided into three separate republics. Old Salé, on the north bank of the river, fell under the spiritual and political authority of Muhammad al-Ayyashi, a young man distinguished for his piety. Legend tells of how the day came when he set aside his Koran, found himself a trusty horse, and rode off to make *jihad* with Spain and Portugal, becoming a great hero in Moroccan folklore.

Driven from Spain by Philip II, the Hornacheros arrived in Morocco around 1610 to establish the second republic of Salé. They came from Hornachos, in Spanish Estremadura. They were Moslems, spoke Arabic, and were said to have gained significant wealth in Spain from such ignoble pursuits as banditry and forgery. The religious leaders, poets and intellectual set of Old Salé considered the Hornacheros to be nothing more than a mob of ruffians, not worthy of settling in the city of shrines and verse. The outcome of this slight was to see the Hornacheros establish themselves in the Casbah, on the southern bank of the Bou-Regreg River.

The third group to arrive were the Moriscos, or Andalusians, who the higher echelons of Old Salé considered even less savoury than the Hornacheros, with their Hispano-Arabic language, alien-sounding names and general lack of means. They had to settle on land beyond the Casbah, in New Salé, an area that is today Rabat.

While the three republics, which were each governed by a Divan (a council of corsair captains), engaged in regular quarrels with one another, and more than the occasional exchange of cannon fire, it was the plunder of infidel shipping that so greatly inspired them, and for which, particularly the Casbah/Rabat republics, gained significant notoriety as the Sallee Rovers.

The circumstances of many of the Barbary pirates were to prove obscure. A good number of them were Christians who'd converted to Islam, or "turn'd Turk" (Turk then being a collective expression for all Muslims). Peter Easton (1570-

1620), formerly a Somerset farm labourer, commanded a fleet of forty ships. By 1612, he was raiding as far north as the coast of Newfoundland. Later, he was to enter the employ of the Duke of Savoy, purchasing himself a title and marrying a lady from a noble family. Then there was Henry Mainwaring (1587-1653), under whose leadership the pirate republic of Mamora thrived, until the Spanish came along and overthrew him. Following a life of piracy, he took the Royal pardon, became a gentleman, and in the process of transforming from poacher to gamekeeper, he wrote a treatise on how to suppress piracy.

Even the aristocracy weren't above dabbling at the business of a corsair. Sir Francis Verney (1584-1615) is said to have lost an argument with his stepmother concerning his inheritance and, in a fit of pique, turned pirate. In 1609, a message winged its way to England from the English ambassador to Spain, telling of how Sir Francis had ... "*taken three or four Poole ships and one of Plymouth*". By 1615 he was said to have succumbed to a ... "*truly bad end*", the lot, naturally enough, of many a pirate.

One of the more infamous of the Sallee Rovers was Jan Janszoon van Haarlem (1570-1641), from Holland. He converted to Islam in Algiers, called himself Murad Reis and married a Moroccan, despite the fact he already had a wife and family back in Europe.

Murad Reis sailed as mate for Suleiman Reis, though when the boss was killed in 1619, Murad settled in Salé, an excellent base due to its proximity to the Straits of Gibraltar, and from where they could intercept the East India and Guinea traders, and not forgetting ... "*ye Spaniards returning from the Americas loaded with much gold*".

When independence was declared in Salé, and the new republic formed, as a measure of the esteem in which

Murad Reis was held he was elected the republic's first Admiral. As a result of his accumulated spoils, and the new lofty position, the Dutchman formerly known as Jan Janszoon van Haarlem was to become a wealthy man. Nevertheless, such accomplishments were not to curb a worthy session of high seas pillage.

In 1627 Murad Reis engaged a Danish seaman who claimed to know the way to Iceland. With three ships and a crew of Moors they set forth to Reykjavik, the capital of Iceland. Having only managed to plunder Reykjavik's local market of its supply of salted fish, Reis set about rounding up the local population, no doubt hoping the pale-skinned northerners would fetch a pretty penny on the slave markets of North Africa.

Between the sixteenth and the nineteenth century the pirates captured an estimated one and a quarter million Christians, whom they ransomed or sold into the slave trade. From 1618 to 1626 alone, the golden years for the Sallee Rovers, six thousand were taken.

In time, the reign of the Barbary corsairs dwindled as the strength of the European navies increased. And while the threat to the geographical missionaries of the African Association still existed during their passage from England to the west coast of Africa, it was to a much lesser extent than hitherto.

The French conquest of Algiers in 1830 is said to have been the terminal event for this colourful slice of history.

By the time we reached El Jadida, the former Portuguese fortified city of Mazagan, we were one hundred kilometres south of Casablanca. It was clear the crème de la crème of Morocco's highways was firmly behind us. From here we experienced life on the real road. And it wasn't pretty. The driver of every bus might as well have had horns, a pointed chin and filed teeth. If all the cars were driven by escapees from an asylum, then the truckers were as spatially aware as a lush at last orders. Cyclists, seemingly high on a cocktail of Rif marijuana and reckless abandon, happily meandered between exhaust-belching trucks and the copious potholes. Above all, though, it was the pedestrian who suffered the most perilous of existences. It was as if their lives ranked no higher than the traffic cones, and were all the more hazardous for being mobile. On this country's road network, even donkeys appeared content to flirt with the afterlife.

Naturally, such hazards of the road all served to put a brake on our progress along the coast, a drive already made tiresome by the relentless rain. In his book, *Travels in the Interior of Africa*, the explorer Mungo Park makes reference to seeing the mountains beyond Mogador (better known today as Essaouira) as the brig *Endeavour* carried him south to the Gambia in May 1795. During Park's time Mogador/Essaouira had for hundreds of years been a major trading port for goods between Sub-Saharan Africa and Europe, and for a while was known as the port of Timbuktu. Originally a Phoenician trading settlement, in more recent years it has become a refuge for surfers and backpackers.

Arriving in Essaouira we'd already been driving for an hour in darkness, something we'd promised ourselves not to do. The roads might be bad during daylight, but at night the chance of an accident increases one hundredfold.

By seven o'clock in the evening, in desperate need of a refreshing beer, we were relieved to spot an hotel sign winking at us from the dark. Busily seeking the entrance to the car park, it was only at the last minute did we spy the policeman's reflective glove appear spookily from the roadside. After Christine pulled up, a fulsome, glistening yellow and black raincoat waddled to the window. Wisely, the policeman's partner remained under the cover of the trees, cradling his hand-held radar. It was obvious which one of them had drawn the short straw, and the man approaching us seemed all the more surly on account of it.

'Why are you doing 50 in a 40 zone?' he demanded, rainwater cascading from the peak of his cap.

There were no mitigating circumstances. We could have hardly told him we were hurrying to a cold beer and a warm bed. It was a straightforward case of *mea culpa*.

There followed a lecture about the perils of speeding in general, and then another one, relating more specifically to the rain, breaking distances and poor visibility. During the entire rebuke the road remained entirely deserted, absolutely nothing to distract his flow. Which posed the question as to why they were here in the first place, on such a murky night. If nothing else it was a heartening display of dedicated police work because, by the time he'd talked himself out, the man was thoroughly drenched.

We waited expectantly. There would be a demand for recompense and, to be perfectly honest, he'd earned it.

'*Bon!*' the policeman concluded, dismissing us with a flick of his soggy glove.

THE FOLLOWING day we reached Agadir.

A blue sky had at last forced the clouds to retreat inland and for the first time since leaving England our thoughts turned to camping. Despite the persistent cold wind the time had come to give all the toys we'd fitted to our car their first, thorough test. Due to the usual grinding delays prior to the departure on a trip such as this, there had been no time to test anything. Not the most ideal of situations considering the places we were going to. The big challenge facing us right at that moment was to find that perfect campsite, the one we'd been dreaming about for so many months, a place we could hole up for two or three days, giving us chance to get to grips with the kit we'd brought along.

This was to be a weighty moment for the simple reason I've never been an enthusiastic camper. I guess this might rank as a considerable flaw in an overlander. For me it never ceases to conjure notions of Victorian privation: damp underclothes, leaking accommodation, cold showers, and squatting in draughty wooden sheds – and that's if you're lucky. Alarmingly, there are a couple of other attributes I'd read should come easily to the overlander: the capacity to embrace uncertainty and, secondly, an ability to laugh in the face of adversity. Goodness knows what the person was thinking when they wrote this; neither of them fitted my idea of orderliness and expectation.

Camping, however, was a different matter. There was to be no avoiding it, and we'd invested enough thought and money into preparing the Hilux, so I felt confident everything should work out fine. I was mentally prepared for any hurdles to come.

We stopped on the cliff-top overlooking the sea and as surf-dudes skimmed the rollers beneath us I unearthed the guidebook, settling on a campsite beside the beach, a few kilometres to the north of Agadir. A campsite beside the beach was what we'd always promised ourselves to kick off our adventure.

I flicked the gear lever to D and set off brimming with hope.

Imagine a sandy cove, the cover of a few trees, a starlit night, a fire to warm the soles of your feet and the sound of pebbles clicking in the surf. It was a vision to melt the heart of the most pessimistic of campers. This was my dream, that we would enjoy the length of the Atlantic coast, tucked between rolling dunes, swimming in the early-morning surf, grilling our fish over an open fire.

Following a half-hour cruise along the coastal road the sign for our campsite emerged boldly from the roadside: Camping Atlantica Parc. In two hundred metres, we turned left off the road and swung into the entrance. I pulled up beside the reception to behold a vast sea of white campervans bristling with an array of aerials and dishes and pop-up windows – plot after plot after plot. Our romantic cove set among the dunes had suddenly become a campervan metropolis, a Winnebago City. The guidebook had directed us to a place where the European caravan club shelter from the northern winter blues. French, German, Dutch, Scandinavian, they were all here, in their regimented plots, divided by trimmed hedges and electrical cabling, and variously including tethered dogs, potted plants, caged budgerigars, sagging clothes lines, bicycles, scooters, assorted garden furniture and the evidence of a bewildering range of hobbies at various stages of realisation.

It was too late in the day to go elsewhere. The suburbs of Agadir certainly held no appeal. We were stuck.

We checked in at the office and were directed to our plot. I climbed the ladder to the roof of the pickup and set about unzipping and removing the waterproof cover from the roof-mounted tent. With the cover off it was simply a case of lifting one half of the base until it extended horizontally over the back of the pickup. Fully opened, the tent served a useful second function of creating a shelter over the kitchen arrangement at the back of the vehicle. Elastic guy ropes inside the tent did the work of springing the canvas upright, and an extendable ladder hinged to the base dropped down to enable access. It was perfect. Even two rank amateurs like us could achieve this exercise within a couple of minutes, and with much less effort than a conventional ground tent.

From the roof, I had an unrestricted view of camping suburbia. The plot on our right was vacant, the other side inhabited by a Belgian in a bulging T-shirt, his white, stick-like legs poking from a pair of shorts. He was observing me, appearing to fret over why his neighbour was intruding on his privacy in such a manner. He returned my greeting with a nod, shuffling out of sight beneath the awning attached to his enormous campervan. 'You big softie,' I muttered accusingly.

With camp established Christine soon had a vegetable couscous chopped and prepared and the pot on the gas ring. By seven o'clock, with daylight long gone, the temperature dropped and the rain started to fall again. It sent a chill down my spine in more ways than one.

We pulled on extra jumpers beneath our waterproofs, retreating with our chairs and table to huddle beneath the base of the tent, exchanging disconsolate glances as the blobs of water bounced half way up the ladder.

'It'll be over in a minute,' Christine said encouragingly.

Only, it wasn't. During the night, the deluge was ceaseless. And yet, even the sound of the rain failed to mask the barking dogs or, at some un-godly hour, a group of Swedes drunkenly roaming from one camping car, located in a far corner, to another, located in the corner diagonally opposite. By three o'clock in the morning my antipathy bubbled to the surface. I growled inwardly, turning over for what might well have been the millionth time. Lying there, I pondered when the first drops of rain might penetrate the tent, resisting the temptation to reach up and touch the canvas.

It didn't take long before all the pondering and the dripping water got the better of me and I could no longer delay the inevitable: I needed the bathroom. Immediately, a multi-stage operation swung into motion. The zip had to be located and opened with the minimum of noise (not such an issue on account of the rain). The toes had to probe the cold night air to find the rungs of the ladder. The shoes had to be uncovered without the aid of a torch, because I'd forgotten it in the tent. The coat had to be found, the mud slopped in...

Partially clothed I plodded through the parallel lanes of Winnebago City, executing a series of ninety degree turns, passed the rows of dripping hedges, growling dogs and half-finished hobbies, an eye on a distant, feeble light. It was right at that moment I hated our rather overweight Belgian neighbour, tucked up in his campervan, with its toilet and TV and shower. For a few seconds, I actually toyed with the idea of breaking in.

When the sun appeared by mid-morning the next day we snatched the opportunity to lay everything out to dry. Ten minutes later it rained again.

The previous day two motorcyclists had appeared in the campsite, their bikes laden with a remarkable quantity of luggage. Intrigued, I ambled to their plot to pay them a visit. I found them rolling up their mud-smeared tents and preparing to get underway. After they'd finished packing their kit their knees and elbows were caked in mud. They were a father and son team, the father explained, on their way from the north coast of Norway to the Cape of Good Hope. Their theme was Cape to Cape. They'd been on the road for three months and appeared unconcerned as to how much longer it would take to go the rest of the way to South Africa. A wife/mother was back in England handling all the logistics, he admitted, and both father and son grinned rather sheepishly. I found them in remarkably good spirits, all things considered. I wished them luck for the rest of their journey.

'Cheers,' the father uttered, strapping a muddy bag to the back of his bike.

The weather forecast pinned to the wall in the reception of the campsite promised more rain to come. There was no debate required, we were getting out of here. We packed away our damp equipment and went in search of a hotel in Agadir. Neither of us wished to experience a repeat performance of the previous night. In fact, I wasn't sure the tent could even withstand it.

If one is to believe the Moroccan proverb, "Slowness comes from God and haste from the Devil", then clearly we were possessed. Instead of exploring the Atlas Mountains, as we'd planned, and where the snow was already closing the higher passes, in our rain and wind-driven haste, we'd arrived in Agadir way ahead of my schedule. I reached for my notebook and section marked Lists, running my finger down the scored-out items. We should have been at an unpronounceable place in the Atlas Mountains. The weather was to blame for our dilemma – the devil's haste was in the wind.

I scored out Traverse of the Central Atlas with two thick lines – we were never going to make it. The next item referred to collecting JP and Susie from the airport, except they were still forty-eight hours away from arriving. There was nothing for it. We were caught in a yawning void that, quite frankly, Agadir was incapable of filling. It was time for some local exploring.

After checking out the location of Agadir airport, Tafraoute and the Ameln Valley were firmly in our sights. To get there we went south, along the N1 coastal road, searching for the track leading to the hills. Attempting to equate the information displayed on our Michelin map with our surroundings meant dismissing a series of goat paths in favour of a stony track that, after ten minutes of rough driving, delivered us at a place displaying a distinct similarity to an abandoned quarry.

'I don't think this is the right way to Tafraoute,' Christine said.

'I don't suppose it is,' I replied.

'This is a quarry.'

I hummed to myself, raising my eyes from the map to gaze at a hillside plundered by something extremely destructive. I had to agree with her: we'd definitely arrived at a quarry. Things were not going well on the navigation front. According to the Michelin 741 we had travelled little more than a pencil length into the African continent. Ghana was still a lot of pencil lengths to the south. As lead navigator, I had to do better than this.

'I think we missed the turning,' I concluded.

For some reason my mind felt particularly woolly, hence all efforts at navigation lacked even the most fundamental skills of reading a signpost. We retraced our steps, stopping at a settlement to buy a loaf of bread. The road to Tafraoute couldn't have been more clearly indicated. We found the signpost at a very large roundabout several kilometres back up the road. We'd driven past it an hour earlier.

On our way to the Ameln Valley we crested the 1100 metre-high Col de Kerdous, by which time the reduced temperature had us reaching for our coats. Here we weaved along narrow roads, passing rust-coloured cliffs, tilled fields, picturesque villages, orchards of almond and argan trees. The people of the Ameln Valley are known throughout the country for being an enterprising crowd. Not content with hiding away in their dramatic surroundings, many a grocer in Morocco's busier city streets hails from the Valley of the Almonds. The production of argan oil, processed from the fruit of the argan tree, has become a valuable commodity in the semi-arid valleys of the Anti-Atlas. Its application in the food and cosmetics industries has flourished over recent years. Goats have also developed a taste for the argan fruit. A flock of the animals scaling the upper branches of a tree in search of the fruit makes for an incongruous sight.

By late afternoon a post on the roadside indicated the turning to Tafraoute, a village popular with tourists for being at the centre of what is judged to be some of the best trekking and climbing in the region. Enclosed within an ochre-coloured rock landscape, the place undoubtedly displays its full glory at sundown, when the last of the sun's rays turn the jagged ramparts into impressive, glowing spires, and the long, spiky shadows cloak the rest.

Making our way to the village, we wavered at the entrance to Tafraoute's campsite, observing an icy northern wind whip veils of dust in a vicious dance. A single tent pegged out in a far corner rippled under the onslaught. The door to a wooden hut marked "*Les Toilettes*" creaked as it swung back and forth.

'This doesn't look great,' I muttered, the memory of our night at Camping Atlantica Parc all too raw.

'There's a hotel up there,' Christine said.

I followed her gaze to the rather monastic-looking building commanding a position on a hill overlooking the village.

'So there is.'

Just then a young man appeared in front of the car, the manager of the campsite, we presumed. He stared at us, until a gust of wind swept the hood of his burnous clean from his head. We waved at him, turned the car round, and ventured up the hill.

Lugging our bags through the front door of the hotel, it was soon apparent how the cloister theme continued inside. For all intents and purposes the property had been purged of life. I felt like a repenting monk returning to lick his wounds. The very moment we dropped our bags at the front desk the receptionist appeared. He bore an uncanny likeness to Lurch, manservant to the Addams Family. Should Lurch have handed our passports to a goblin perched on a monkey's skull, who then proceeded to copy the details with a quill plucked from the tail feathers of a Griffon vulture, I wouldn't have been in the least surprised – uneasy maybe, but not surprised.

We completed a form in exchange for the room key dangling from Lurch's bony finger. '*Bienvenue*,' leaked from between his pale lips.

We mounted the steps to the first floor, the bitter wind I'd hoped to leave outside the front door burnishing our cheeks. At least carrying the bags up the stairs warmed us up a little. Along the corridors, we searched for our room. At each turning I imagined owls watching us, bats biding their time, arachnids eagerly awaiting nightfall. Perhaps this noise was the spirit of a ravishing Berber princess tapping to be freed from these walls.

The room, when we found it, had three beds.

'Maybe Lurch and the goblins are joining us,' I murmured.

The wind had the doors and windows rattling in their frames. We shivered and Christine retrieved a number of blankets from the cupboard and laid them on a bed. Thankfully, several flocks of sheep had gone into their manufacture. We were going to need them.

In Tafraoute, Maison Tuareg is lauded as something of an institution where rugs are concerned, even if their salesman, a warlock shrouded in a djellaba, needed to tweak his technique. We were heading for the village when the shadow broke from an alley – WHOOSH! – and there he was, as if popping from the spout of a genie's lantern, an odious bundle of verbose mutterings blocking our every move. With the odd curse and a mucus-clearing grate of the throat, he was not in the least dissuaded by our polite excuses. What we'd anticipated as being a pleasant stroll to the local bar for an aperitif quickly spiralled into a diplomatic spat. There was no way, we explained, that we were taking half a dozen of his rugs all the way to Ghana.

'Ship them!' he spat, striking like a viper. 'It's very cheap to ship them.'

I could tell from the smirk how he thought he had us on the ropes with that one. I squared my shoulders, attempting to stand a little taller. *Get stuffed you f*****g a******e*, I was ready to tell him. Instead, I came out with: 'We've only come for a drink.'

'We have drink in the shop. Very good tea. And beeeuuoootiful rugs.'

Drinking tea for an aperitif was hardly what we had in mind. But the warlock didn't want to hear it. Irked that a sale might slip from his claws, he changed tack.

'You foreigners never want to engage with the locals,' he snarled. 'You're not interested in our culture. You're rude...' Etc, etc.

Despite his charmless performance, we promised to call

on the way back. Less than satisfied, he whirled and vanished, the hem of his djellaba leaving a flurry of dust.

Later, after a drink in the village, we stuck to our word. The man inside the shop was a much more polished affair than the sorcerer we'd fallen across earlier, though a practitioner of enchantment, none the less. He entertained us for the next hour or so with a fine display from their collection. For all that, we still departed from the establishment rugless.

Back at the hotel, and with the last remnants of the sun's warmth having slipped beyond the mountains, we resorted to wearing thermals beneath our clothes when venturing to dinner. It wasn't long before a steady stream of guests joined us, sporting their thick jumpers and padded jackets. Apparently, we weren't the only ones feeling the cold.

We studied the menu while the waiter bustled furiously between the tables, scratching orders on a notepad, which he tore off and sent fluttering through a doorway. Christine opted for the vegetable couscous. I went for the highly-recommended Tagine Berber. As the wind buffeted the windows we washed it all down with a Cabernet Sauvignon from Meknes, a town in northern Morocco. After dinner, and feeling suitably fortified, we huddled over a game of Scrabble in the bedroom, which I ... almost won.

During our absence from Agadir both the weather and the temperature had thankfully improved. We spent some time driving around the southern suburbs, searching for a hotel not too far from the airport. The squawking flesh, throbbing metal, choking fumes and hooting horns of the metropolis all came as quite a shock after the peaceful Ameln valley. Almost abandoning any hope of finding a hotel, purely by chance we came upon a charming little place called Hotel La Pergola. With a roaring fire and plenty of chintz, the restaurant radiated an appealing, old-worldly feel. The contents of the menu and wine list were equally rousing. Circumstances were improving, particularly as we'd learnt how the property was owned and run by a French family from the Loire valley. We felt quite certain they'd know a thing or two about eating. And they did.

As much as I hankered to indulge in the wonderfully seductive, come-hither-and-get-drunk feel the restaurant so warmly emitted, we did have a midnight rendezvous to keep.

BY TWO O'CLOCK in the morning, via a route covering a good deal of North Africa, Jean-Pierre and Susie stood before us in the airport arrivals hall, all their bags present and in one piece. It was good to see them. Finally, we were a team. JP, snug in his brown tweed jacket, reading glasses perched on his forehead, beamed when he told us all the airports they had set down at in the last twelve hours. Susie was less enthusiastic.

Little was left of the night by the time we returned to the Hotel La Pergola. A flash of the headlights roused the watchman from his slumber beneath a tree. He groped to his feet, opened the gate and waved us in. We parked and instantly retired to our rooms.

After breakfast the next day, and with a hope of establishing some order to our lives over the coming weeks, we stood round the Hilux discussing where we should pack our belongings. Faced with all our equipment, it was as if the car had assumed the proportions of a Corgi die-cast model. Where on earth were we to fit everything?

With the aid of drawers and bulkheads, the rear of the vehicle had been sub-divided into spaces according to various designations: luggage, kitchen utensils, fridge, water tank, compressor, gas bottles, medical equipment, folding chairs, food, library and, rather larger than it should have been, a wine cellar. Tucked behind the wine cellar were additional pockets of storage for items such as a high-pressure air line for the tyres, a tool bag and a jack. And still there wasn't enough room. The luggage space, for a start, was too small.

After a lot of pushing and shoving and strapping down, we succeeded in getting everything either inside or up on the roof. By the time we were loaded, it was already past midday.

Our final task before departing was to commandeer the waiter, who knew a man, who knew another man, who had a cousin who sold wood. It was not far, he assured us. He kicked his scooter into life. *'Suivez-moi!'* he called, and with that he was off.

We followed the scooter through a series of backstreets, the car rocking lazily as it dipped in and out of the potholes. It was soon apparent our waiter had never visited the woodman on anything other than his scooter because, to our increasing alarm, he led us through a labyrinth of gradually narrowing streets. Just as we imagined becoming forever wedged in the suburbs of Agadir, a gaping doorway displaying a store of chopped wood appeared miraculously beside us. We squeezed out, haggled over the price with somebody's cousin, and loaded fifty kilos in the last available space on the roof-rack. Finally, we were ready for the open road.

By late afternoon we descended along a valley onto a broad, arid plain. A track going off to the right disappeared beyond a cluster of rocky mounds occupying an otherwise barren plateau; it offered a possibility as an overnight stop, if not a very appealing one. By then we were running short of options, resigning ourselves to the fact that the track we'd passed a few hundred metres back up the road was quite possibly the best we could hope for. With roughly half an hour of sunlight left we spun the car round and headed for the cluster of rocky mounds.

There was a bitter mountain wind blowing down the valley. It howled across the plain, meaning we had to take time sheltering the car as best we could. It was a lost cause. The ground was too exposed, the wind eddying in any shelter we tried to place ourselves. We might have left the rain behind, but now we had the wind to contend with. I cursed our luck as I clambered up the side of the Hilux and unfolded the roof tent. We hurriedly zipped a ground tent to the unfolded base. At least the ground tent afforded us some shelter from the worst of the icy wind. Guy ropes were stretched and tied to the biggest stones we could find. When we'd finished, the canvas fluttered and cracked in protest. I'd never anticipated weather quite like this. To counter it definitely called for a raid on the wine cellar.

Gripping our glasses of red wine, wrapped in our warmest clothes, we huddled by the fire, turning the chicken on the grill, a pot of vegetables boiling by the side. Occasionally, the headlights of a truck passed in the distance. When it came time to eat we retreated inside the ground tent, dragging the table and chairs with us.

Warmed by two bottles of Spanish Rioja, JP unearthed some Havana rum and a bottle of Spanish brandy. Life turned rosier, cosy even, as we huddled together. We made a lot of toasts. It took quite a few before the howling wind and flapping tent assumed a more benign presence.

Later, up in the rooftop tent, I barely slept a wink. Everything shook and creaked. By five in the morning the wind gusted so violently I feared it was close to tearing the tent, with us inside it, clean off the car's roof. There was nothing for it – we had to get out of there before we were blown out. I descended the ladder to the lower tent and nudged JP from a deep sleep. Susie was already awake. JP shook his head groggily. He'd been dreaming a wonderful dream about a ship, out at sea, in a storm. I might have laughed if my teeth weren't chattering.

'Then we've well and truly foundered,' I managed through numb lips.

In the darkness, we folded away both tents to minimise the damage. What was left of the night we spent cramped inside the car.

As the sun crept over the horizon a pink and lavender sky took colour. I unfurled my shivering limbs from under the steering wheel and ventured outside, shuddering in the new day. I hopped from one foot to the other in the hope of inducing some warmth, only to be almost blown over. The freezing wind was still gusting strongly. Everything I stood up was knocked down again. Even the steel cooking grill had been swept off the stones we'd built around the fire. It lay a couple of metres from where we'd left it before turning in. I stooped to remove the rock from inside the plastic washing-up bowl and it too was snatched by a gust of wind. It wheeled in the direction of the Sahara Desert like a piece of red, circular tumbleweed. I chased it for a while, until the rush of blood provoked the most dismal of headaches. Maybe I'll find it later, I reasoned, in Bou Izakarne.

Not far down the road from our campsite we stopped at a service station, drawn there by the smell of fresh coffee and an urgent need to thaw out. The first two coffees were a real morale booster. It was busy inside the café, the locals craning their heads toward the news burbling from a TV up in the corner. Images of Barak Obama flashed up on the screen. He was to be the new president of the United States of America.

When we'd stopped shaking we left the café, clambered back in the car and set off down the road.

Just before Tan Tan Plage we pulled in at Les Deux Chameaux, a comfortable *auberge* with an adjoining compound catering for overlanders. None of us had the heart for a second night's camping. Instead, we opted to throw our gear in a couple of rooms inside the *auberge.*

The only other clients at the inn was a French couple. They were in the bar talking with the owners. Their campervan occupied a lonely corner of the compound at the back, sagging on its springs, the deepening shadows falling short of masking the dark stains gathering beneath it. They looked a curious pair. His features, what could be made of them behind the furious beard, gave the impression of having been hastily chipped from a lump of flint, and then framed within a dull bush of dreadlocks and faded beads. The T-shirt and cut-off jeans barely qualified as rags. He was shoeless, his age indeterminate. She, on the other hand, behind a veneer of weariness, was in the prime of her youth. Her clothes, mottled and dusty, hung from her like dewlaps. Her skin displayed a similar ochre tone to his.

'We're going home,' she said, with more than a hint of relief in her voice.

They were coming up from the south – from out of Africa. What kind of people had they been when they went in to Africa, I mused? What size, what shape, what state of mind? What had this continent done to them?

In Joseph Conrad's *Heart of Darkness,* the protagonist

Marlow must visit the Company's doctor prior to his departure for the Congo. The doctor produces an instrument described as being like a calliper, and asks to measure Marlow's skull. With a morbid fascination, the doctor carefully notes the results, telling his client how, whenever permitted, he records the crania of all those heading out to Africa, even though he suggests "*...the changes take place on the inside...*"

And when they return, Marlow questions the doctor, what then?

"*I never see them again,*" the doctor tells him, adding how it would be interesting for science, "*...to watch the mental changes for individuals, on the spot...*"

The doctor regards Marlow with a level of curiosity, telling him his pulse is good, "*...good for out there...*" and he asks him if there is any history of madness in his family.

Might that French couple have qualified as scientifically interesting to Joseph Conrad's doctor I wondered? Had their skulls enlarged or shrunk? What was going on inside them?

'It's the dust,' the girl lamented, tousling her hair. 'And the filth. You can't escape the filth.'

The inside of their van was the same ochre colour as their flesh. I ran a finger over the external bodywork. Beneath the dust the vehicle was painted white.

'Benin was the worst,' she said. 'But it started in Mali. I wasn't able to cook anymore. Everything was covered in thick dust. We got very sick in Ouagadougou. We were ill for days.' She tugged absently at the folds in her clothing. 'I hate this place. Look at the filth.'

Apparently, he goes to Africa every year. It was her first time. She vowed never to return.

In the late afternoon, we drove down to the port. Row

upon row of rusting fishing boats were lashed together, seemingly abandoned, save for the seagulls which soared above the forest of masts, hoping for better days. Though their flags were blackened, shredded and thus unidentifiable, it seemed likely that most of these trawlers would be registered in Spain. The Spanish fishing fleet has been one of the principal beneficiaries of the European Union fisheries agreement with Morocco, an arrangement that has allowed access to these waters for the bloated European trawler fleets who have already plundered their own stocks. There was the likelihood, under the very same EU agreement, that these trawlers were fishing the disputed waters of the Western Sahara, just to the south of Tan Tan. It is a situation much criticised by human rights groups. Even the EU's own lawyers describe it as quite possibly illegal. However, over-fishing in European waters, and the political fallout, continues to be something of an issue. Far easier, therefore, to make questionable arrangements with Morocco.

THE WESTERN SAHARA came under Spanish control in the late 1800's, becoming a province of Spain in 1934. By the 1960's times had moved on; the "winds of change" swept fiercely across Africa. Nationalist movements emerged throughout the continent and the people of the Spanish Sahara, as the province was then known, were as keen as any African to be rid of their colonial masters. The Popular Front for the Liberation of Saguia el Hamra and Rio de Oro (Polisario, for short), named after the two administrative sections into which the Spanish had divided the colony, was established in 1973 to represent the rights of the Sahrawi, the collective name for the people of the Western Saharan tribes, including the Tekna, Chnagla, Oulad Delim and the Reguibat.

With Spain's dictatorship crumbling and the country suffering political turmoil, it had little stomach for a prolonged guerrilla war with the Polisario. Spain heeded the International Court of Justice's ruling to recognise the rights of the Sahrawi to self-determination. Just as the Spanish and the United Nations were preparing for a referendum King Hassan II of Morocco, believing the Spanish Sahara belonged to Morocco, ordered 350,000 of his subjects to occupy the province. It was known as the Green March.

In the event Spain backed off its plans for a referendum, negotiating a settlement with Morocco and Mauritania, effectively partitioning the region. Thereafter it became known as the Western Sahara and by the time of the Madrid Agreement, already many of the Sahrawi had taken flight, hastened, it is claimed, by the Moroccan air force deploying napalm and phosphorous against them.

The Polisario gathered the refugees in a hastily formed desert settlement near Tindouf, across the border in south-west Algeria. From Tindouf they declared their former homeland to be the Saharan Arab Democratic Republic and vowed to fight for it.

For the next fifteen years, aided by Algeria and other, covert sponsors, the Polisario waged a highly successful campaign against its new masters, causing Mauritania to relinquish all interests in the Western Sahara. Morocco, on the other hand, and with the help of France and the US, strengthened its grip on the region by constructing an extensive sand wall covering a distance of more than seven hundred miles.

By 1991 the United Nations had brokered a ceasefire,

attempting to cajole Morocco into a referendum on independence for the Sahrawi. With voter eligibility being a major stumbling block, today the situation continues to be unresolved. For as long as the Western Sahara remains under the de-facto administrational control of Morocco, they will continue enjoying the rights to exploit the fisheries, the significant phosphate deposits, and whatever oil may eventually be found within the offshore boundaries. In 2023, some 175,000 Sahrawi refugees are estimated to exist under dire conditions spread over five camps. The actual figure is unknown, due to political disputes between Morocco and the Sahrawi authorities. However, the situation in Tindouf is among the most protracted in the United Nations High Commissioner for Refugees (UNHCR) history. The sense of hopelessness among the young places them at high risk of radicalisation.

THE NEXT DAY we entered the Western Sahara, though there was no physical evidence to suggest we had done so. The only difference was the increase in the number of police and army checkpoints we encountered. The wind was the same, if appreciably warmer. It caused a film of dust to hang over the desert. During the morning, we passed the turning to Tarfaya, also marked on the map as Cape Juby. More than eighty years ago, Cape Juby, for a short time, was home to a famous author and pilot.

In 1918, the Frenchman Pierre-George Latécoère founded the Compagnie Générale d'Entreprises Aéronautiques (CGEA), establishing an air route from Toulouse to Dakar that specialised in delivering the mail. In 1927, he sold the bulk of the company to Marcel Bouilloux-Lafont, a French businessman based in Brazil. The company changed its name to Compagnie Générale Aéropostale, known more generally as just Aéropostale, and it went on to expand its services throughout South America. Aéropostale's first trans-Atlantic mail flight, from Dakar to Natal (Brazil), occurred in 1930 and took nineteen hours and thirty-five minutes. From the north of Morocco, the planes hugged the coastline, putting down at Casablanca, Agadir, Cape Juby (Tarfaya), Port Étienne (Nouâdhibou), St Louis and Dakar. It was a particularly perilous route between Cape Juby and Dakar, over a vast expanse of sand and unruly tribes, and is a place where a great number of pilots were lost.

Antoine de Saint-Exupéry was a pioneer of these international postal flights. In 1927, the company made Saint-Exupéry manager of their Cape Juby staging post, where there was only a god-forsaken Spanish fort surrounded by ocean and desert. Saint-Exupéry wrote of being, "*...trapped by the Sahara, like flies in amber.*" During his time at Cape Juby Saint-Exupéry led reconnaissance flights searching for missing Aéropostale pilots, negotiating their release from the Sahrawi tribes, who had often shot them down in the first place. He wrote the first of his novels, *Southern Mail*, during his time at Cape Juby, though delivering the script was not without its setbacks; it is said that Lola, a monkey belonging to his good friend and fellow pilot Jean Mermoz, ate several pages of his first draft.

In *Southern Mail* the pilot Jacques Bernis leaves a love affair in Paris to fly the mail plane from Toulouse to Dakar. The cockpit was open to the elements. He had no radio or radar. He lands in Casablanca, his red cheeks massaged by the wind, his grease-blackened hands, leather flying suit and heavy boots dripping with rainwater, his hair pasted to his forehead. During the night he'd navigated, "*...by the white ruin of the waves...*" Leaving Agadir, Bernis gradually enters the desert proper and, "*...before him lay the dazzling whiteness of this lawless wilderness...*" He follows the coast, entering a becalmed land of "*bare rock*" and "*serried dunes*", the ground ahead "*...charged with mysterious menace.*" Each time the engine misses a beat Bernis reflects how little he knows of himself; should the plane go down, how might he cope with thirst, loneliness and the cruelty of the Sahrawi tribesmen? *Southern Mail* is a wonderful insight into a trail-blazing age of aviation.

I gaze from the side window of the car at the same land those pilots flew over and get an understanding of the trust they placed in their machines. What must it have been like flying out here in their day? Much has happened in the world of aviation, and yet so little in this landscape has changed.

By early evening we'd made it to Boujdour, discovering a recently opened campsite beside the beach. We booked one of the chalets, the fierce wind still a considerable deterrent to camping. Judging by the standard of the chalets it was obvious somebody had spent a considerable sum of money on the infrastructure, even if the investment, on that day, wasn't enjoying much return. Save for a small party of Spaniards next door to us, we were on our own.

On account of the political insecurity and general banditry, the closure of south-west Algeria to all but the most intrepid tourist had resulted in the Atlantic route becoming one of the two main arteries for overlanders heading to and from central Africa. We had expected to cross paths with more European travellers. Apart from the French couple at Tan Tan we hadn't met anyone else. It made us speculate if the banking crisis in Europe hadn't forced a lot of people to change their plans and stay at home.

We had left Europe in what the papers were describing as financial melt-down. Often, I found myself speculating whether there would be a bank left standing when we got back. Out here, we were blissfully unaware if the world had taken a turn for the worse. And, anyway, there was nothing to be gained worrying about it. Instead, we chatted with Pepe, our Spanish neighbour. He owned a tourist resort in Barcelona.

'My place is called Camping Pepe,' he announced with a flourish.

Each year, when the summer season finishes, Pepe packs up his car and heads for Africa.

'I go to the Cameroon,' he said. 'And we kill *muchos* bongos.'

Watching his master lifting an imaginary rifle to his shoulder and taking aim, the Jack Russell lounging beside Pepe's feet sprang to life with a bark, though what interest a Jack Russell has in a bongo I had no idea. It certainly couldn't retrieve one for the simple fact that a bongo is a large antelope, more than a mouthful for Pepe's terrier.

'Bang!' the Spaniard called, lowering his imaginary rifle with a grin. The dog yelped, scampering in the direction of Pepe's dead bongo. 'I have a lodge and a hunting concession...' he rubbed his thumb and forefinger together with a cunning smile, '*...y muchos Americanos*.'

The Spaniard had two vehicles, one driven by himself, the other driven alternately by his wife and his sister-in-law. Some years they make the journey a couple of times, he said. It all depended on the demand for shooting bongo, a creature seemingly considered a worthy prize by men who measure their manhood by the size of a creature's antlers. I didn't bother asking Pepe how many he had above his fireplace, because I could see JP's eyes were glued to the generator in the flat-bed of the pickup truck, bringing a glow to the Spaniard's face. JP loves an engine. Any old engine will snatch his attention. He tapped an affectionate knuckle against the engine's manifold.

Pepe stepped forward. 'It weighs three hundred kilos,' he announced. 'I decided to weld it to the bed of the pickup for the journey.' The Spaniard puffed out his chest. 'Nobody can ever steal this *máquina*.'

JP put a match to his pipe and blew out a cloud of smoke. 'I suppose they could always steal the pickup,' he countered.

Pepe sniffed the air, choosing to ignore his flawed logic. Meanwhile, the terrier trotted back to us, a dripping tongue lolling from its muzzle. Sensing how he'd been duped, the dog launched itself at his master's boot, growling and snapping at the laces until they were thoroughly dead.

For supper, the staff of the campsite offered to cook a plate of freshly caught fish. When it was ready they knocked at the chalet door.

'Dinner is served,' they chimed.

They led us to what appeared to be the provisions store, inviting us to take our places at the table. The plate of fish arrived with some ceremony and we tucked in hungrily, surrounded as we were by shelves of cleaning products, mop heads, toilette rolls and other, less obvious items. The fish tasted very good, our appetite not in the least diminished by the pungent smell of bleach. With a little rummaging behind him JP uncovered an opened carton of wine on the bottom shelf. It was wrapped in brown sticky tape and propped between two suspicious-looking white tubs. As we'd finished the last bottle of our own wine, he tucked in unhesitatingly.

'How d'you know it doesn't contain more of this cleaning fluid?' Susie asked him.

'It's perfect,' he said, smacking his lips.

I tried it. It tasted foul.

THE NEXT DAY I'd planned on reaching Dakhla, to camp for the night somewhere near to the town.

'This is the turning for Dakhla,' I announced as we approached the junction, allowing the car to roll to a stop beside the signpost.

JP lifted his glasses to his forehead and lay down the book he'd been reading. In the back the girls also put down their books. Together we stared at the haze in front of us.

'What shall we do?' I asked.

Dakhla is 40 kilometres along a peninsular, not a long way, though a journey requiring us to retrace our steps. Such was the monotony of the Atlantic route that it made me reluctant to even consider driving over the same section of road twice, no matter how short. I felt we'd become rather entrenched on this section of the journey, our progress lent further urgency by the constant wind, and the matter of trying to escape it. While a long and boring one, the road through the Western Sahara was largely straight and very smooth and, in spite of the fact that the near-distance constantly shimmered in a haze of dust, at least it enabled us to maintain a steady 110 kmh. We were covering a lot of distance quickly. I was loathe to break this rhythm.

'Perhaps we should go to Dakhla,' JP said.

'We don't have to go there,' I stated. 'It was only –'

'But it's on your list,' Christine said.

'I don't mind,' piped Susie.

'You said we should stick to a schedule,' added JP.

'We have to be in Essakane by a certain date, therefore we need a schedule. But we could easily drop Dakhla. There's still a long way to go.'

'Well, we shouldn't become undisciplined,' Christine said.

'And it's a very nice schedule,' JP muttered.

There was a snigger from the back of the car and I looked from one to the other. It seemed my careful planning was being looked upon with a degree of contempt. I didn't know why I'd bothered.

I put my foot to the floor, accelerating past the turning for Dahkla.

On the Atlantic route, with little traffic to worry about, and even fewer life-forms, the only thing to remain cautious of was the many police checkpoints and their mobile speed-traps. The Moroccan police seemed to have taken to the speed-trap with a boundless enthusiasm, wielding hand-held radars with as much savagery as if they were Darth Vader's lightsaber. Appearing in the distance as an unrecognisable blob, with each metre travelled a lurching shape emerged, the arms and heads and legs joining together and gradually growing in authority. Having reached the checkpoint we usually witnessed an impressive array of guns, which you ignored at your peril. With the last one hundred metres to run, a hand would shoot skyward, a finger pointing to the roadside. At each checkpoint we exchanged pleasantries, and handed over a single, pre-printed document called a *fiche,* on which we'd written details of our passports and the car's papers. The *fiche* worked as a remarkable piece of bureaucratic fast-tracking, avoiding the need for each of us to pull out our papers.

A few kilometres after the turning to Dakhla we pulled off the road by a line of shacks and placed an order for meat, which a fellow cooked on a warped section of greasy chicken wire. When it was done, he wrapped the meat in a strip of paper torn from a discarded cement bag.

For lunch, we left the main road and crossed a stretch of rough land to the edge of the cliff, finding some rocks to sit on. Chewing on pieces of sinewy mutton (and doing my best to avoid the remnants of cement dust) we regarded the Dakhla peninsular from a distance. The coastline was beautiful, the sea turquoise-blue and most inviting.

After lunch, we drove down to the beach and swam in the sea. Tucked away in a cove, it seemed we had the perfect campsite for the night, until the cold wind did its old trick, stirring the tufts of grass and kicking up the sand. We unfurled the awnings and put the kettle on to boil, certain a cup of tea would help us make up our minds about what to do next. Just as we'd poured the tea a local guy rocked up on his scooter, two kids perched on the seat behind him. The kids ran across the beach and splashed into the sea. The guy hung back making small talk. He told us smugglers worked this part of the beach every night. If we camped here we might not get much sleep, he said.

'Fish, mainly,' the man told us when asked what the smugglers landed.

'Nothing too wicked, then,' JP said.

Beyond where we were parked the area was scattered with the evidence of the smugglers' activity – several fish heads here, a pile of fine bones over there, bundles of green netting stashed beneath the boulders, the occasional fishy whiff.

We drank our cups of tea and decided to heed the scooter man's advice; perhaps it was better if we didn't get in the way of the smugglers. The policeman at the last checkpoint had talked of a hotel one hundred and forty kilometres before the border with Mauritania, so we were of a mind to try and find it. We packed up and continued our journey.

After two or three hours' thundering down the road we arrived at our destination in the dark, numb and tired. Viewed from the car, the hotel gave the impression of being half finished. This tendency to leave buildings unfinished was a state of affairs more prevalent the further south we ventured. Here, at this particular hotel, it was as if aspirations of a second floor had simply evaporated in the late afternoon, leaving in its wake a series of rough concrete pillars, vertical iron rods and an occasional wall to support the starry night sky.

We unloaded our bags and checked in, finding the rooms okay, providing one applied a few simple principles:

#1: Do not inspect the sheets too closely.

#2: NEVER uncover the mattress.

#3: Keep your bag zipped at all times to minimise ingress of wildlife.

#4: Wear flip-flops while you shower.

The communal toilets were definitely not a place to linger.

When we sauntered down to the outdoor restaurant we found the three Spaniards and their Jack Russell already ensconced at the next table. The moment we sat down Pepe leaned over, so as to divulge in some secrecy how he'd stashed away fifty litres of hooch in both his vehicles. He swore the Mauritanian customs had no chance of finding it. Bright-eyed, the terrier was sitting expectantly on a chair beside his master, the picture of innocence; you'd never in a million years take him for a hooch smuggler.

We'd heard the Mauritanian authorities allowed no alcohol to pass their borders, so after dinner, unlike Pepe, we retreated to JP and Susie's room to plunder the rest of ours.

The next morning, we left for the border just after sunrise. "The early bird catches the worm" is not an adage that applies in any measure to the Morocco/Mauritania border. At Fort Guerguargat, an hour down the road, life had ground to a standstill. In the roadside café, we fortified ourselves with a strong, grainy coffee and gawped at the long line of cars.

'Ok, we might as well make a start,' I said. I'd heard a lot about this border. It was going to be hassle all the way and I wanted to get it over with.

We ambled along the line of cars waiting to cross the frontier, stopping at the wall enclosing a substantial compound. JP handed our passports to one of the three youths, border touts, slouched over a table in the shade of the wall. Just as they did at the docks in Tangier, the touts performed an unofficial role, assisting the traveller for a small reward. These three were filling out travellers' exit forms, which we could have completed ourselves in a quarter of the time. It was tiresome, though better to play the game. Much of what they wrote down was incorrect.

'I can't understand why they tolerate this,' I grumbled. 'Morocco's a modern, thriving country and then you come across this.'

'Take it easy,' JP said.

Very soon the sun got the better of me and, much like everybody else, I resigned myself to staring at the little mound of earth the toe of my shoe had gradually formed. The sun was fierce that day and there was insufficient shade for us all. There so rarely is at an African border. Be it a tree, a wooden hut, a crumbling veranda, there's only ever sufficient shade for the officials – or the touts. At least that's how it always feels. Maybe it was the heat aggravating me that morning

'Occupation?' the youth snapped, not bothering to look up, his biro quivering over a white box.

JP had to check which passport the youth was working on before replying. It was Susie's.

'Dentist,' he told him.

Slither, slither, slither, went the biro.

When each of us was in possession of a completed exit form JP dropped a handful of change in a tin on the corner of the table.

The uniformed official standing at the side of the table hooked a thumb at the next hurdle, somewhere inside the compound. We stepped over the chain blocking the entrance and walked on.

Having deposited our travel documents with a man packing a machine-gun, we joined the crowd loitering eagerly by a small, open window. We jostled so as to hear when the character inside called out our names. It was all slightly sinister. That faceless head, that dark silhouette bobbing up and down in the gloom, I suspected, held more power than many of us were happy with.

After clearing Morocco, you are advised not to stray from the six-kilometre-long "corridor", an ill-defined route of inter-weaving tracks meandering through no-man's-land, for fear of triggering land mines laid during the guerrilla war between Mauritania and the Polisario. I'd read conflicting reports as to how easy the track was to follow. The line of vehicles up ahead of us was marginally reassuring. Providing the guy at the front, in the battered Transit van, wasn't suddenly possessed by reckless suicidal tendencies, it was more than likely we should all remain in one piece.

Many broken and stripped cars lay abandoned along the corridor. Most likely they would never be removed. There was certainly no chance of a recovery service making an appearance. I suppose, if you do have the misfortune of suffering a serious breakdown out here, it's a matter of carting away what you can. The rest must be left to the scavengers and the ravages of time.

After all the terrible things we'd heard about them, we actually began to consider the Mauritanian authorities were not so bad after all. Perhaps it had something to do with the recent *coup d'état* – a new broom, and all that. Only a cursory inspection of the car was all they required.

'Where is the alcohol?' they demanded.

'Definitely no alcohol,' we told them.

I thought of Pepe and all his whiskey. The Spaniards were nowhere to be seen. I hope his dog hadn't tried to kill the customs officer's shoelaces. That could have been awkward.

And then, just as our passage was proceeding all too well, matters drifted downhill. After the vehicle inspection, I was obliged to join two officials in what can only be described as a concrete cell. They closed the door, indicating a plastic chair on which to perch, which I did, because the back of the chair flapped uselessly like a large slice of bleached skin. With all the zeal of a train-spotter banished to the desert, one of them proceeded to scribble our names in a large book, a compendium of names and car registrations. The mood subtly changed. Setting aside his biro, the scribe reached for the last of our passports, thumbing the pages. Watching the eyes narrow and harden, he put me in mind of Colonel Douglas Mortimer (Lee Van

Cleef in the Spaghetti Western, *For A Few Dollars More,*) just as he lets the saddlebag of weapons unfurl down his horse's flank, and he knows for sure his target, an eye-twitching, buck-toothed murderer two hundred yards along the street, is good for a five-hundred-dollar reward.

'You have something for me,' the colonel drawled.

'Have I?'

'*Oui.*'

By then I had a good idea why the fellow before me had been so unceremoniously shown the door. I assumed he hadn't given them enough of what they wanted. The game of verbal ping-pong began.

'Give me that mobile telephone,' he said.

'I can't.'

I told him I must keep the telephone, so as to remain in contact with my family. I reckoned he might empathise with that. Strangely enough, he did. Though I have to admit, at this point I weakened. I'd had enough of this morning's charade, and all the heat and pieces of paper and jostling that went with it. I'll never know how much time the five Euro note bought us. It was worth every centime.

'This must be our secret,' he hissed, waggling the limp note, his head inclining in the direction of the door.

Next on the list were our fifteen-day visas. I bought them at the immigration hut, yet another in a series of concrete cells. These agents of the state were marginally less sinister than the two I'd just left behind. Again, our details were entered in a book. The money for the visas was handed over, passports were stamped.

After immigration, a man in a blue robe sprang from nowhere. The blue robe wanted to sell car insurance and urged me in the direction of a lean-to constructed from planks of wood haphazardly nailed together. In an instant I was shoved in the small of the back, propelled through the crooked doorway, left to find my balance amongst the streaks of darkness and light, and the dancing dust.

By that point I was not only rendered temporarily blind, I was also deeply confused, given that the extent of my French vocabulary could be said to rank alongside that of a parrot.

Was it an insurance broker slowly emerging before me? A uniformed insurance salesman was a new experience. The gold-coloured pips on his epaulettes winked when they caught the streaks of sunlight. Maybe he was their star broker. He had three pips on each shoulder. I told him I needed fifteen days' cover for the pickup outside and, in return, received a severe dressing-down.

WHOOPS!

As my eyes adjusted to the darkness, the badge on his shirt removed all doubt: DOUANE. He was a customs officer, and a senior one, by the look of him. I groaned inwardly. It had been a long and arduous morning, including far too much sun for an Englishman to cope with. My brain was fried.

'*Je suis un imbécile*,' I declared, slapping my forehead in what I hoped was more a look of contrition than a parody of Inspector Clouseau.

'*Tout à fait!*' he grunted.

I might not have understood a word he said, but the tone of his voice was enough for me to know we would not be crossing the border without his say-so.

'*Oui. Bien sûr*,' I interjected during a moment I judged opportune.

I held his cold stare, calculating whether he needed the same inducement as Colonel Mortimer two huts back. I've never been comfortable with the idea of bribing border officials. Not only does it risk backfiring, it feeds a crooked system.

Thankfully, the customs officer snatched a pad from across his desk, filled out a sheet and tore it free. I breathed a sigh of relief.

'*Alors, vingt-cinq Euros*,' he barked, slipping the fee for the *laissez passer* into his trouser pocket.

3

MAURITANIA

A LOSS OF IDENTITY

On the forty kilometre stretch of road between the border and Nouadhibou we were stopped by two military checkpoints. They inspected our papers all over again.

The town of Nouadhibou, population 80,000, is the heart of Mauritania's economic activity. At anything up to three kilometres long, the trains lugging phosphate from the mines deep in the deserts of Mauritania are thought to be the longest trains anywhere in the world. Certainly, it took a good deal of time for them to clear the railway crossing. I'd read somewhere that they pull more than two hundred wagons. We didn't count them.

One of the principal economic activities in Nouadhibou is hinted at by the pervasive smell of fish. Some of the richest fishing grounds in the world lie off this coastline. The name Nouadhibou roughly translates as "The place where the jackals get fat", though "The bay of the abandoned ships", might be equally fitting. Hulks of rusting ships lie along the shoreline, a veritable wasteland of davits, gunwales, hawsers and poop decks. Alongside its standing as the possessor of the world's longest trains, it could feasibly include a second declaration: keeper of the world's largest cemetery for the mercantile marine. Where unwanted ships are concerned, it seems Nouadhibou is the home of the dodgy insurance claim.

For some time, we hunted up and down Nouadhibou's sandy streets, eventually finding the Auberge du Lévrier in the middle of town. Housed within a small compound, the bedrooms and ablutions looked in on a square of packed earth. In one corner of the square a pair of naked legs poked from beneath a vintage overland truck and in the other, a communal Bedouin tent gave shelter to a number of mattresses. As we pulled up, the naked legs grew a torso, and then a grease-smeared face, which eyed us with a degree of curiosity. The registration plate bolted to the front of the vintage truck indicated it was from Poland.

It was pleasant enough at Auberge du Lévrier, except the dry border crossing meant we'd purged our stash of alcohol, and the hour of the aperitif was nearing. With a degree of certainty that the inn's charm would improve one hundredfold with a drink in our hands, JP and I went in search of beer.

'Go to the Chinese restaurant,' Ali Baba, the owner of the *auberge*, had suggested. 'In this town, the Chinese have everything.'

We followed Ali Baba's advice. Though finding the Chinese restaurant was another matter altogether. Either we were not being understood, or "Little China" had temporarily vanished from this corner of the Sahara. No amount of questioning the locals wandering the edge of the road took us any closer to our goal. Quite clearly, little China was not a place frequented by the bourgeois of Nouadhibou. We returned to Ali Baba's in a state of minor anxiety, given we were facing three to four days' abstinence, the length of time I estimated it taking us to reach Senegal.

By late afternoon a young Mauritanian called Vetten arrived at the inn, plonking himself in the centre of the Bedouin tent like a storyteller of old. He announced to his audience, namely us, that he had an eco-camp in the Parc National du Banc d'Arguin, a major breeding ground for migratory birds, and a World Heritage site of some 12,000 square kilometres. He took a file from his bag and we flicked through his album of photographs depicting golden beaches, a calm sea, Bedouin tents, a seabird gliding above the waves, a fish cooking over an open fire. It looked idyllic. As the park was located on the coast between Nouadhibou and Nouakchott, our next port of call, we agreed to pay a visit.

That evening Vetten drove the four of us to his home on the outskirts of town. He'd invited us for supper, telling us on the way how he lived with his extended family in one large house. He parked his car down a dark, narrow alley and ushered us towards a door.

The family home was large. We were led through a series of corridors and across internal patios, finally arriving in a spacious room at the back of the house, where the striking rugs and banquettes contrasted with the plain white walls. His family derived its living from the fish trade, he explained, as we settled ourselves on the floor.

If the size of the house was any indication, then clearly

Vetten's family were very successful in the fish trade. An ample dinner of mixed fish (and chips) was prepared and served by his sister, during which time family members, from the youngest to the oldest, drifted in and out of the room to meet us. While we chomped through our food Vetten talked at length about his eco-camp located in the park, which he assured us was the closest thing to paradise we would encounter anywhere in the world.

'It is my one great passion,' he affirmed. 'Mauritania will become the tourists' choice of the future.'

When the plates were cleared away, and the mint tea poured, Vetten steered our conversation in the direction of toilets and, more specifically, what constituted the most suitable toilet for an eco-camp. I wondered if this was leading to a joke, except he looked terribly serious. It was as if we might have been a gathering of international luminaries – a kind of underground, free-thinking alternative to Thomas Crapper. It was obviously a matter plaguing Vetten's mind, and one requiring sound, blue-sky thinking. Surely a bunch of overlanders know a thing or two about bush toilets, he must have been thinking. Vetten assumed the role of chairman and we settled against the banquettes to listen to what he had to say.

He lowered his voice an octave or two when he said: 'An eco-toilet should have no flushing parts. And paper is forbidden.'

This was radical talk for us Europeans, though not unexpected, in the circumstances. Humbled by such a bold announcement, the committee was swept up in the chairman's exposé on drainage and the positioning of a toilet relative to its surroundings, the latter having more to do with reducing man's encroachment on the environment, than any ancient spiritual beliefs. As the camp in question was located on the beach, within metres of the shoreline, the chairman resolutely believed in letting the sea do most of the work. Why interfere with the course of nature, he challenged?

'Absolutely!' we trumpeted.

After a short discourse on the amount of time required for human waste to decompose, the committee was dismissed with the suggestion that we might wish to go for a drive through the town.

'What a great idea!'

We clambered eagerly to our feet and filed through the house. Returning along the corridors and across the internal patios, I couldn't help reflecting on what a curious presentation Vetten made of his camp. I pondered over what on earth we should find there. I'd never before heard of a resort being promoted on the basis of its latrines. I suspected a sturdy shovel would be a definite bonus. We were well prepared. We possessed two of those.

Vetten drove us to a Spanish bar overlooking the port. It had as much atmosphere as the interior of a shipping container. Expats of various shapes, sizes and colours shored up the bar, growling in foreign tongues. Messrs Spielberg/Lucas would have gone a long way to recreate such a scene. The place was devoid of any humour; these men at that bar were here simply to forget that they were here. On leaving, we profited from the opportunity by filling a plastic bag with extra cans of San Miguel.

The noise of the town penetrated the Auberge du Lévrier for much of the night. The taste of exhaust and the dust dried your throat. I didn't need the wail of the muezzin to wake me. I'd been counting camels in the dark way before the mosque opened its doors. We were all up early, infused with a certain buzz about visiting the Parc du Banc d'Arguin, intrigued by what we'd heard of Vetten's eco-camp. Armed with three GPS waypoints and a rudimentary sketch, we were assured by Vetten that we had more than enough information to lead us directly to his camp.

Somehow, I just didn't believe him.

'I've called ahead,' he announced breezily. 'Everything will be ready for you.'

Vetten had to stay behind in Nouadhibou, to spend the day with his family. It was Tabaski, a religious holiday commemorating the willingness of Ibrahim to sacrifice his son, Ishmael, as an act of obedience to God. According to the scriptures God commanded him to spare the child at the last moment, calling on him to sacrifice a ram instead. Tabaski, therefore, is a very bad day if you're a sheep – and especially alarming if you're a male sheep.

As we loaded the last of our things in the car, a Datsun saloon arrived in the compound of the *auberge*, a black-faced man-sheep trussed on the back seat. It was his last ride. The man of the house, for tradition dictates that it is he who has to slit the ram's throat, hauled the poor creature from the car and, to the accompaniment of much bleating, dragged it through the front door. Any old fool could see that the man-sheep knew the game was up. By the time we climbed into the Hilux, the bleating had already ceased.

Due to the festival, there was little traffic on the roads in town. The people, dressed in their flowing robes of white, yellow or pale blue, formed long processions making their way to various gatherings.

We left the town and the ceremony behind us and headed south on the new tarmac road. On the way, I kept a wary eye out for the bandits and terrorists the British Foreign Office had warned of. When I last looked, the FCO Travel Advisory webpage had still been reporting a high risk of kidnap by terrorist groups throughout Mauritania and they advised against visiting pretty much all of the country. Al-Qaida in the Islamic Maghreb (AQIM) was reported to be active in Mauritania. We could only hope that on the day of Tabaski the kidnappers were all eating men-sheep. And then tomorrow...well, tomorrow would be another day – *Inshallah!*

In 2007 four members of a French family had been shot by Islamists associated with AQIM, resulting in the cancellation of the 2008 Paris to Dakar motor rally. In September 2008, AQIM fighters boldly crossed from Mali to ambush a Mauritanian military patrol near the city of Zouerate, in the north of the country. The mutilated bodies of all twelve soldiers were later recovered from the desert. It was chilling news, though we remained optimistic a heightened state of security existed following the recent *coup d'état*. Such reasoning didn't stop me, for a while at least, watching the road ahead through the binoculars, glassing the dunes, sweeping across the vast shimmering plain, lingering on the black strip of road running through it. I soon bored of the exercise. We didn't meet another car all morning.

After many kilometres of nothing but desert, a black pebble mutated into a roadside shack and, a little closer still, the shack came with the added detail of a man butchering a sheep. The sheep was trussed to an overhead beam, the man tearing the skin from its back, so that the top half was marbled pink and the bottom half still had its trousers on.

JP pulled over and went to see the man, who straightened, his hand swiping a bloody trail over his brow. Did he want to sell us a leg of sheep? JP asked him.

The man grinned, an expression that looked much like a fissure suddenly appearing in a rock. He nodded enthusiastically. He was very happy to sell a leg of his sheep at an inflated price to a bunch of *toubabs* (the name in West and Central Africa for a white European). What a silly question. We sat in the shade while the man finished butchering the sheep. When he finished, we had to remove most of the tins of San Miguel in order to get the leg into the fridge.

It didn't take us long after that before we found our first marker, a cluster of masts by the roadside, the starting point for our trek to Vetten's camp. I tapped the three waypoints he'd given us into the GPS, including the one for the mast (as a precautionary measure), and off we went, the compass needle guiding us west. Somewhere out there was the sea. How could we possibly go wrong?

With JP at the wheel we raced toward the bleached and quivering horizon, swerving to avoid the clumps of thick, low bushes, and the deeper tyre tracks of previous vehicles, indications of soft sand ahead. Every now and then the Hilux slowed, the engine labouring as it sank that bit deeper in the sand, and then it was away again, the ground solid beneath us.

After twenty minutes an escarpment running north/south rose from the sand, blocking any further progress. It ran each side of us for as far as the eye could see and our first GPS waypoint was some way on the far side of it. All other tyre tracks had suddenly vanished. Somewhere between the escarpment and the cluster of masts beside the road we had made an error.

JP brought the vehicle to a halt facing down the dune. We got out and attempted to establish our position. Everything looked the same. It is unnerving how quickly that happens; total disorientation. We turned Vetten's drawing through 360°; it was no clearer. We discussed the possibility of sticking to the bearing and trying to get over the escarpment, a series of sand ridges, but the ground in places appeared too soft. We could have been stuck in there for a long time – forever, perhaps. There was nothing for it but to return to the mast and make a second attempt. We got back in the car, though not before all of us pulled on a hefty draught of water, to replenish what we'd just lost.

With JP still at the wheel, me pointing in the direction of the compass arrow, all of us giving advice, arguing, stopping again to get our bearings, becoming despondent, and then elated, until finally, forty-five minutes later, we found ourselves at a collection of Bedouin tents by the sea, which we assumed to be Vetten's slice of paradise.

I felt the deep sand had given the Hilux a good testing. It had passed with flying colours. Even JP, died-in-the-wool Land Rover man, and for whom driving a Toyota is akin to manning a Donald Duck float at a lord mayor's parade, grunted a form of approval at its performance.

We climbed out and stretched our legs, for once appreciating the cool wind after the heat inside the car. The camp looked deserted. And then a man popped up from between the dunes.

'Is this Vetten's camp?' we asked him.

The man nodded. He squinted at us, his face a blank. Despite Vetten's assurance earlier in the day, quite clearly, he hadn't a clue we were coming.

'I haven't heard from Vetten in weeks,' he announced. Not that he seemed the slightest bit bothered.

'Does he never come here?'

'Not much.'

THE FOLLOWING DAY, rather than hurrying off to Nouakchott, our next port of call, we decided to stay put, to swim in the sea and try and catch some fish.

I wandered to where the surf washed over the beach. The water was wonderfully cooling, the saline air more than a relief after the dusty drive. If this was Vetten's vision of paradise, then it wasn't a bad insight: beautiful beach, crystal clear sea, not a single German and his imperious towel, not even a lobster-coloured, drunken Brit wallowing senselessly in the dunes – not anybody, in fact. But then, when all is said and done, paradise doesn't really exist as a place you can go to. And if it did, after a short while, doubtless it would be unbearable. Paradise exists only in the mind, a state of being, as close to home as your own back garden, on a warm sunny day, after a glass or two of decent wine among good company.

The guardian of the camp had had more practice than us at catching fish. By the end of the day it was three nil to the hosting team. He brought us a sizable Dorada, and another fish, which none of us could identify. We knocked up a fire and when they were cooked, stripped the bones clean with our fingers. It was just like Vetten's photos.

The guardian joined us while we ate, squatting a short distance from the fire. He asked where we were going and when we told him, he smiled broadly.

'Essakane!' he cried, a twinkle coming to his eye.

Our host was a small man, wiry, with little hands and feet. His name was Mohamed Ali and he was a Tuareg who came from a settlement very near to Essakane.

'It is a beautiful place,' he said. Except finding work was difficult and so he'd made his way to Mauritania, to run Vetten's camp, and to catch fish for the punters. Tourists are the future, he said. Then he talked of the banditry in the region to north of the River Niger, and in Mali generally. He said Gao had become quite bad. That was not so good for the tourists.

'You should not go there,' he warned.

Gao is a trading town on Mali's eastern border with Niger. It lies beside the Niger River and was a place JP particularly wanted to go.

'It'll be fine,' JP said. 'My friends are in Gao. They're all Tuaregs.'

Despite my new African fortitude, I wasn't so sure. A scan of the chat sites on the internet before we'd left had already underlined how the north of Mali was getting hot where banditry was concerned. After the music festival at Essakane we planned following the route north of the Niger River, all the way to Gao. On the other hand, no way did I relish the chance of being kidnapped, shot at, or robbed. We'd come out here to have a bit of fun, not to be constantly glancing over the shoulder. I tried to assuage myself: what could a Tuareg, hidden away on the Mauritanian coast, possibly know about bandits so far away in Mali?

As it turned out he was right on the money. And he wasn't the last one to warn us about the road to Gao.

'You could go by camel to Timbuktu,' Ali suggested. 'It's not far in a straight line, and much better than a car.'

'Not likely!'

A combination of camping, sand and camel riding – no bloody chance. I'd read Michael Asher's book, *Impossible Journey*. In 1986, he and his wife Mariantonietta became the first Westerners to travel by camel from Nouakchott, the capital of Mauritania, to Abu Simbel, in Egypt. It took them forty-two days to reach Timbuktu. Thirteen months later they arrived beside the Nile. It read like a journey into hell, cementing my determination never to sit astride a camel, and certainly not to ride one across the Sahara Desert.

The sea was wonderful to swim in as a prelude to a new

day. Susie was first into the water, her Nordic genes easily the measure of the chilly, early morning surf. The rest of us allowed the sun to establish itself before venturing in. To float on your back staring up at the blue sky was hugely invigorating. To wash ourselves off we fixed a twenty-litre bag of water with a shower attachment on the roof of the car, letting the sun gradually warm it. By lunch time it was a perfect temperature.

Vetten's eco-camp really was a special place, even if it wasn't that tidy. Garbage disposal did not rank highly on his waste management plan. I'm surprised it hadn't featured on our agenda after dinner at his house. And despite the long discussion about eco-toilets, no toilet, flushing or otherwise, existed there. He was a curious chap, Vetten. Had his family, obviously wealthy and presumably well connected, secured him this concession as a means to keep him out of mischief? Or was it his way of demonstrating to them his worthiness? Who knows. I was right about one thing, though. You certainly needed a sturdy shovel. It was then a matter of finding a quiet place in the dunes – and whistling while you went.

The following day a strong wind blew up and after a breakfast of cold, gritty fish we retraced our route (very successfully, it has to be said, despite the sand storm) to the main road.

We arrived in Nouakchott by late afternoon.

After driving around town for some time, ending up in the hustle and bustle of the busy market, we eventually found our overnight stop. This was a decent place, run by a French girl who gave classes on yoga. She was very Zen, gliding about her property, and always with a smile. The property itself was set within a small compound, amongst the diplomatic district of Nouakchott, though that's not to suggest any grandeur concerning its surroundings. It was a smoggy, filthy, chaotic city wherever we went.

Nouakchott is the capital and largest city of Mauritania, and at the time of our visit the ruling High State Council was still under the governance of the military junta, after a coup in August 2008 unseated the first freely elected President Sidi Ould Cheikh Abdallahi, and his prime minister.

Somewhere close to two thirds of the country's population of three million people live in Nouakchott. And so do quite a few Chinese, quietly investing in various infrastructure projects, as they are doing in much of Africa, including expanding the cargo handling facilities in the port, and a new railway which will supposedly link Nouakchott with the phosphate mines at Bofal, near the Senegal River. They'd also just laid the new road we'd driven along from Nouadhibou, for which we were most grateful. The old coastal route through the dunes is no longer the only way to reach Nouakchott from the north.

In Mauritania, half the population still relies on agriculture and livestock for its livelihood, though recurrent droughts in the seventies and eighties forced many to the cities. The economy of Nouakchott is structured on salt, fish, cement, copper, insecticides and carpets. For Mauritania as a whole, the great hope for the future is the exploitation of offshore reserves of oil and gas.

There is also a darker side to Mauritania, an apparent unwillingness to move away from the tradition of slavery. Estimates suggest some six hundred thousand, twenty per cent of Mauritanians, are held as slaves. Chattel slavery, where one person owns another, has existed here for hundreds of years. It is said there is no need to bind them in chains for, after several generations, their minds are attuned to a life of servitude. According to the United Nations, the adoption of law 2015-031 criminalising slavery and slavery-like practices addressed many of the gaps in Mauritania's previous anti-slavery legislation. Though the UN recognises there is still some way to go.

In the tiny courtyard where we settled for the night we were soon thrown together with an eclectic mix of travellers. There was the usual collection of young backpackers, plodding in and out like overburdened snails, their skin a dark patina from overexposure to the sun and the grime of the road. Two French couples, who'd just concluded the sale of one of their French registered vehicles to a local businessman, were celebrating over a bottle of wine. Another group were making their way down to Benin and Togo. They thought they might have to sell one of the cars on the way back, as a means of financing their trip. In fact, Europeans selling cars in West Africa, though not strictly legal, was a recurring theme all the way to Mali.

Our couple of nights on the beach had easily seen off the San Miguel, so it was a matter of getting out into the town to find our aperitif. This time we did locate the Chinese restaurant, where we consumed unpronounceable tins of beer amongst fading scenes of fire-breathing dragons, stick-like warriors, paper lanterns and arched bridges floating between forests of red and golden trees.

I was woken before dawn by the muezzin, refreshed and happy to be nearing the end of the long coastal road that had brought us all the way from Tangier, and which would deposit us, later that day, at the border of Senegal and the infamous frontier town of Rosso. Before that, however, we were to discover Mauritania had one last prank up its sleeve.

Stopping for lunch we drove some five metres from the road into the sand, to benefit from the shade of the acacia trees. After the obligatory sardine and raw onion sandwich we were ready to get back on our way. Barely had reverse been selected than our three and a half tonne Hilux was axle deep in the sand. Three of us variously did our best at the wheel, but it was to no avail. As soon as the tyres of your 4x4 spin in the sand, it's pretty much game over. It was time for the shovels, the sand ladders and a considerable amount of shoving. After a good half an hour of digging, and with the assistance of two locals, we eventually liberated the car. We thanked the two locals, jumped back in and continued toward Senegal, giggling at our foolishness.

Less than five minutes down the road I was about to suffer the mother of all rude awakenings. I happened to pat the breast pocket of my shirt, an involuntary habit I'd developed in Mauritania. I sprang bolt upright in the seat.

'It's gone!' I cried to incredulous looks.

'What's gone?'

'Back there,' I gasped, 'in the sand...my passport.'

In view of the country's political and security issues, there was a profusion of military checkpoints punctuating the road south. For ease my passport had come to live in the pocket of my shirt. And now it had gone.

Back at the scene of our mishap I stared, momentarily dumb-struck, at the extent of churned sand we'd left behind. How deep could the passport be buried? What if a tyre had shredded it?

I dropped to my knees, not wishing to linger on the consequences of a passport with several pages ripped from it, the remaining pages quite likely stamped with the black tread mark of an all-terrain tyre. That's if we found it at all.

We hastily formed a line, burying our arms to the elbow, sifting the sand between our fingers, painstakingly working up and down over the stretch of ground. As I forced my hands through the sand, with increasing difficulty I dismissed visions of returning to Nouakchott, of trying to find the embassy and putting in a request for a new passport. What embassy? The complications didn't bear thinking about.

It didn't take long for the locals to drift back. They watched us grovelling in the sand, variously screwing up their faces and rubbing their chins, murmuring about the crazy *toubabs.*

The digging seemed to last an age. Tops from Coke bottles were about the most we came up with. It seemed hopeless. We would have to start all over again. My shirt was pasted to my back, sand coating my forearms. I was clambering to my feet when, all of a sudden, JP's hand shot upwards, my passport gripped between his fingers.

'YESSS!' Struck by a wave of relief I grasped him in a bear-hug. The passport was in remarkably good condition. I dusted it down, flicking through the pages to find none were missing.

'Let's get out of here,' I said.

We arrived at Rosso, the Senegalese border, by late afternoon.

The border officials, and the touts who insinuate themselves into the system at Rosso, have a bad reputation for both lightening your wallet and burdening your mood. This lot made the Moroccans seem like pussycats.

We'd been warned along the way not to take the border at Rosso, on account of the touts' aggressive tactics. The alternative was to follow the course of the Senegal River westward, along a dirt track, out to a place called Diama, where a less challenging border crossing exists at the entrance to the dam. Travellers can then cross over the dam to the southern bank of the river.

The crossing at Diama was our preferred option, and I'd

even checked Google Earth to make sure we knew where to find the turning in Rosso. Our plan was hatched. We were firmly in control of our destiny. Or so we thought.

Arriving in Rosso, a pack of touts circled us from every direction, from out of the crumbling buildings and discarded trucks, the mountains of shredded tyres and rusting forty-gallon drums. It was as if they leached from the very earth, swarming over the car. With their faces pressed to the windows they shrieked of how an overweight lorry had broken the road leading over the dam at Diama.

'C'est fermé! Le barrage est fermé.'

Was our carefully prepared plan already in ruins? How could we know if they spoke the truth? Everybody knows blocked roads are a daily event all over Africa. We sat there a moment, weighing our two options. To drive out to Diama and back was a long way to go, if the dam was really bust. And yet we knew, in our heart of hearts, that these scoundrels were most likely lying.

'The ferry is leaving!' they shouted, tapping on the windows. 'The last ferry today.'

A hundred metres up ahead, the entrance to Rosso port displayed about as much affability as the gaping jaws of one of the river's crocodiles. There were yet more touts eyeing us by the open steel door leading to the port. Beyond them I could see the quay, a mass of people crowding a couple of cars. We rolled forward. We'd done so much driving already – it was as if in that moment our spirits weakened and wordlessly we acquiesced. As we steered toward the port the touts loped beside us, licking their lips, sensing a kill.

So much for being in control of our destiny.

'I don't want to get out of the car,' Susie said. 'Look at them...it's crazy here.'

She was right. It was crazy. After parking on the quayside, I could barely open the door for the amount of bodies round the car, impatient, frenetic, hungry. Everything I'd heard about Rosso was precise to the finest detail; a whirl of shoving and grasping, of demands and counter-demands, of haggling and fixing, of dilated eyes and oily, desperate faces, of outstretched hands, of aggravation in a sultry heat, and the wreak of acrid sweat.

JP and I jostled our way to a building housing the ferry office, customs and immigration. Demands were made, money handed over, a boat passage and vehicle insurance purchased, and our passports stamped. Each administrational procedure meant several people received their cut. And that was before we'd reached the Senegalese border, on the other side of the river.

The ferry left the quay the moment we drove on board. I leapt out to berate the youth who sold us the car insurance. He owed me money and I wanted it back.

Everything to do with this place angered me. I couldn't restrain my frustration any longer – the red mist was up. Even the policeman standing amongst us lamented the behaviour of his countrymen, though he seemed not in the least inclined to make a stand.

Rather foolishly, I'd allowed my temper to snap. The touts were closing ranks. JP stepped into the fray, the old Africa hand, puffing on his pipe, calming the rabble.

Rule # 1 at Rosso: Never incite the rabble – especially when outnumbered, and particularly when in the middle of a crocodile-infested river.

AVOID irritation more than exposure to the sun, the doctor opined to Marlow in Joseph Conrad's *Heart of Darkness. Du calme, du calme. Adieu.*

4

SENEGAMBIA

"DONNE-MOI UN CADEAU!"

The distance from the border to Saint-Louis was an axle-snapping, wheel-squaring one hundred kilometres. All the breaking and the swerving did nothing to lighten our mood, and yet we felt the need to put distance between ourselves and Rosso in the shortest possible time.

Our sour introduction served to confirm the travellers' stories about Senegal. We could only hope it wasn't a portent of things to come further down the road. Not that we intended spending too much time here. For us Senegal was a transit to and from the Gambia, where we planned a few days downtime at JP's house on the beach. When doing our research on the internet, many of the travellers' blog sites bemoaned the attitude of the Senegalese customs and police, both at the borders and along many of the principal roads. It seemed that most European overlanders had taken to giving the country a wide berth, exasperated with the belligerent attitude of its officials and their constant demands. Instead, they were taking the route from Nouakchott to Kiffa, in the east of Mauritania, and then cutting south straight to Mali. The country wasn't doing itself any favours. The question was: did anybody in Senegal care?

The town of Saint-Louis is situated on the Île de N'Dar, an island in the estuary of the Senegal River. It is reached by crossing the Pont Faidherbe, a five-hundred-metre-long iron bridge designed by Gustav Eiffel, a man better known for the Eiffel Tower in Paris.

Established as the first French settlement in West Africa in 1659 by Louis Caullier, it was to be more than one hundred years later, by which time it had become a bustling trading port, that Saint-Louis came to be named after King Louis XIV. Its expansion thereafter continued rapidly, the city most probably at the zenith of its political and commercial importance in 1895. With the creation of French West Africa, Saint-Louis became the capital of France's empire, so that today, the architecture, the cool, shaded patios, the wrought iron balconies and the huge wooden doorways, all hinted at its once colonial grandeur. Despite being named a UNESCO World Heritage site in 2000, the infrastructure, and a good many of the classic buildings have been left to crumble.

After rumbling over the Pont Faidherbe we entered Saint-Louis' grid-system of narrow roads. Being a relatively small place, it wasn't too long before we had found Quai Giraud and a guesthouse going by the name of Sanu Keur.

Sanu Keur is run by Jean-Jacques, a Niçoise, and was to be the perfect antidote to a long day on the road, not to mention the wicked assault on our wallets. The property's point of focus was a large internal courtyard of potted plants and palms, and it was there, within moments of unloading our bags and signing the registry, that we retired to the cushioned, wrought iron chairs beside the well. It would be later, after a sufficiently soothing gin and tonic, when we lugged our kit up the wooden stairs, weaved across the rickety landing, and swayed at the open doorway to our quirky rooms.

In the morning, we wandered the litter-strewn streets of Saint-Louis, eventually arriving in Place Faidherbe. Apart from a statue of the famous French governor, Louis Faidherbe, there were also several brightly coloured buses parked nose to tail, and a gaggle of uniformed school children in search of '*...des cadeaux...*' In Place Faidherbe we also found a local fisherman. His name was Idrissa. He was sitting on a wall quietly watching the world drift by.

Idrissa explained how he lived on the Langue de Barbarie, a peninsula joined to Saint Louis by the Mustapha Malik Gaye Bridge. The Langue de Barbarie had at one time been inhabited by the freed slaves, since then becoming a thriving fishing community called Guet N'Dar. Idrissa was keen for us to visit the fish market, so we might absorb at least some of the flavour of local life.

As we strolled beside him, dodging the cyclists and handcarts and the general to and fro of pedestrians crossing the bridge, he told us something about himself. The business of fishing was not as easy as it used to be, he lamented. Foreign trawlers were fishing closer and closer to the coast, in waters traditionally worked by the artisanal fleets.

'Nothing is being done to stop them,' he said, claiming a lack of will on the part of the authorities had resulted in the depleted stocks they were now seeing. 'It is hard for all the fishermen to make a living when there is less fish to catch.'

Idrissa aspired to reach Europe. '...a land of opportunity,' he asserted. He ardently believed that it was only in Europe where he would find decent work and good money, and a means to pay for his family. He'd tried to reach Spain twice on a pirogue, the narrow, wooden boats used by the fishermen, and each time he'd been rounded up by the Spanish and sent back.

We spent most of the morning with Idrissa, absorbing something of life in Guet N'Dar's busy community. Much of what we saw involved women leaning over cooking pots, women mending fishing nets, and yet more women going about their business, carrying a lot of things on their heads bound up in colourful cloth. The men, by contrast, huddled together on up-turned boxes, chatted and smoked cigarettes. They seemed a contented bunch, always quick to engage us in friendly banter. Groups of kids observed our approach with big round eyes and runny noses. They chirped like birds after we'd passed.

After half an hour of meandering through the tight, sandy streets of Guet N'Dar, we reached the fish market, which happened to be closed, a fact that had slipped Idrissa's mind when we set out, and the reason, no doubt, for the men to be idling away the day on their up-turned boxes. In spite of this setback, we returned alongside the river and tried to imagine what it might have been like in the hustle and bustle of a normal day.

It was here beside the river, Idrissa explained, where the women gutted the daily catch and then dried or smoked the fish, prior to it being sent in trucks to Dakar. Despite the place being entirely deserted our senses were certainly left with a keen idea of what it was all about; the smell of rotten fish alone was intense. Even so, we ambled amongst the riot of steel barrels and woven baskets, around the clumps of hessian and canvas sacking shimmering under layers of fish scales, ducked under lean-to shacks with their makeshift gutting tables and broken plastic chairs, and stepped over the piles of abandoned fish heads, pools of oily water and yellowing skeletons.

Passing the Pont Faidherbe on our return we stopped to bag a few photos of this impressive bridge. For JP, bagging the Faidherbe was a satisfying moment. Up to now his photographic subjects had consisted principally of infrastructure, with particular emphasis on bridges, ferries, rolling stock, fuel stations (and their attendant pumps), trucks, marine diesel engines and the occasional government building. Being more absorbed by the hard facts of how a subject worked, JP's library of photos displayed only marginal aesthetic appreciation of the places we'd been. In the hands of the authorities, the camera's memory stick might easily have provoked a good degree of suspicion. Did they have among them an imperialist saboteur? We could only hope no soldier bothered to look at it.

Fortunately, as a tourist attraction, a photo of the Pont Faidherbe was positively encouraged. There is a certain mystery surrounding the Pont Faidherbe. Local lore tells of the bridge originally being destined for the Danube, though unspecified events dictated its arrival here in 1897. JP didn't rush the shot, either, due in part to his temperamental camera, which refused to work after sundown and, in daylight, ensured many of his subjects had the appearance of being snapped whilst tumbling from the top of a twenty-storey building.

Later that day, negotiating the suburbs of Louga, we were nabbed by the police.

Having taken a wrong turn down a boulevard clogged with buses and trucks and all manner of obstacles, I'd profited from a break in the oncoming traffic by making a U-turn, a manoeuvre requiring me to drive over the central reservation. Why not? Everybody else did. Only, the whistle that followed such rash behaviour was shrill and long and its authority quite unmistakable. We were enthusiastically flagged to the side of the road by a policeman's truncheon and I, as the miscreant, marched inside the hut at the edge of the busy road. The interior of the hut was dark, oppressively hot and very untidy.

'This is a big fine, *Monsieur*,' the policeman muttered, slumping in a chair at a desk littered with piles of grubby paperwork.

For some minutes the policeman conducted a conversation with his colleague, who was slouched at an opposite desk sporting an identical pile of grubby paperwork. He was in no hurry. This was all part of the softening up process, and so I took advantage of the moment to surreptitiously delve in my bag, pretending to look for something, and all the while attempting to part the smaller denominated notes from the larger ones, making them easily accessible. I could hardly negotiate from a position of strength if I was observed leafing through wads of CFA, in order to pay whatever fine he deemed appropriate.

All of a sudden I was aware the talking had stopped. I ceased rummaging and looked up. The policeman had one eye on my bag, the other on me. I had a strong sense he knew what I was up to.

'*Combien?*' he snorted.

How much? I was taken aback by his opening gambit. What did he mean, how much?

'It's your fine,' I replied in my faltering French. 'You say how much.'

His eyes rolled with theatrical boredom. '*Cinquante mille!*' he snapped.

'*Cinquante mille?*'

'Eh!' he exclaimed, looking away. Muttering to his colleague, he slid a piece of paper from one pile to the other without even looking at it.

'*C'est trop cher*,' I told him.

Another piece of paper moved from one side of the desk to the other. The policeman cast me a sideways look, '*Trente mille, alors!*'

'*Trente mille?*'

We settled on five thousand CFA, about five pounds and twenty pence. The money went straight in his pocket.

'Where are you going?' the policeman asked, the official business satisfactorily concluded.

'To Ghana.'

'EH! Ghana is a long way.' He smiled broadly, ushering me from his office.

Outside the hut, the policeman leapt among the oncoming traffic, his truncheon thwacking a gap in the hooting line. I was quick to take it.

'*Bon voyage!*' he bellowed with a wave.

By evening we'd arrived at La Somone, a town just to the south of Dakar. La Somone is on the Petite Côte. Located at the quieter end of what is known as Senegal's Côte d'Azur, it is nevertheless a favourite destination for the French holidaymaker. If the hotel we stayed the night at was rundown, its location beside the beach was unrivalled. A Senegalese man sauntering along the shoreline told us how the whole of the coast was one long party in the summertime.

'Now it is quiet,' he said. 'But the French, they like it here very much.'

In many ways, it seemed both extraordinary and

saddening the number of Senegalese piling into those wooden pirogues, filled ten to the dozen, risking their lives on the precarious journey to mainland Europe, in search of the land of milk and honey. Senegal has one of the strongest growing economies in West Africa. On the face of it, here was a country of opportunity, with a vibrant people capable of making something of it.

Wandering back to our hotel, the sun already melting into the Atlantic, I glanced over my shoulder. The sea spume masked Dakar and Gorée Island some forty kilometres across the sea to our north-west. Many of the African Association's early explorers commenced their adventures from the old fort on Gorée Island. It gave them their first taste of the privations to come.

In June 1788, a select group of gentlemen gathered for dinner at the St Alban's Tavern, a public house close to London's Pall Mall. Aristocrats and politicians, industrialists and soldiers, adventurers and explorers, though their social standing and interests varied, they were bound by a longing to validate tales of an African city paved in gold, a city rumoured to be the capital of a mighty empire.

This was the age of Enlightenment. Remarkably detailed images of the moon had been studied and digested, the Arctic Regions trampled and analysed, and Australia pawed and dissected, yet no accurate maps existed of Africa much beyond the coastline. What they unfurled before them presented swathes of blank paper, accompanied by drawings of mythical beasts.

The assembled company resolved once and for all to overcome such ignorance, and on that very evening in 1788 the African Association was conceived for the specific purpose of promoting the discovery of the interior parts of Africa.

Before the year was out two geographical missionaries were commissioned to pursue the committee's ultimate goal: the discovery of the fabled city of Timbuktu – Africa's El Dorado.

John Lucas carried instructions to head south from Tripoli across the Sahara Desert. Lucas was a man already acquainted with the ways of North Africa. In his early twenties, Lucas had been captured by Barbary corsairs during a voyage from Cadiz to England. Sold to the court of Moroccan Emperor Sultan Sidi Muhammad, he spent the next three years there before securing his release. Making his way home via Gibraltar, General Cornwallis, the Governor of the Rock, persuaded Lucas to return to Morocco as British vice-consul. The young man had been returning to his father's wine business in England. Instead, he agreed to go back to the emperor's court, where he remained for a further sixteen years of his life.

The second man to be retained by the committee was to sail for Egypt and make his way from the east. His name was John Ledyard, a man already famous as the newly independent America's first explorer, and for whom ambitious journeys were manna from heaven.

Despite both men's undoubted qualities neither of them was to be a match for Africa. By late November 1788, and after three months spent in Cairo preparing his passage, John Ledyard suffered a recurring problem of the bowels, a predicament most travellers to Egypt are familiar with even to this day. Confident of his preparations Ledyard was keen to get going and had no time for personal weakness. Self-administering an overly generous dose of sulphuric acid, he chased it down with a tartar emetic, a toxic substance he no doubt hoped would remedy his ailment. And, in a manner of speaking, it did. His intestines steadily disintegrated and within days he lay dead.

John Lucas fared little better than his colleague. With the aid of the Bashaw of Tripoli's donkey, and in the company of a couple of wily traders from the Fezzan, Lucas managed to reach the coastal town of Mesurata, some two hundred kilometres in the opposite direction from Timbuktu. Several months after having left England he arrived back in London, declaring how he no longer wished to be an explorer.

As I stared in the direction of Gorée Island, I tried to conjure up a connection with Major Daniel Houghton, the African Association's third geographical missionary. Houghton had been suffering a run of bad luck. There were rumours of mounting debts. In 1778, he'd had to sell the company in his father's old regiment to keep the bailiffs from the door. Scouting for employment, he settled for a job in Madras as an engineer. However, on the way to India war broke out between Britain and France, forcing his boat to put in at Gorée Island, then occupied by the British military. The departure of the former Fort-Major, having either died of disease, or bought himself a promotion in a less hostile climate, meant Houghton was offered the position the moment he stepped ashore. Most might have run a mile from this accursed outpost. Houghton had a wife and children to feed: he grasped the opportunity with both hands.

He remained on Gorée Island from 1779 to 1783, and while there made forays to the Gambia, witnessing first-hand the valuable trade conducted by Europeans along the river. Back in England he approached the British Government in the hope of garnering support for his ideas of forging trade links further inland. He also made the case to the Committee of the African Association, and in Houghton they felt sure was a man who could further their goals.

Engaged by the African Association, Houghton returned to Africa in November 1790. He carried specific instructions to proceed up the Gambia River for as far as he was able. He was to then travel overland to Hausa. On the way, he was to mark the rise and course of the Niger River, all the way to its end, and to determine to the best of his ability the whereabouts of Timbuktu.

'How many men should I have at my disposal?' would have sounded a reasonable question from Houghton.

'We rather thought you'd have a go on your own,' Henry Beaufoy, secretary of the African Association, declared,

The task being asked of Major Houghton was quite extraordinary – almost suicidal. Most men would have likely declared it impossible. Houghton, however, was hungry to better his lot.

'When can I start?' was no doubt the major's enthusiastic response.

Following a three-week voyage from England Major Houghton's vessel dropped anchor at the mouth of the Gambia River. He set about loading gifts into a pirogue and immediately reacquainted himself with the King of Barra. Having secured the king's blessing Houghton sailed upriver to the premises of Dr John Laidley, a British trader based at Pisania. There, Laidley assisted the major in securing the services of a translator and a servant, finding him a number of pack animals, and the stores needed for the start of his journey. Within days of reaching Pisania, Houghton was once again on the move. But his progress was to be dogged by calamities.

After a few days ride the explorer and his small party arrived at the town of Medina. Feasting on roast mutton and an abundance of palm wine, King Jatta requested the major identify a suitable location where a fort might be built for the monarch and his court. Houghton grasped the task with his usual enthusiasm, passing long days in the saddle scouting the local countryside. Finally, he fell in love with Fattatenda, a place of grassland, streams and bounteous game. Whilst penning a letter to his wife, outlining the new life he'd dreamt up for his family in Fattatenda, a fire raged through Medina. In the ensuing inferno, the major lost much of his stores, and worse still, all his scientific equipment. Now, no matter where he went, he could no longer accurately record his findings.

Some might have called it a day and gone home – not Major Houghton. He recovered what equipment he could still put to use and plodded eastward, in the direction of Barra Kunda. In Barra Kunda he sought out the blacksmith, where he hoped to replace his destroyed musket. A less desperate man might have left the relic presented to him on the shelf it came from. When the major later pulled the trigger, the weapon exploded in his hands. His equipment destroyed by fire, a musket disintegrating in his hands – what more could possibly go wrong?

If the explorer hadn't previously believed in bad luck visiting in threes, then he soon must have. For as he lay on his bed that night, shards of steel and wood being plucked from his flesh, his interpreter stole three of his five pack animals and hot-footed it back to the coast.

Undeterred, Houghton and his manservant joined a slave trader's caravan heading east. In the ensuing days, he shed his European clothes in favour of robes and bought himself supplies with beads, buttons and poems he'd written on scraps of paper. Along the way, he came face to face with Mumbo Jumbo, witchdoctors and juju; dodged the packs of hyenas and prowling lions out in the bush; drank water from a *soofroo* full of sludge, beetles and fluke; ate couscous and gristle and gnawed old bones; lanced his boils and dressed his sores. On the way, he mingled with groups of *solinama*, recently circumcised adolescents, who sang him songs. Later, he met an Arab, who told him the Niger flowed eastward (which was contrary to everything he'd heard in London), followed later by *jilly keas*, itinerant singing men, who warbled tales of war barring the road ahead.

In between scribbling in his journal, the major trudged, rode and limped through the Great Wilderness, after which he waded the River of Gold, making a beeline for Ferbanna, and the King of Bambuk. Thankfully war between the kingdoms of Bondo and Bambuk had by then ceased, though he stumbled through the gates of Ferbanna sweating, delirious and barely remaining upright. When the major recovered from his fever, he spent many hours in the king's hut fattening up on corn beer and mutton.

Bambuk had lost the war against Bondo, the king informed the explorer, on account of their inferior weaponry. His opponent, the King of Bondo, purchased his muskets from the British traders plying the Gambia River, while Bambuk's armaments were traditionally supplied by the French, who had a fort at St Joseph, on the Senegal River. The Revolution sweeping France had disrupted the supply of weapons and the merchants of death no longer visited. On hearing this, Houghton sniffed opportunity. He penned a missive to the African Association. Back in London, Henry Beaufoy MP, Quaker, and member of the Society for the Abolition of Slavery, barely disguised his enthusiasm at the opportunity to sell a few guns to the Africans. Houghton, with an eye to his future plans, was happy to oblige where he could in any forthcoming commercial enterprise. But first of all, he had a river to find.

In Ferbanna word spread concerning the explorer's quest to reach the Niger. Many a local scratched his head, perplexed by this strange *nasrani* dressed in the robes of an Arab. Were there no rivers in Britain to admire? they asked him. In the market one day a trader by the name of Madegammo sidled up to Houghton. He offered to lead the explorer to Timbuktu. Only, his price was too steep. Houghton negotiated hard: if the trader got him to Timbuktu, and safely back to Pisania, he promised the good Dr Laidley would discharge the explorer's obligations. Madegammo agreed to the deal.

Major Houghton, cock-a-hoop at the arrangement, swapped his two asses for a horse, and the rest of his charred goods for a purse of gold dust. The following morning, he was on his way once again.

The details of what became of Major Houghton after leaving Ferbanna are sketchy. It seems he crossed the kingdom of Kaarta (the kingdom of Kaarta was in modern day Mali, some two hundred kilometres to the east of Kayes) arriving at a settlement called Simbing. From there he sent Dr Laidley a note: he was in good health, had been robbed of virtually everything he possessed, and was continuing to Timbuktu. There was no mention of what had become of his guide, Madegammo.

Three years later, during his own quest to discover the Niger, Mungo Park followed in Houghton's footsteps. He learnt how the major had turned north after Simbing, in the company of a party of Moors. The direct route to Timbuktu had become too dangerous, on account of tribal warfare. Park speculated that after being robbed for a second time and then abandoned by the Moors guiding him, the

Irishman had tried to find his way back to Jarra. On the way he reached a well, but the people who controlled the well refused him water. Whether Houghton's indomitable spirit was finally crushed by the elements, or at the hand of murderers, is to this day unknown. Sadly, the riches he'd dreamed of in Fattatenda for him and his family were never to be realised.

AT THE GAMBIAN BORDER, we were met by a former bouncer from a night club in Leeds. As we pulled up beside the immigration office, a grey, single storey building, he chuffed towards us like a small locomotive. He was the archetypal heavy: broad-chest, no neck, a menacing gaze and his clothes a size too small. His name was Aboulaye. He was an old buddy of JP's.

Having tired of knocking heads on a wet Saturday night in Yorkshire, Aboulaye returned home to the Gambia, bagging himself a job in the republic's immigration department. He was a genial fellow, despite first appearances. After a round of vigorous handshakes, he gathered our passports in a manner that was a hundred times more obliging than the immigration officers we'd met hitherto and, in the blink of an eye, we were legitimate, fully subscribed tourists of the Republic of Gambia.

After clearing customs and immigration, guile and determination ensured we made the last ferry of the day to Banjul. An unruly gathering, including a queue of lightweight trucks, overloaded pickups and the ubiquitous *Sept-place* taxis, lined the quayside at Barra, waiting to board. We noticed the groups of youths meandering through the crowds. One after the other they approached us, wanting money for their fictitious football teams.

'We need shirts,' they cried, 'and boots...and footballs.'

Others didn't even bother with this apparently common ruse. They just wanted the money, plain and simple.

Throughout this horde of waiting passengers there seemed a general understanding that not everyone was going to make it aboard the approaching ferry. I gripped the steering wheel as fiercely as the rest of them. There was no room here for a well-mannered Englishman among this lot. In Africa, the faint-hearted are left on the quayside. That evening Sally, the wife of one of JP's employees, had promised us a supper of *yassa poisson*, a local favourite of spiced fish. We needed to gain a few places in the line if we were to keep our rendezvous with Sally, and so we deployed our secret weapon. Aboulaye lumbered into the crowd, hustling with unseen people. Pondering the likelihood of having to camp in the bush surrounding Barra, an arm popped above the heads, waving us forward.

The ferry eased into the shallows. The ramp slapped down on the riverbank. The pedestrians and vehicles surged forward.

All aboard!

We arrived at JP's house in pitch darkness, slowly descending the track leading to the beach. His was the only dwelling on the beach and the last three hundred metres required a blast across the sand, our headlights revealing a line of baobab trees running parallel to the escarpment. We were happy to have made it, relieved to feel the warm wind blowing humid and sticky off the sea, to see the silver waves crashing along the shoreline. A lantern glowed brightly beside the open doorway to the house. The embers of a fire warmed a cooking pot. A whiff of spices, burning charcoal and seawater hung on the breeze.

With the headlights doused the house became a backdrop to flickering shadows. The lady leaning over the pot straightened, the light from the lamp catching the whites of her eyes, and her teeth as she smiled.

'This is Sally,' JP said as we clambered from the vehicle.

THE NEXT MORNING, we visited JP's ice-making plant on the escarpment above the beach. He'd established the plant some years ago, carting all the equipment, the generators, ice-makers, piping and tools from Europe in a shipping container. He sold the ice produced by the plant to the local fishermen and they used it to preserve their catches, in the process ensuring their businesses were more profitable.

We met him there later in the morning, for by the time the rest of us had risen and dressed, JP had been long gone. We found him roaming the cluster of buildings with what might as well have been a post-coital pipe clamped in his jaws. The oil coating his hands and forearms was additional evidence, if any were needed, that his affairs of the heart had well and truly been renewed.

JP was surrounded by his three staff, guys who had been with him through the thick and thin of a challenging environment, and who did their best to keep the show on the road during his long absences in Europe. He broke off whatever he was discussing with his men and gave us the guided tour. In the main building, among the ice-makers and compressors and storage bin, wove a complex web of piping and electrical wiring that never ceased to amaze me. I hold a deep admiration for people like JP, who can come to a place like the Gambia and single-handedly create something like this.

The very last building we visited was the grand finale, the place where the principal objects of JP's ardour were to be found: his harem of generators. They presented themselves freshly painted and polished, still as immaculate as I remembered them from the last time I was here.

'They're working perfectly,' he said, grinning broadly.

'And they look splendid,' I told him.

After the tour, I wandered to the tool shed. I wanted to see if he still had it. Inside, the old Ducati motorcycle lay against the wall. 'What's this still doing here?' I called to JP.

'Ah! Someday I'll get around to fixing it.'

'It has to be a classic. You can't just leave it here.'

'It needs new brake pads and a few other things.'

I rubbed a hand through the dust on its red fuel tank. 'We should fix it up. Then we could ride it back to Europe. That would be a hell of a thing to do.'

'We should do that. One day.'

Outside the tool shed JP's Land Rover stood beneath a lifting frame, a gaping hole under the bonnet where the engine should have been. The last time I'd been in the Gambia with JP we'd used this vehicle to get us around. 'And the Landy?' I asked.

He emptied the bowl of his pipe beside the front tyre. 'There's never enough time for everything,' he said.

From the edge of the escarpment the four of us watched the brightly coloured pirogues fishing beyond the reef. Closer to us, a line of dromedaries bearing half-naked, whooping tourists loped along the shoreline.

'That's Pepe's Camel Safaris,' JP said. (No relation to Camping Pepe, the bongo hunter of Barcelona.)

Apart from the village, JP's house, and a couple of circular huts acting as unofficial bars, the beach was deserted for as far as the eye could see. While it seemed idyllic, what with the pace of development along the coast, the future was uncertain. The fate of the coastal community was similarly in question. It seemed their livelihoods and their traditions were being squeezed, eroded from overfishing on the one side, and on the other, by the unceasing march of the tourist infrastructure. If the resort hotels continue their expansion, in time, the bay will become increasingly sought after by developers. How could the local community resist them? The simplicity of their lifestyle would be gone forever. And what of JP's ice plant and the role it serves? Would the developers also bring to an end the hard work of a pioneering businessman?

Later that day we drove to Banjul, the capital city of the Gambia. On the way to the city we were stopped at two police checkpoints. In contrast to the more despotic elements of Gambian officialdom, there was an almost child-like manner to the police, both men and women, to whom we handed our papers. They tittered as they leafed through the pages. 'Have you a present for us?' they asked.

'Not today.'

'Ah! Never mind.'

Each occasion we drove along that road it was the same characters on duty. When we came to leave, two days later, we were on first name terms with them all. This was the tourist face of the Gambia – the light touch. With the coastal resorts developing so fast, the country has come to rely on the tourist dollar. Be it birdwatchers or adventure seekers, family holidaymakers or big-game fishermen, in a country which counts peanuts as one of its chief exports, tourism is a key component in swelling the coffers. Even sex tourism gets a look in in the Gambia. In contrast to the norm, however, it's the white, middle-aged women who are the predominant predator, observing from their sun-beds on the beach the daily parade of muscled young Africans hoping for a ticket to Europe. In West Africa, it seems everybody is looking for a way out.

In Banjul, having made a number of left and right turns down sand-blown streets, circled the only two roundabouts in the country, elicited a lot of honking of horns, and attracted a notably dark glare from a policeman, we managed to find a place to park in the busy harbour area, shunting ourselves between two trucks.

Banjul can be visited in half a day; it is compact, and there's not much to it. Highlights are few and far between. When you learn that the Ministry of Tourism considers a large concrete arch, Arch 22, to be one of them, you know you're not in for much of a treat. Beware, however: only the Head of State is permitted to drive beneath Arch 22. Penalty for abuse is probably to rot in the prison we'd passed on the way in.

As we loitered in the shade on the corner of Nelson Mandela Street and Ecowas Avenue, swigging from bottles of coke, I was not convinced the phrase "it's seen better days" could be applied to sepia-toned Banjul, for I was pretty sure it hadn't. There was a more than even chance it had always been a non-entity. I reckon Major Houghton most probably saw it at its best, in 1790, when there was nothing more than an orchard of fruit trees.

Many of the Gambia's private enterprises have followed a trend of relocating down the coast, away from the capital. They've left behind a smattering of crumbling colonial-era buildings, some seedy hotels, a few shipping offices, a lot of warehouses, and the usual collection of Indian and Lebanese retail outlets, their suitcases, wood carvings, leather belts and trinkets busily marching into the street, forcing pedestrians to totter between a chaotic road and the open sewer running beside it. Having said that, the guidebook's description of a sleepy seaport belies the hotbed of activity occupying its streets and alleyways, not to mention its principal market, Albert Market, where the human flow naturally washed us.

Back at the car we discovered a truck blocking our exit. It wasn't a problem. We'd been travelling for three weeks by then, increasingly able to resign ourselves to events. We were cool. We waited in the shade, watching them unload the truck with a remarkable turn of speed. In the blink of an eye a sea of undulating, king-sized foam mattresses extended in a single wave across the street, from the back of the truck to the depths of the warehouse. They laboured with all the diligence of an army of soldier ants carting away a loaf of sliced bread. On the side-lines a fat Lebanese barked orders.

'We need one of those,' JP said.

'You mean a mattress?' I asked. Just to be on the safe side.

'Yeah, a mattress.'

When it came to wild-camping, the sleeping arrangement for JP and Susie was no more than a rudimentary affair. It consisted of unravelling a canvas awning attached to the side of the roof-rack, securing it with a series of poles and guy ropes, fixing a mosquito net beneath it and then laying the mattress on the area of cleared ground. It was not such a tiresome procedure, except the inflatable mattress we'd brought for them from Europe refused to remain inflated. So far, the Atlantic wind had sent us scurrying for the cover of a roof and four walls, making camping altogether too unpleasant to consider. We expected more opportunities for wild-camping the further we pressed inland. In fact, our budget demanded it. We therefore needed to ditch our inflatable mattress for something more durable.

With a comfortable foam mattress firmly in mind, on the way out of town, we made a stop at the Banjul Bed Emporium, a warehouse with every conceivable bedroom appliance this side of Mumbai.

'We need a mattress,' we told the Indian salesman who came to our assistance.

'We've just received a fine shipment of mattresses from Europe,' he announced. 'Here we have a spring unit, knitted fabric cover, 25mm memory foam filling, five-year g–'

'What about those?' JP pointed at the pile of foam mattresses almost touching the roof. They were very much like the ones we'd watched being unloaded from the truck in Banjul, and vastly more practical than the salesman's proposal.

'Oh, yes, sir. No problem. If this is your ardent wish. They are also a very fine mattress.'

'I'm sure they are.'

'Would sir like a fabric cover?'

'Yes please.'

Watching us from the warehouse doorway, the transaction completed, the salesman suppressed a whimper at the sight of JP chucking his and Susie's new bed, complete with natty nylon cover, on to the roof-rack. We doubled it over, lashing it to the top of the storage box.

It was a relief to stop for a day or two in the Gambia, to grab the opportunity of some routine maintenance, get some order back in the car, read a few pages of a book, to catch up with some much-needed clothes washing. When the girls went to the village to buy bread and eggs, and JP worked at his factory, I gathered a pile of my dirty clothes, brimming with good intention. Washing my clothes was a chore I'd been putting off for too long. I rubbed my chin, circling the bowl of clothing, regarding it from different angles. How was I going to do this with the least possible effort?

It's amazing how much we take for granted a simple thing like running water – or, god forbid, a washing machine. At JP's house, you could wait by the kitchen sink until the termites gnawed your toes off – you would never see a drop of water from the tap. In the outside washroom, you could flush the toilet until the metal rod attached to the ball-cock ground to the size of a matchstick – all you'd achieve was a pathetic squeak. At JP's house water had to be drawn from a well, manfully, with a hemp rope attached to a rubber bucket fashioned from an inner-tube, which quivered as you hauled it up, thus losing half its load.

With no running water and no electricity, it's incredible how much longer it takes to complete the most mundane of tasks. I fixed a clothesline at the side of the house, between a tree and a rusty nail, gathered two empty buckets and made for the well.

That night we went to Aboulaye's house for dinner. We took a gift in the form of a bag of kola nuts bought at Albert Market. Aboulaye's family lived together in the traditional African way, that is to say, four generations of them all existing under the same roof. The single-storey house was in the centre of an expansive compound. We sat outside eating oranges and chatting about our journey, and life in general in the Gambia.

BRITAIN DECLARED the Gambia a British protectorate in 1820. There's a quaint story describing a man-of-war sailing up the river firing its cannon either side; wherever the cannon balls fell on land, so they marked the boundaries of the territory. Unsurprisingly then, the Gambia is a very narrow country. Initially the colony was administered from Sierra Leone, another former British colony further to the south. Sierra Leone was established in 1787 as a haven for freed slaves.

Gradually, with the trade in slaves brought to an end, and the exchange of valuable goods such as ivory and gold much diminished, the administration had to search for other means of generating income to support the colony. They turned to groundnuts, establishing a thriving trade which to this day remains a major export. Finding little else of commercial viability, the British tried to swap the Gambia on a number of occasions. They had no takers.

By 1965, at the time of independence from Britain, the future might have looked extremely dire had it not been for two factors; the international price of peanuts was going through the roof and tourists had taken a liking to the beaches. During a ten-year period, from 1966 to 1976, the number of tourists arriving in the Gambia increased from three hundred to twenty-five thousand. And if the tourist industry provides employment for the local population, it has also sprouted an odious bunch of hangers-on known as "bumsters", young men unfortunately caught in a world of high unemployment and no welfare. They attach themselves to tourists like molluscs to a rock, selling everything from sex and drugs to rock and roll.

Despite its limited scope for future development and opportunity, seventy-five per cent of the labour force was employed in small-scale agriculture. Deforestation was a chronic problem caused by industrial loggers, smallholders clearing land for livestock, charcoal makers selling their bags at the roadside and women simply needing to keep their cooking fires alight. Neither was education providing the much-needed impetus for the majority. An education system was available to all children, always subject to a family's ability to pay the fees and associated costs. Then there was the hurdle of the parents' unwillingness to release their children from domestic chores, and the lack of opportunities for their offspring to earn an income following their schooling.

If a family has insufficient funds to go round, it will be the boys who are favoured over the girls, with many of the girls not reaching secondary level education. Despite government initiatives, literacy for boys was at forty per cent and for the girls it was even lower.

AFTER THE SUN WENT DOWN, Aboulaye led us inside the family house, where an enormous platter of fish, salad and rice was awaiting. None of the family joined us.

'Please enjoy it,' Aboulaye said. 'You are our guests.'

The next day I had the maps spread across the bonnet. We had to be in Essakane for the 7th January and despite the Michelin map 741 showing a major road running all the way from the Senegalese border to within a couple of hundred kilometres of Timbuktu, we had absolutely no idea of its condition and, as a consequence, no clue how long it would take us to get there. The harsh seasonal weather, coupled with the enormous loads some of the trucks were hauling across country, resulted in the roads disintegrating extremely rapidly. The road from Senegal through to Mali was held up as one of the busiest freight routes in West Africa. It was time to get moving. Our sojourn in the Gambia was coming to an end.

We left JP's house by mid-morning the following day, heavily loaded with fresh supplies. Even our one hundred litre water tank was pressed to the rim, this extra load exacerbating my growing obsession over the weight we were expecting the Hilux to carry. Sneaking a look at the suspension, I could see there was no upward curve left in the rear leaf springs; on the contrary, they exhibited a notable sag. Already both the rear U brackets holding the cluster of leaf springs had struck the underneath of the chassis, popping the rivet that attached the bracket to the lower leaf spring. The situation wasn't critical, just an indication of the stresses we were applying to the suspension. I re-set the brackets, fixing them in place with several straps cut from an old inner tube. I followed that by packing chunks of tyre, a plentiful commodity on African roads, including a redundant pair of flip-flops, between the leaf spring and the chassis, to cushion any further impact. It was an awful bodge; it would have to do.

During our preparations of the last twenty-four hours we'd heard of difficulties obtaining supplies further up the river. The rumours proved correct at Brikama, where we tried to buy a loaf of bread. Earlier in the morning there had been a riot due to a wheat shortage. No matter where we wandered in the market there wasn't a crumb to be had. In fact, there wasn't very much of anything. What we did find was a *fourneau* – hundreds of them, to be precise; big, small and all sizes in between.

Fourneau is the French word for stove, though such a label might be a tad overdone for the contraption I tied to the roof-rack. That said, what the *fourneau* lacked in looks was amply compensated by its efficiency. It was a basic, one-piece barbeque, knocked together from reclaimed tin. Its height was not much more than thirty centimetres, and its maximum width slightly more again. A square column, one side open for ventilation, was set on a flat base. Above the column was a square container, the four sides tapering inward to a vented plate, on which the charcoal burnt. Its principal advantage over the standard campfire lay in the short time it took to get it to a cooking heat and the ability to rotate it to catch the wind, thereby controlling the flow of air, and subsequently the heat of the coals. In West Africa, every household worth its salt has a *fourneau*. This simple contraption proved to be one of our best pieces of kit.

Shortly after leaving Brikama we encountered yet another police checkpoint, this time manned by a particularly gruff character. He asked us where we were from and where we were going. Two of his colleagues observed us from the roadside, carbines hanging from their shoulders.

'Have you something for me?' he uttered somewhat menacingly.

There is never an easy way of telling men with guns you have no intention of giving them anything. Generally, we had learnt that an equally abrupt response often did the trick, even if it detained us a little longer. Despite their firepower and ill-humour, we felt it necessary to continue making a stand against their demands.

'Nothing,' we responded, softening it with a smile and a shrug of the shoulders.

'Give me all your documents,' he growled.

After Brikama the tarmac road was strafed with potholes, some as deep as bomb craters; a B52 couldn't have done a better job of taking the road apart. The rough condition forced us to reduce our speed to no more than twenty kilometres an hour in order to preserve our vehicle. Potholes make the perfect Sleeping Policeman, unless you are the driver of a car belonging to one of the NGO's, the non-governmental organisations, all of which clattered past with indecent haste.

After a couple of hours in an African version of a cake

mixer, we rumbled off the main road, following a track towards the river. Beside the river, we found Tendaba Camp, formerly a hunting lodge during the 1970's.

Tendaba Camp sits between the river and a rowdy village and could have occupied a gang of joiners and plumbers for several months. That said, to slump in a seat at the bar adjacent to the Gambia River, a bottle of chilled Jul Brew beer cooling your hand, was to really appreciate the beauty of the setting. It was then a matter of trying to ignore the screeches emanating from the United States Peace Corps, an over-excited group of college graduates who'd all but raised the Stars and Stripes in their sheer dominance of the place.

At the bar, we met a guy called Robert, a British expat who'd established a business in the Gambia two years ago. From his camp outside Banjul he ran escorted bird-watching tours. He was doing pretty well, by all accounts. At precisely four o'clock in the afternoon he ushered his four clients, a shambling collection of floppy bush hats and high-powered cameras, on to one of the camp's small boats.

'You want to get out there,' he called over his shoulder. 'It's wonderful.'

We took Robert's advice, hiring one of the boats for ourselves. It was exciting to be out on the river, to imagine that I was seeing pretty much the same as Daniel Houghton had observed on his trip up to Pisania, just over two hundred years ago. I speculated on what might have been going through his mind as he journeyed up the river. Was he in the least fearful of what lay ahead? On engaging Houghton's services Henry Beaufoy had described him to the committee as appearing inaccessible to fear. Yet, completely alone, he was heading into a vast land that was largely unknown, a world of hearsay, of obscure kingdoms and cultures, of skirmish and banditry, with no backup, and carrying the burden of responsibility put upon him by the African Association, not to mention his own ambitions. I should imagine he was terrified.

With a twist of the throttle, our boat driver urged us across the river, to the northern bank, and we entered the Bao Bolong Wetland Reserve. In the soft breeze and warm sun, we chugged lazily along the network of waterways, beneath the canopy, where Brown-Necked parrots clicked and warbled, through mangrove forests, salt marshes and savannah woodland. At one point a croc slipped silently beneath the surface ahead of us, the ripples swelling outward, disappearing beneath the prow of the boat.

The 220 km^2 reserve is home to both Nile and Dwarf crocodiles, hippos and manatees, and its verdure refuge to the Gambia's rarer birds, such as the Pel's fishing owl, the African fish eagle and ospreys. The land-based predators are noted as hyena and jackal and, if you look *exceptionally* carefully, perhaps even leopard.

By the time we returned to camp it was dark and our stomachs were rumbling.

In the dining room the Peace Corps had annihilated the buffet.

A PATTERN of sorts quickly emerged, delineated by the changing colours of the road. For a kilometre or two the colour was grey, the tarmac virtually un-blemished. Grey signified harmony, the chance to read a book, to doze, to look out of the window without butting it with your head. Grey was progress – the world was good.

Then it was black, a few metres at most; an ill-omen. Black was lip-curling; it made the shoulders knot, brought a groan to the throat. Black was the broad skid marks and chunks of shredded rubber just before ochre.

Ochre was always several centimetres lower than black, and arrived with a thump. Ochre was the colour of the earth and it stretched in a dispiriting line for kilometre upon kilometre. A fine, orange mist hung over ochre, creating a setting that echoed the aftermath of a bomb-blast. Traffic, what there was of it, weaved from side to side, avoiding the myriad, tiny islands of grey, dipping in and out of the holes and gullies, tyres churning the earth to a powder that masked the colours of the grasses and the trees. To see ochre was to be tossed back and forth at twenty kilometres an hour. It was infuriating and sapped the spirit. Ochre invoked a creeping mania.

At Soma, we turned north for the ferry, for a while following a dirt road cutting through a broad expanse of cleared forest. Petrified tree trunks poked out from the mud, slender and twisted, a memorial to their own existence – dead but not allowing themselves to be forgotten. Later, a man-made inferno was busily ravaging swathes of grass and woodland, while kites whirled and twisted in brown thermals, ever watchful over the fleeing prey. In the wake of the firelighters, the earth smoked, and the trees lay felled and blackened and ready for cutting. What a sight! There was no regard for trees in the clamour for land and the need to fuel the cooking pots. In that fleeting moment, I glimpsed a microcosm of the world. If the earth could weep, surely man would drown in its tears.

At the end of a laterite road lined with traders' shacks the Gambia River flowed silently through this land. It was something of a relief to see it, a therapy that softened the mood and calmed the mind. We followed the horde for as far as we could, waiting beside a group of women dressed in skirts and blouses of vivid colours – lilacs, yellows, greens and reds. By their feet blue plastic bags – mamma sacks, as they were called – bulged with goods. A youth sported a woollen hat pulled down over his ears, even though the temperature was near to thirty degrees centigrade. We bought mangoes and oranges from the woven baskets held aloft, and tepid tins of coke from a toothless man sitting huddled over his cool-box.

Out in the river the blue-hulled ferry, *James Island* painted in tall white letters on its side, approached the quay. A man wearing a white hat and blue coat stood erect at the end of the partially lowered ramp, guiding the captain with movements of his outstretched arms. He had the bearing of a man of great importance, which of course, in the scope of things, he most certainly was. The wall of passengers kept a respectful distance behind him. On the riverside, there was no shortage of customers waiting to board. The Africans are constantly on the move.

The Trans-Gambia highway on the north bank of the river was a much better proposition than its southern brother. At least there the aid money had been put to the correct use. In little time, we were opposite McCarthy Island, where a short ferry ride lands you at the former colonial trading station, Georgetown.

We turned off the road and into the bush moments before the ferry landing, making an overnight stop at the Jangjang Bureh Camp. No matter if it was overrun with puppies and monkeys, beside the river made for a wonderful place to relax and to forget about Gambian roads.

'I think I'm going to bring my boat out from Copenhagen,' JP said between puffs on his pipe. 'I could bring tourists up here from Banjul. I think they'd like it out here.'

'Imagine,' I said, picking up on his theme. 'You could

overnight at Tendaba Camp before moving on to here. And maybe you could set up some fly-camps as well. Do a bit of trekking, bird-watching...take a week over it. What a great adventure. When shall we start?'

'I need to get the boat fixed,' JP replied.

'Ah! You mean it doesn't float or it doesn't start?' I asked.

'It's in a yard.'

'Yeah, along with all the other things,' said Susie.

'What about that truck of yours, the Landy Forward Control?' I probed. 'Last I heard there was a tree growing through it.'

'That's in Spain with my friend, Pete.'

'Does it work?'

'I need to do a few things to it. The engine's sweet; there's nothing wrong with that Perkins engine. And the diffs should be in great shape.'

'And the little Peugeot 504 cabriolet?'

'That's in Spain, too. That could be a nice car. And the Laverda motorbike. I think she's pretty rare. She has a beautiful little engine.'

Susie rolled her eyes. 'You've got to get rid of some of these things, Jean-Pierre,' she said.

Even though JP nodded his head in agreement, it was patently obvious he would not be parted easily from his beloved machines.

The beds inside our round bungalows were the shape of an eighth of a circle, the same shape as the Laughing Cow cheese we'd been eating for more days than we cared to count. It was an observation none of us had overlooked.

During the night, I heard a hippo laughing. He was thrashing in the shallows of the river. I wondered if he was dreaming, and what might make a hippo laugh in his sleep? Maybe it was I who was dreaming. At dawn a monkey rummaged in our thatch roof, scampering back and forth. Each time he moved, particles of dust flashed as they broke the beam of sunlight.

After breakfast, we retraced our route to Wassu, stopping at a police checkpoint to ask the young officer for directions to the border. As if caught by a violent gust of wind the policeman took a sudden step backward as we pulled up beside him, his face crumpling in a look of incomprehension. He gazed for several seconds at Christine sitting in the driving seat. Then at Susie occupying the front passenger seat.

'Good morning,' JP said from the open back window.

The bobby stepped sideways, eyeing JP with a degree of curiosity. 'What are you doing?' he asked.

'We're going to the border,' JP told him.

'No. This is not what I mean. I mean, what are *you* doing...in the back of the car?'

'I'm going to the border.'

'And you let a woman drive you there?'

'Of course! Why shouldn't I?'

'But...'

'You mean you never let your women drive?' Christine asked.

The officer sniggered, shaking his head. 'Never,' he said to JP.

'So, which way is it to the border?' Christine pressed, her fingers drumming the steering wheel.

A second policeman came to stand beside his colleague and was told of our plans. He made a point of resting his hands on the sill of the rear door when he addressed JP. 'Are you going to Senegal?' he asked. In his world, this was clearly not a question for a woman.

'Yes,' JP replied.

'For Senegal, you follow the road to Maka Gouye. It's very easy.'

Follow the road to Maka Gouye – this was easier said than done. Thus far, not one of the dirt tracks exiting the Trans-Gambia highway had displayed any signposts. The tracks simply vanished in the bush without designation, ignored by the wary, travelled by the assured.

'Where *is* the turning to Maka Gouye?' we chanced.

To achieve an answer there was a further trading of words between the two officers, a vague wave or two, some chit-chat about a river and a big tree, and an exchange with a man pushing a bicycle heavily loaded with chopped wood.

'The turning to Maka Gouye is before the bend in the river,' the second officer announced with a flourish. 'Not far from where we are standing right at this moment.'

'Thank you very much.'

'Have you a present for us?'

We were soon to discover that there was no such turning before the bend in the river. And as for a big tree, no tree looked any bigger than another. We took a chance down one of the many dirt tracks, keeping north when the track divided. After about five kilometres the thick bush opened and the track converged with two others beside a pock-marked concrete wall. We stopped a short way from the wall and stood for a moment in the fierce sun. A dog barked. Washing hung limply on a line. Nobody came to enquire what we were doing. We poked around, pushing open the door in the pockmarked wall. Inside the compound stood a bungalow and a topsy-turvy row of buildings built against the outer wall. Chickens pecked at the spare ground. The dog was vociferous but nowhere to be seen. Somebody had definitely been there and now they'd gone. About to leave, we saw the outline of a man sitting in the shade, his sandaled feet planted in the sunshine.

'Is this the border?'

'This is the customs, Monsieur.' A beckoning hand flashed in the sunlight.

The man pushed himself from the chair with what appeared to be the greatest of effort. I couldn't be sure if it was the chair that creaked, or the man's joints. The sandals, seemingly too heavy to lift, left a slug-like trail in the dust as he walked. We followed the man to his office, where he lifted a stamp from the open drawer, rolled it back and forth on the ink pad and placed it sparingly on the papers for the car. He didn't seem to care if we were smugglers, or even if we had a car. He slid the *laissez passer* halfway across the desk, abandoning it beside a typewriter covered in a film of scum. I placed the money beside the document, each taking our due, as if exchanging Cold War spies at Checkpoint Charlie.

'You must go to the police in Koungheul with your passports,' he said, ushering us from his office. We left him to shuffle back to his chair in the shade.

For the next two hours, we struggled to find a way through the bush, the compass our surest guide in that labyrinth of tracks. Save for a single village, whose occupants were of little guidance, and the occasional lone farmer toiling a stretch of scorched land, we saw no one. Our efforts finally yielded the Dakar to Tambacounda road, due in part to hearing the distant noise of growling trucks.

In Koungheul the police weren't interested in our passports, or why we were there.

'Do it in Tambacounda,' they said.

Their attitude was a pleasant change after the Gambia.

In Tambacounda the police weren't interested, either.

The mild irritation of our presence caused the aging, overweight officer to crease his forehead.

'Get them stamped at the border,' he rumbled.

It seemed curious that we should get our entry and exit stamps at the same time and place. Yet, who were we to question such logic – especially in the police station? Behind the policeman, a large cell of wretched, wild-eyed prisoners challenged us. Taut fingers tugged at the bars of the cell and flesh squeezed between the gaps – the town's flotsam and jetsam washed up at the sluice. It was as if the hum, the murmur of their voices, seeped from the walls. The cell to the right contained a single woman. Her clothes were ragged, her hair like black, windblown candyfloss. As we turned our backs to leave she struck up in a guttural, incomprehensible tongue.

In the softening light, we drove out of town, checking in at Le Relais de Tamba, a motel-style property on the outskirts of Tambacounda. The comfortable bedrooms surrounded a swimming pool that, after a day of forty degrees centigrade, required balls of steel to tackle. Parked outside Le Relais de Tamba was an English-registered Mercedes Unimog, converted to an overland vehicle. It had a certain look about it that I felt no bandit would bother to mess with. Sarah, the owner, opened the door to show us the accommodation module behind the cab. It was constructed by the coach-maker Willoughby. Inside it was akin to a small apartment, a quality piece of workmanship, and offering every comfort you could hope for. Sarah was on something of a pilgrimage, she said. She was visiting Mali in memory of a good friend, who had recently died in a motorcycle accident on the road to Bamako. Paul, her companion, lived on the roof in a tent.

'We are not...together,' Sarah announced primly.

Paul was a plumber by trade, and a climber in his spare time. He was going to scale the Hand of Fatima, a rock-face rising two thousand feet above the plain in eastern Mali.

The dusty town of Tambacounda, a trading crossroads of repute, was a hive of noise and activity, no evidence there of the malaise gripping the Western world. We took the opportunity of exchanging an empty bottle of gas, and replenishing the fruit and vegetables at a row of traders' stalls.

The route to the Malian border, and onward to Bamako, is one of the busiest in West Africa. Unsurprisingly, the condition of the road laid waste innumerable trucks and vans, overloaded in their eagerness for profit, or just sheer incompetence. We soon learnt that branches stripped from the surrounding savannah and positioned strategically in the road, indicated yet another breakdown around the corner. Often, we found travellers huddled together in the shade of trees, away from the road, surrounded by their belongings, whilst two or three men laboured beneath a van chocked up on tree stumps, a collection of oily parts strewn beside them. On that road, it wasn't unusual to see a truck driver stripped to the waist, single-handedly hauling the differential to the side of the road where, by hook or by crook, it would be stripped, repaired and put back together again. Not always would somebody come to help. He might be there a day; it might take two weeks. It was for those reasons the side of the road was a storybook of man on the move: makeshift shelters and old campfires; abandoned shoes and cloth fluttering in the breeze; burst tyres and scuffed, oil-stained earth; scavenged carcasses of domestic stock and overturned vehicles; plastic bags clinging to branches and heaps of empty tins catching the sun's glare.

By four o'clock we reached the customs control, a

building set below the road beside the junction. Outside a limp flag barely reached the top of the pole. The drab building shaded a number of men in olive-green uniform. From the junction, a line of trucks led to an iron bridge crossing the Falémé River; Mali stretched out beyond it.

At the border control a queue of drivers were waiting to be processed. We observed them for a while, pondering our next move. It was getting late, perhaps only another hour of sunlight.

We decided to delay our paperwork until the following morning. It would have been dark by the time we'd cleared both borders and the time of darkness is never a good moment to enter a strange country. Searching the map, we identified wild country to the west of the road leading to Bakel. We thought we might secure a place to camp out there.

We drove north for a few kilometres, turning off the road when we were sure there was nobody around to see us. For a while we followed tyre tracks to the west, and then veered north again, weaving between the trees, positioning ourselves in the lee of some low hills. We were camped where the borders of the kingdoms of Bondo, Bambuk and Kasson had converged. I liked to think Major Houghton had been exactly where we were camped – and Mungo Park after him. The land at which I stared cannot have changed since those days and I fancied I could see Park urging his horse through the trees, his assistants Johnson and Demba, and a host of others, in tow. The area was dotted with old campfires – rings of blackened stone. There was no half-burnt wood or tins or paper. Not even a discarded tab end.

We fired up the gas cooker and started a small fire in the last of the light. JP and Susie laid their new mattress beside the car and unfurled the awning. Aperitifs were poured. JP smoked his pipe. For a moment the land, and the khaki-coloured hills, turned a shade of pink. And then the light went like the flick of a switch.

During the night, not long before the wind masked all other sound, the call of jackals drifted from far away. When the wind calmed, a couple of hours before dawn, I heard the muffled sound of hooves, the metallic click of the bit, voices, ropes creaking. It was only my imagination – the ghost of young Mungo was riding through our camp.

IN JUNE 1795 Mungo Park jumped ashore at Jillifree, a village some thirty kilometres upstream from the Gambia's present day capital city of Banjul. Two days later he sailed upriver to seek out Dr Laidley, the African Association's Man in Africa, where, despite the bad air (the *mal' aria*) rising like steam off the rivers, killing the human population in huge numbers, the explorer found Laidley in rude health, his trade in gold, slaves and ivory flourishing.

Within a week of arriving at Pisania, and while out observing an eclipse of the moon, the Scotsman himself succumbed to the "vapours" (the scourge of the mosquito having not yet been discovered). For days he sweated, trembled and rambled, his eyes the weight of musket balls and what must have felt like an axe cleaving open his forehead. Laidley administered various potions, for he'd witnessed Park's symptoms often enough. He assured his guest that all he was suffering from was the seasoning, nothing more than the body adjusting to its new environment, and that in a couple of months he would be as right as rain.

Four months after arriving in Africa Park regained sufficient strength to resume his journey inland. He travelled with an interpreter called Johnson, a Mandingo who had lived seven years in London, and Demba, a lively young manservant from Laidley's own household. They joined a coffle (a caravan of slaves) run by Serawuli traders heading home and, by mid-December, had reached the Kingdom of Bondo.

Where Houghton had taken to disguising himself in robes Park had no time for such nonsense. On his way to an audience with King Isata, Park strutted through the streets of Fatteconda clad in a broad-brimmed hat, blue frock-coat with yellow buttons, a figure-hugging waistcoat and nankeen breeches. Mungo handed over supplies of gunpowder and tobacco, though it was the explorer's umbrella and frock-coat that particularly caught the monarch's eye. King Isata, having relieved the Scotsman of his outer garments, pressed his guest to buy some slaves. The explorer shook his head, telling the monarch he was there only to meet the people. The king peevishly fingered his *saphies* – his lucky charms – for he'd never heard of such queer talk. Why should any man walk the length of Arica merely to meet the people? The sole reason King Isata ever left Fatteconda was to plunder and kill.

While the king scowled at this curious visitor, his wives caressed Mungo's skin, tugged his hair, counted his fingers and pressed his nose. Johnson stepped forward to translate, telling Park that the king's wives thought he was very white. They wondered if he washed in cow's milk.

Two days before Christmas Park and his entourage were back on the trail. The explorer might have lost his blue frock-coat and umbrella to King Isata, but at least he'd gained a bag of gold in exchange. The young Mungo might have rightly allowed himself a smug grin as he trotted deeper into the hinterland of Africa. So far, his expedition was proceeding rather well. All that was set to change.

As he passed through the kingdoms of Kajaaga and Kasson Park's goods were to fall under the covetous gaze of such characters as King Batcheri, Demba Sego Jalla and Tiggity Sego. Gradually his store of gold, tobacco, beads, gunpowder, rolls of cloth and pistols were spirited away. Weighing less by the day, Park and his assistants forged on, surviving on guile, kindness and by knocking at the door of Dr Laidley's debtors.

In the Kingdom of Kaarta, the court of King Daisy was to be the last bastion of generosity for weeks to come. The king slaughtered a sheep in honour of his guest and begged him not to continue with his quest, advising Park that the Kingdom of Kaarta was at war with Bambarra and that the Scotsman, if he continued, was sure to be killed as a spy. The explorer would hear none of it. To appease Daisy, he agreed to make a diversion by heading north, to Ludamar and the land of the Moors.

'The land of the Moors?' the king exclaimed incredulously. 'Then may God preserve your soul.'

Park didn't much like the sound of these northern hooligans and he rested some days in Kemmoo to recover his strength before this imminent encounter. When he crossed the frontier of Ludamar the explorer was surrounded by a gang of Moors, immediately seized in a vice-like grip by a turban-topped warrior, a scar the width of a firebreak streaking through his beard. 'We have orders to take you to Benowm,' the Moor growled at the Scotsman. For the moment, all Park's ideas of a refreshing swim in the Niger River, followed by a wander in the souks of Timbuktu, had to be put on hold.

For nigh on a week Park trudged north in the company of his captors. Slowly but surely the meaningful landmarks, a settlement of tents, the crooked trees, the shrubs and the tufts of grass bending to the wind, the watering holes and all the things suggestive of life became fewer in number, replaced by the sensuous curves of the dunes, the jagged edges of the rocky knolls, dust devils, the vertebrae of camels and the vast plains devoid of relief.

Cresting a dune Park's heart sank into his boots. Ahead of him a collection of flapping tents lay strewn over the bleached plain. Herds of emaciated goats, camels and cattle filled the spaces in between. Robed figures meandered back and forth as if in slow motion. People crowded the wells, filling earthen vats strapped to the backs of asses. What vegetation existed had been stripped bare, left to poke from the earth like the hands of a skeleton. The call of the herdsmen and the cry of children, the bleat and low of animals, the thud of the *paloon* and the clang of the blacksmiths hammer all drifted to Park's ears.

He was led directly to the tent of Ali of Ludamar, who reposed on a black leather cushion and clipped hairs from his top lip. Ali had the few bundles of goods the explorer still possessed emptied over the sand in front of him. When the compass sparkled in the sunlight Ali snatched it up, confounded as to why the needle constantly pointed toward the Great Desert. When Park explained that it pointed to his mother, so that he might always find his way home, the instrument flew from the sovereign's hand like a hot coal; the king wanted nothing to do with a white man's juju.

Nobody was allowed to be indolent in Benowm, save the Moors themselves. Even explorers had to be gainfully employed. Park was given the role of court barber, though when he sliced open the young prince's skull he was banished to his hut, all of his pleas for release rebuffed.

'Queen Fatima is desirous of meeting a white man,' Ali

told him. Until such time as she arrived in Benowm, he would go nowhere.

For the next three months Park didn't fare well at the hands of the Moors of Ludamar. He found them rude and ferocious, their constant torment intolerable. He suffered terribly from the meagre diet and the lack of water, the repeat fevers and delirium, the scorching heat and the sand-winds, the threat of execution or removal of his eyes and, not least, the slow psychological corrosion born of the thought he might never be released. When he finally met Queen Fatima he persuaded her to allow him to travel with Ali and his warriors to Jarra. In the confusion of gathering war clouds Mungo finally made his escape. By then he was both mentally and physically exhausted.

After escaping the clutches of Ali, Park took out his compass and trudged in a south-easterly direction, in the hope of stumbling across the Niger River. He proposed following the river until reaching Timbuktu, though he had no food, no water and no real clue where he was going. Almost without hope, and no more than a few days from Jarra, he climbed a tree standing little higher than his horse. Swaying in the branches he beheld a wilderness of sand and shrub. There was no sun, only an ashen sky and he believed he'd as good as arrived at the end of the world. Distraught, he slithered down the tree, leaving behind shreds of his shirt. Mungo no longer cared. He had what felt like tapioca and crushed glass swimming in his eyes, his lips were fused by a layer of crust and his skin was as wrinkled as the ears of an old elephant. He sank to his knees, a whirl of memories filling his head: emerald-coloured lakes in a sinking June sun, the sweet odour of roses, herding long-horn cattle in the rain, catching butterflies in Sumatra, knocking on Sir Joseph Banks' door in Soho Square, mangrove swamps appearing over the prow of *Endeavour*, Johnson tying a live chicken to the branch of a tree to appease the Spirits of the Woods...

Mungo fell backwards, wheezing. His feet turned numb, and then his hands, followed by his legs and arms and torso. He was done for. The Bean-Nighe was beside him...the "washer women"...the omen of death. The buzzards gathered in the treetops, hooked beaks and naked necks poking from their cloaks. Sure that he was now finished, the explorer started mumbling the Lord's Prayer. And then a fat drop of warm water whacked him in the eye.

Plop! – Plop! – Plop!

The rain drops gouged divots in the earth...more and more of them. The drops became a deluge, and then a flood in which the shrubs turned green, grass sprouted in tufts, trees straightened, the earth sighed and fish slithered out of the mud. Park cackled and the vultures cawed as life returned to the Sahel. The explorer had been saved by the rain.

It took Park a further three weeks to reach the banks of the Niger River. When he got there, he threw his hat in the water and whooped with delight. It was absolutely true what he'd been told numerous times on his journey: the river really did flow east. The only thing left for him to do was get the hell out of there, and tell the world what he'd discovered.

Back in London Park became famous. He wrote a book, *Travels in the Interior of Africa*, met the king, spoke at dinners, and mingled in high society. When the rush of adulation soured, he took himself back to Scotland, becoming a local doctor, a husband and a father. Ultimately, he never settled to his new life. Business in Africa remained unfinished. The termination of the Niger remained unknown; the whereabouts of Timbuktu was still a mystery.

The explorer returned to Africa in 1805, leading an expedition sponsored by the British government. The expedition team included forty-four Europeans, of which thirty-four were soldiers. Only twenty-five per cent of the party remained alive when they reached Bamako, on the banks of the Niger. A combination of disease and hostile engagements had wiped them out. Nevertheless, Park persevered with the construction of a vessel (only one of his six carpenters remained alive), and a modified pirogue, heavily fortified with bullock-hide shields, steadily materialised. As they laboured alongside the banks of the river, every few days another of his men succumbed to fever and died. Some of the bodies were dragged into the bush by wolves before they could even be buried. When the vessel was finished, Park christened it HMS *Joliba* (after the Bambarran name for the river) and loaded it with provisions and an arsenal of weapons. As the three slaves rowed them out into the river only five members of his team remained alive.

By now the Moors had so thoroughly got inside Park's head he couldn't even conceive the idea of putting ashore to visit Timbuktu. Instead he sailed straight past. Any canoe displaying the slightest intention of intercepting them was blasted from the water. Everyone, in Park's mind, had become the enemy. According to Amadi Fatoumi, Park's guide, and the only survivor of the 1805 expedition, Park's vessel was attacked shortly after crossing the frontier at Hausa and those not killed in the skirmish drowned in the rapids at Bussa.

5

MALI

A FOLLY IN THE SAND

I ran over a mobile telephone on the road from Bakel to Kidira. It was early morning, the sun still low in the east. I didn't see the blob of plastic until the very last minute. It made for an unusual addition to our list of road kill.

The Senegal Department of Immigration was to be found in the backstreets of Kidira, in a small, unassuming office. As we turned to leave with our completed paperwork, a Swedish motorcyclist clomped through the doorway, perspiring in his heavy leather boots and padded jacket and trousers. Even at that early hour the sultry heat was up. We asked him where he was going.

'Nairobi,' he asserted. 'Through the Central African Republic.'

I shuddered. He might just as well have announced how he was about to climb into a cage of lions, armed only with a Swiss army knife. The Central African Republic was a country that seemed to have been at war with itself for as long as I could remember. His BMW was parked outside the window. It was covered in boxes and bags and spare tyres.

'Can you get through the CAR?' I pondered aloud. I never cease to wonder at the places people choose to go.

'We'll see,' he said, offering a slightly maniacal grin. I must admit, he looked the type who might jump into a lion cage armed only with a Swiss army knife.

'By the way,' I started, 'have you lost a mobile teleph–'

The rest of the words evaporated on my tongue and I shrank from the Swede's steely glare. Perhaps I shouldn't mention the flattened mobile phone. His was a look leaving me in no doubt he would get to Nairobi.

'Never mind,' I mumbled. *Bon courage, mon ami.*

By mid-morning formalities had been dealt with on both sides of the border without a hitch. Despite the advice of the Paris Automobile Club, our *carnet de passage*, the internationally accepted temporary vehicle importation document, had yet to see the light of day. At Mali customs, just as with the other countries we'd passed through, it was far easier to buy their own temporary import document, than attempt to cajole them into looking at the carnet. Here, it cost CFA 15000, the equivalent of about fifteen pounds. The money joined a nest egg in a metal box in a drawer.

The tarmac road from the border stretched before us in a smooth black line, a stark contrast to what we'd left behind in Senegal. It was the tonic we needed for a long day's drive. Youssou N'Dour's album *Nothing's in Vain* played in the CD player. I turned up the volume and sooner than expected we arrived in Kayes, a hot and dusty town nicknamed "the pressure cooker of Africa" on account of its searing temperatures. Kayes has the distinction of being promoted as the hottest town in Africa, with average daily temperatures of 35° centigrade. The cause is attributed to the high concentration of iron in the surrounding hills, which reflects the sun's heat. The journey from Tambacounda to Kayes had taken us twenty-four hours to complete. In 1796, it took Mungo Park eighteen days.

Kayes lies at the western boundary of what was once the Ghana Empire (not to be confused with today's Ghana, the country to the south of Mali). Founded by Soninke-speaking peoples in the tenth century, the Ghana Empire is considered to be the first of the great Sudanic empires. Early accounts of it are attributed to Arabic chroniclers and geographers of the eleventh century. The kingdom covered an area of today's north-west Mali, and its power was based on its control of the gold fields of Bambuk and Baré. Arabic geographer Abu Ubayd Abd Allah al-Bakri wrote of the city of Ghana as being divided into two towns, one comprising Muslim merchants from the north, including twelve mosques and various imams, muezzins and scholars, and a second town some six miles distant, home to the monarch's court, where the king resided amongst sorcerers, religious idols and the tombs of his forefathers.

While the rulers of the empire clung to their animist beliefs (the attribution of a living soul to plants, inanimate objects and natural phenomena), their success in integrating both Islam and the Muslim traders within Soninke society was key to their prosperity. This happy state of affairs drew the covetous eyes of the Almoravids, Berber's who ruled Morocco to the north. The Almoravids wished to seize control of the gold supply for themselves, and to convert the *kafir* rulers of the Ghana Empire to Islam.

Whether the Almoravids ever conquered the empire is disputed by historians. Along with drought, they weakened its dominance of the region during a time when the empire's easterly neighbours grew in economic power – the Ghana Empire's death knell had chimed.

To this day, the Soninke attribute the collapse of the empire to the legend of Bida, a seven-headed snake who guaranteed the kingdom's prosperity, provided the snake was offered a virgin girl once every year. On the eve of the sacrifice legend tells of how the girl's suitor rushed forward and slaughtered the snake. With a dying breath, the snake pronounced a curse on the kingdom. Thereafter, the rainfall ceased, the lands dried and cracked, the cattle perished, and the Soninke dispersed over distant lands.

Languishing for many years as a forgotten corner of Mali, thanks to the construction of a railway running between Dakar and Bamako, the fortunes of Kayes improved during the twentieth century, becoming a major centre for gum arabic, a gum exuded by certain acacia trees and used in glues and incense, and by the pharmaceutical industry.

Stopping for lunch at a restaurant in Kayes, we toyed with the idea of staying the night, enabling us to explore more of what the town had to offer. After all, it had once been the French capital of Upper Senegal and Niger, and a considerable colonial trading hub. Even to this day Kayes remains an important commercial centre for Mali. We pulled out the guide book and scouted the local accommodation. However, it soon became apparent, on account of a cultural festival, there was no accommodation to be had anywhere in the town.

We pushed on, crossing the bridge over the Senegal River, and headed east. Marginally downriver from this bridge Mungo Park crossed to the other side in what he described as a "dangerous passage-boat". It overturned shortly after leaving the shore, pitching him full length into the water.

The improved road conditions put a smile on all our faces. There was not a pothole to be found. Not even a dimple. We were cruising through a country of savannah and rolling hills. For kilometre upon kilometre the road sliced an unblemished path through the bush. Every now and again a settlement, marginally set back from the road, appeared in a clearing. They were no more than a cluster of circular mud huts with conical, thatched roofs. Many seemed deserted, save for an outline of a lone figure hiding from the sunlight, a pall of smoke spiralling upwards from a cooking fire, or the patches of recently tilled land.

We came upon large herds of cattle and sheep stripping bare the countryside, as if in competition to establish which of them could wreak the most destruction on a land already chronically overgrazed, and this in a country that raises more goats, sheep and cattle than any other in West Africa, save for Nigeria. Never far from their animals were boys with switches loitering in the shade of the trees. When we passed them, shouts of '*toubab!*' and '*cadeaux!*' carried in the dust devils pirouetting across the road. Periodically, bloated livestock lay dead in the stain of their own fluids, amongst conspicuous skid marks, shattered glass and discarded vehicle parts.

Though as much a part of domestic life in Africa as goats and cows, it was rare to see a chicken as road kill. They've adapted well to the intrusiveness, becoming extra-ordinarily agile in the process. An African chicken covers fifty metres quicker than you can crow "cock-a-doodle-doo". When in full flight from the wheels of a speeding car, they strike a great similarity to a furiously peddling cyclist, hence they are known as *poulet bicyclette*, or bicycle chicken. As a consequence of this constant bustle back and forth, to eat a *poulet bicyclette* demands a keen hunger, a sharp knife and a healthy determination.

Not far from each village, vast areas of land had been cleared of trees and scrub to make way for cultivated fields, the axe and hoe sparing only the willowy palms, the stout baobabs, the occasional acacia and the Karité tree. The Karité tree is a valued resource in West Africa. The oil-rich nuts of the Karité tree are roasted and then pounded, placed in large cauldrons and cooked over an open fire. The nuts ooze a rich oil, and when cooled it has the soft, creamy texture of butter. Known as Karité, or shea butter, it is commonly used in cooking. The European cosmetics industry has a particular liking for it.

The road ahead was punctuated by clusters of traders' shacks, established to service the abundant travellers. More often than not they materialised from a shroud of dust, exhaust fumes and charcoal smoke. At one such watering hole we all clambered from the heat of the car for a break. The dry, hot wind quickly un-stuck the shirt from my back as I watched a mini-bus thundering down the road towards us, the shape of its cargo wobbling in the heat shimmering off the tarmac. It was just like one of the many we'd come across all morning. The mini-bus slowed to walking pace, touting for business. A ticket-boy hung from the open sliding-door, his hand thrust outward, the composition of his fingers and thumb apparently signalling their destination, his sharp calls and hisses competing with the general roadside clamour. The mini-bus was painted white and green, with BAMAKO EXPRESS in blue letters down the side. An orange tarpaulin covered the roof cargo, from which poked the head and neck of a bleating sheep. Inside, a cluster of human heads, some wrapped in brightly-coloured cloth, others in woollen hats, waited patiently for the journey to recommence.

Out on the roadside, in less time than it took to angle my hat against the sun, we were mobbed by banana hawkers, girls thrusting bags of nuts at our mid-riffs, knots of grubby kids screeching to shake our hands, meat-sellers with a bargain, a chancer or two, and even patrons of the numerous cafes offering coffee and tea, their shelves stacked with chocolate, Johnson's baby shampoo and bars of Coal Tar soap and Colgate toothpaste. Each one of them vied fiercely for our attention. We exchanged words, a jostle, a scowl – *'j'ai déjà des fruits....merci...non, pas pour moi...les noisettes?...ca coute combien pour le petit sac?...non, je n'ai pas de stylo pour toi...eh, arrêtez... pardon...excusez moi...donnez moi un petit sac de noisettes, alors...oui...un café ?...oui, Monsieur, pourquoi pas...'* and so it went on.

JP immediately set a bearing for the butcher's stall. There, a youth wafted flies from the mottled carcasses hanging beneath a corrugated-iron roof propped up by four spindly poles. Behind him, a second youth hacked a chunk of meat into cubes on a trestle table. With each whack of the blade a swarm of flies briefly left their feast of dried blood. When he'd finished chopping, the youth picked over the cubes, feeding them one by one to a blackened grill. He already had his eyes on JP, no doubt calculating the price a *toubab* might pay for a handful of meat. He shouted at the men gathered round, the several generations who hovered beside the aroma of roasting flesh. They parted to let JP through, exhibiting a collective look of curiosity, deference and perhaps envy.

In the shade of a café, no more than a wooden lean-to,

we perched on a rickety bench, observing the patron's wife produce our cups of coffee. Filling a dented kettle, she set it to boil on the coals. Instant coffee and powdered milk were spooned into chipped mugs and, after the steaming water had been tipped into each of them, she used the spoon and an impressive wrist action to whisk a frothy head on each of the drinks. I'd witnessed earlier how the Africans of the sub-Sahara had a fondness for whisking their coffee, requiring a particularly vigorous motion to achieve the right composition. This appeared a similar tradition to the tea being tipped from teapot to glass and back to teapot. Much like the frothy tea, the "sub-Saharan" whisk did zilch in raising the coffee game.

Wobbling on our bench and slurping coffee-flavoured froth, we were immediately distracted by the arrival of a white Hummer with shiny chrome wheels. Scattering the crowd, it slew to a halt and three sharply dressed and self-important fellows stepped out. They were what Africans the continent over call the Big Men. Men who'd muscled their way to the top, securing for themselves power and money and the trappings to go with it. Through wraparound sunglasses and a settling dust they absorbed the mayhem and sultry looks. Nobody was of a mind to go near them, let alone sell them nuts and shake their hands. If the Big Men had a *bon-bon*, nobody wanted it. After a moment or two, and I suspect having made less of an impression than they might have wished for, all three padded over the road, staring down an approaching taxi. They settled on an equally rickety bench at the opposite Café Lean-to. Our host shrank to her haunches beside the steaming kettle, stroked her jaw and eyed the competition.

Ambling back to the car after refreshments, we beheld a perfect example of African ingenuity – a trailer bolted to the back of a Chinese manufactured motorcycle. The rear wheel of the bike had been removed, the drive chain extended to a sprocket on the trailer's axle. Within the trailer were two lines of wooden benches for the passengers, and a tubular frame to support an awning. The bike had a patterned rug folded over the seat and the word FRUTTI painted on the yellow fuel tank. The owner stood beside it dressed in a mustard-coloured robe and a blue skull cap. He bought the bike in a wooden crate, he told us, from a dealer in Bamako. It was cheaper to buy a motorbike in a crate and assemble it himself, he said. And so he had. Then he added the trailer – truly an engineering masterpiece!

He was making plenty of business ferrying people up and down this road. 'Life is sweet,' he enthused. 'Long may it continue, *inshallah*.'

Shortly after Sandaré we slowed to a crawl. With not a soul in sight we darted from the road and into the bush, weaving through the tangle of bushes and trees, until the swathes of burnt land joined to become one and the blackened shoots, branches and twigs crackled beneath the tyres. A sooty mist clung to everything. Judging ourselves far enough from the road, we settled in a small clearing where the burnt foliage would least bother us. There was barely half an hour of sunlight remaining. It was time to make camp.

With the minimum of noise, we unpacked the table, chairs, cooking pots, the all-important aperitif, and gathered brush-wood to start a fire. A group of women, their chatter filling the stillness, passed through the bush some hundred metres off the bonnet. We stopped what we were doing and whispered, waiting for them to pass. To give away our presence was to submit ourselves to an intrusive audience for most probably a good part of the night. For them it would have been bush TV – a soap opera about *toubabs* and their myriad possessions – and a good laugh. Stay quiet, we hissed. Let them pass.

When the sun sank beneath the tortured branches we lit the fire. The ghostly howls reminded us we were still in jackal country. What lions might be left in Mali are said to have sought refuge on the Senegal border, beside the Falémé River, far enough away for us to not worry about their nocturnal wanderings.

The following day was a long one and we were thankful for the good road stretching all the way to Bamako. It was the heat more than anything that was wearing. We didn't use the vehicle's air-conditioning for the simple reason that the difference in temperature, the constant change from coolness to heat each time we stopped for a break, to change drivers, to drink a frothy coffee, would most likely have proved murderous in the end. Better to acclimatise to the conditions.

We were setting a surprisingly good pace, considering how we'd anticipated the roads through Mali to be in the same appalling state as the Gambia and Senegal. So far, the Chinese had turned up trumps, though we could never be sure how far their largesse might stretch.

By late afternoon we descended from the plain and into the mayhem of Bamako, the capital city of Mali, home to a population fast approaching two million people. It occupied an area of 40 km^2. *Bama*, the Bambara word for crocodile, and *Ko*, meaning river, was a noisy, polluted, chronically congested city, and yet, twenty-four hours later, I discovered it exuded a strangely appealing mood.

After a week of rural Africa, the drive down Avenue Du Fleuve was a wakeup call of shocking proportions. Neither did the traffic let up on Pont des Martyrs, from where we secured our first view of the Niger River, and two Bozo fishermen tossing a net from their canoe. JP reacquainted himself with a river he hadn't laid eyes on for years, not since he and a friend had bought a pirogue in Bamako and paddled all the way to the mouth of the Niger, to the Bight of Benin, and the rollers of the Atlantic Ocean. On hearing such a story, Mungo Park would have turned in his grave.

Our accommodation for the next three nights was located in a rapidly expanding residential neighbourhood. The *auberge* had several bedrooms, a dormitory-style tent on the roof containing twenty beds, and a garden of cool green shade, where dressed-down traveller-types wandered to and fro. Relaxing in the garden, we couldn't help overhearing a young Frenchman trying to sell a single-decker bus he'd driven all the way from Paris. He'd been there a couple of weeks without clinching a deal, he told us later. The tall fellow in smart robes was playing him. He wanted the bus for transporting workers back and forth to a mine based in Niger. The Frenchman was confident a deal was close to being struck. Each day he remained in Bamako, a little more was skimmed from his profit. He had to get back to Paris for the New Year, he said.

It was dark when we left the *auberge* to go for dinner. We stumbled down pitch-black alleys in search of a restaurant that came well recommended. When we got there the patron was absent, apparently ill with malaria. The replacement showed not the least sign of wanting to be there. Though the menu was comprehensive, the fridge was virtually empty. We sent a boy out into the streets to find us beer and settled in for a long wait. In the kitchen, the assistant banged her pans.

The next day, while JP and Susie headed off to meet an old contact in the suburbs, Christine and I girded our loins for a visit to the heart of the city. We took a cab from outside the *auberge*. It was waiting beside the white single-decker bus from Paris.

In a country where 45% of gross domestic product is derived from agriculture, a sector employing 80% of the population, it doesn't help when a majority of the land is desert or semi-desert. Many within the agricultural sector are subsistence farmers cultivating millet, rice, maize, sorghum, yams and cassava. Naturally, the most productive area for agriculture hugs the Niger, between Bamako and Mopti, a town to the east of the capital. Along this stretch of the river and its surrounding wetlands, the main export crops of rice, cotton and groundnuts are grown, including, to a lesser extent, sugarcane, tobacco and tea. Cotton and gold account for around 90% of the country's export revenue. Much of Mali's other exports, livestock, dried and smoked fish, and groundnuts, are traded with their West African neighbours. Processing and refining of agricultural produce, plus the growing mining industry are Mali's principal industrial activities.

Mali's service sector accounts for 39% of the country's GDP. Tourist revenue has been increasing, producing an income in 2007 of $262 million. With four World Heritage Sites and a growing list of cultural festivals, the government has focused on developing tourism as a number one priority.

With the national museum of Bamako promoted as one of the best museums in West Africa, it was a natural draw for us. After fighting our way through the morning traffic, we had our taxi drop us at the door for a leisurely trawl through its various exhibitions, notably a remarkable collection of wood carvings and artefacts depicting Mali's rich history, and a comprehensive account of cloth weaving in the region, including the materials and the techniques they used.

In the afternoon, after strolling back over the Pont des Martyrs, a man squatting by the roadside sold us cowrie shells scooped from a ragged hessian sack. 'They're for good luck,' he assured us, on hearing we were heading for Timbuktu.

When Mungo Park was given five thousand cowrie shells by the King of Bambara, they were worth to him the equivalent of £1. To give some idea of their value at that time, he was able to support himself and his horse on one hundred shells a day. Harvested in the Maldive Islands, cowrie shells had been brought to West Africa by Dutch and British ships trading with India. As well as for decorative and ritual uses, the shells were widely accepted by the Africans as a monetary currency even before the arrival in West Africa of the European traders. The extra volume imported by the Europeans had the effect of devaluing it from three thousand shells to a *mithqal* (the standard measure of gold), to fifteen hundred to a *mithqal*. Despite an ever-expanding supply their value remained at this level for three hundred years, an indicator of how West African and Saharan trade flourished during the latter years of the slave trade.

After paying the trader I weighed the shells in the palm of my hand. Had we rocked up at the supermarket offering our handful of cowries as currency, I reckoned the only thing they might have bought us was a kick in the pants.

Back at the *auberge* we crumpled into the seats beside the bar. I felt myself beginning to cave in from the heat. These weird bouts of vertigo I was suffering had also become more frequent in the last few days. Perhaps I just wasn't drinking enough water.

'D'you want a beer?' JP asked, dropping in the adjacent chair. He put his beer bottle on the table and fished out his camera.

'No. I'm dehydrated.'

'You should drink more beer,' he said.

'I'm dizzy.'

'Great,' he declared, draining the rest of his beer. 'Then you're already halfway there.'

'Mine is not the "everything in the garden is rosy" kind of dizziness.'

'Then you should try a pastis.'

From toothache to athlete's foot, Pastis was JP's remedy for everything.

'No thanks,' I told him.

'Here. Take a look at these pictures.'

JP passed me his camera and I squinted at the screen on the back.

'You've really got to change this thing for a new one,' I grumbled, clicking from an image of contorted fuel tankers parked side by side in a compound. I continued scrolling through a medley of bowed walls, blurred traffic, trees bending at queer angles, a partly constructed building slanting at forty-five degrees, followed by a collection of tables and chairs fused together at the legs. In the next shot, the friend JP had been to visit beamed from above a body the perfect shape of the letter S, while a bottle of Castel beer melted over his left hand. Amongst this pictorial carnage appeared Susie, a plate of grilled fish before her. She was smiling and everything was in the correct place.

Christmas Eve in Bamako felt very strange; the heat and the dust, the calls of the muezzin echoing over the city. It was disorientating. Some places, the odd café, restaurant, and shop displayed tinsel and garish-coloured balls. In

Bamako Santa Claus kept appearing in the guise of an inflatable doll. Wherever we wandered he appeared with an extraordinary regularity. At Square Lumumba, and along Rue Mohamed V, he came in tethered batches; they bobbed above plantations of plastic pine trees.

To get through the bustle of the Marché Rose and the streets surrounding it required a certain resolve and fleet-footedness. Barrow boys wheeled goods from stall to stall, forging a corridor through the crowds. By all accounts there was order in this chaos, though amongst the unceasing movement nobody appeared to be trading – they made effusive greetings, conspired together in small groups, huddled round a teapot, shouted at the barrow boys, shouted at us, watched the world go by, smoked a cigarette, scurried from street corner to street corner, and yet no goods seemed to change hands. Nobody licked their thumb and peeled notes from a wad of cash. Nobody flashed an invoice. Nobody got out a handful of cowries.

Near the Place de la République we stumbled on the market for traditional medicines. Here, witchdoctors sold animal parts – from crocodiles, hyenas, chameleons and monkeys – to the sick and superstitious. Imbecilic wooden masks sprouting wild hair glared from the shadows. Buzzards' talons, pigs' teeth, guinea fowl feathers and matted dog fur hung from leather thongs. It was a sinister place. It smelt of must and blocked drains.

After the bones, effigies and strips of curled skin we sought refuge in a Lebanese restaurant and ordered omelette and a coffee. It was genteel and orderly and, if nothing else, it was a relief to be away from the crowds. Afterwards, along Boulevard du Peuple, to the hum of engines and the chorus of hooting horns, we filled our lungs with the gritty air.

That evening, by the time the manager of the *auberge* and his girlfriend served the Christmas Eve dinner, just about all of us had lost the will to go on. The manager, however, was in glorious flow. Springing from an exotic *mélé de fumée*, he juggled plates with an adroit skill and a ceaseless banter, stuttering and crackling like a Maxim gun on the frontline, its barrels zealously cooled with a blend of Castel beer and cheap Bordeaux plonk.

About thirty guests sat round a long table, most of us withered by hunger and an over-indulgence of complimentary *demi-sec* champagne. We should have been having fun, except the timing in the kitchen had quite literally gone to pot. A group at the far end fooled around and told jokes. They were like a brass band playing on the deck of a sinking ship – but nobody was in the mood to man the pumps. Nothing but a state of self-induced oblivion was going to save the SS Christmas Eve from slipping beneath the waves. Amongst all of us, only the manager seemed to have grasped that. A lanky guy kept clambering to his feet to sing, displaying a curious blend of seasonal cheer and insanity. He rocked and flapped his arms in an act of desperate encouragement. The response was as tepid as the beer. JP wanted to knock him over the head and have done with it. Forget it, I said – perhaps the guy had been on the road too long. I poured JP another glass of plonk and we talked of quiet nights back in the bush. This is all bullshit, he said. Sure, it was.

The next day the Frenchman sold his bus to the mine representative, who immediately jumped aboard and left for Niger. The Frenchman bought a ticket back to Paris, happy that he would, after all, be in the City of Light for the New Year.

On the way out of Bamako we passed lines of trotting

donkeys towing wooden carts. The owners beat the animals with solid lengths of timber to urge them on. We'd seen this often enough on our journey; the lot of a donkey is not a happy one out here. Sadly, our presence usually infused them with a need to hit the animals even harder and more regularly. After each thwack of the beast, they would make a point of looking at us. I felt it was almost a look of defiance on their faces, as if it was us they were wishing to taunt. And, in fact, they were taunting us. Maybe it was all an act of braggadocio. They were good at that. I would have loved to have given the length of timber to the donkey.

In the suburbs, we stopped at a Lebanese-owned supermarket to resupply the larder. Barely had we left the car than a man marched up to Christine, claiming her as his long-lost wife. He still loved her dearly, he declared volubly, and they could start all over again. He took her by the arm, telling her it was time to go home. In spite of his insistence, we persuaded him otherwise. He looked very confused. Security guards ushered the man away, sending him ambling up the street. 'Your car will be perfectly safe with us,' they assured us.

This place was getting crazier by the day.

Inside the supermarket mussels and oysters lay on a bed of crushed ice. In this land of the needy such excess smacked of a kind of madness. We stocked up on basic supplies. After all, New Year's Eve was still to come. Who knew what we would find further down the road – or wouldn't, more to the point.

While packing the car with our goods a Russian-made Hind helicopter gunship loomed over the minarets and thundered up Avenue De L'Unite Africaine, wrapping us in its downdraft. At Nampala, five hundred kilometres to the north of us, the Tuareg rebel leader Ibrahim ag Bahanga had led a dawn raid against a military outpost. There had been four hours of intense fighting and a number of fatalities. The Malian president, Amadou Toumani Touré, suggested in a statement that those who want war can go elsewhere. It was bold, ineffective talk. The newspapers claimed elements high up in the military were responsible for the rebel leader remaining at large. There was a suggestion that both weapons and drug trafficking were involved. In the most recent Tuareg uprising in Mali, between 2007 and 2009, Ibrahim ag Bahanga had refused to take part in a peace agreement signed between the government and his fellow Tuareg. He had formed a splinter group in late 2007, the North Mali Tuareg Alliance for Change, and vowed to continue the conflict.

It was yet another reminder for us that all was not well in Mali.

Up in the sky the Hind gunship dipped its nose, turned to the north and went in search of a target on which to blast its phalanx of weaponry.

Later, we passed a convoy of military vehicles loaded with troops heading in the opposite direction and ate our Christmas Day lunch in the broad shade of a baobab tree, an open sandwich of tinned sardine and raw onion – Seasons Greetings to one and all!

Twenty-five kilometres to our north lay Koulikoro, the country's second largest river port after Mopti and a city of historical note. In the year 1235 Sunjata Keita, the ruler of Mali, then a small state in the Manding Mountains, defeated his arch-rival in a battle just outside Koulikoro. From an alliance of independent Malinké chiefs he created the Mali Empire, a vast kingdom reaching from the Atlantic Ocean to Timbuktu, encompassing modern-day Gambia, Senegal, eastern Guinea and most of Mali. The Mali Empire claimed more territory than any other western Sudanic empire and was to endure for more than a century. Much like the Ghana Empire before it, its wealth derived from the gold trade. Back in Europe, news of the yellow metal mined in Africa caused them to quiver with excitement. And then, in the year 1324, an event of eye-popping magnitude shook Cairo. As the story spread across Europe it spawned a sense of wonderment that endured for almost five hundred years.

When Mansa Musa, then ruler of the Mali Empire, went on a pilgrimage to Mecca, his extensive caravan rested for three days in Cairo, a bustling, sophisticated city. Cairo's citizens, in normal circumstances, would have paid little heed to a gathering of foreign travellers. Mansa Musa was different on two counts: he came from an unknown land in the west, and his pockets bulged with gold.

Very soon the Sultan of Cairo pandered to his visitor's every whim. When it came time for the emperor and his entourage to move on, they were lavished with the best horses, camels and provisions their host could provide. On his return journey through Cairo the emperor marked his appreciation with an orgy of generosity and acquisition. In fact, he so plundered his coffers of gold it took a generation for the value of the precious metal to recover in Cairo.

Such a legend had he become, a picture of Mansa Musa features in the Catalan Atlas of 1375, one of the first sets of European maps to provide significant information on Africa. Sir Joseph Banks and his colleagues at the African Association might have done well to secure a copy of the Catalan Atlas when sending Houghton and Park on their missions. For treasure hunters like the members of the African Association, the Catalan Atlas was the equal to any map Blackbeard or Captain Henry Morgan might have concocted to recover their ill-gotten gains.

By the late eighteenth century the legend of Mansa Musa, as impressive as it was, was not the only historical account doing the rounds in London concerning the splendid fortune to be had beyond the Great Desert. Both al-Idrissi, the twelfth century geographer, and Leo Africanus four hundred years later on, wrote of African kingdoms whose significant wealth and power were founded on abundant supplies of gold. In London, the businessman and traveller Hajj Shabeni had talked at length to Henry Beaufoy of the sultan occupying an enormous palace in Timbuktu, not to mention his habit of showering even the lowliest of his subjects in handfuls of gold dust. Indeed, by late seventeen hundred, gold dust, along with ivory, slaves, gum Arabic and goatskins were commodities the people of West Africa freely traded with the Europeans. Britain, along with other nations, had by then seen sufficient evidence that gold existed there. The very thought of getting their hands on more of it caused their palms to sweat, not least because the merchant adventurers saw the writing was on the wall for the slave trade, at that time West Africa's most valuable commodity.

The growing campaign to ban the slave trade, coupled with the desire to enhance commerce, hastened Britain's eagerness to form greater ties with the rich kingdoms of this mysterious African world, ahead of their rivals if they could. Before all that could happen, there was a small problem to overcome: they had to find those kingdoms.

By the time Daniel Houghton and Mungo Park arrived in the 1790's the Western Sudan had fragmented into a number of warring kingdoms. Life for the explorer was made more treacherous still by the Moors (peoples of mixed Arab and Berber descent) who occupied the Sahel and dominated many of the Black African tribes occupying the banks of the Niger River. Following the crusades there was little love between the Moors and the white Christian explorer encroaching on their patch. A wandering Irishman down on his luck, such as Major Houghton, never deserved to fare well in the eyes of the Moors.

The European traders had been present on the African west coast for almost two hundred years prior to Park's arrival. Very few of them had ventured inland. The West African traders certainly did not encourage them. They preferred to bring their gold, ivory and slaves to the coast. Though Mungo Park met with generosity and kindness in some of the states he passed through, most of the people he encountered had never seen a white man before. Often fearful and suspicious, many believed the slaves taken to the Atlantic coast ended up on the white man's plate. Why else do our people never come back? they regularly asked the explorer.

THE COLONIAL ARCHITECTURE and mud houses of Ségou appeared in the afternoon's softening light. We checked in at a hotel, another Lebanese outpost in Africa, and later took a stroll beside the river. From the terrace of the Hotel l'Esplanade we watched two fishermen sail their canoe, piled with netting, through the sun's orange beam. In 2009, the rivers Niger and Bani presented an abundant supply of fish. However, with a growing population, there is increasing pressure on the stocks. Concern exists as to how much longer the fish stocks will continue providing a valuable food source.

The king of fish in Mali is the *capitaine*. A menu without its presence is like a monarch without his crown. And like all good impersonators the *capitaine* carries off his many guises with aplomb – *papillotte, brochette, croquette, à la bamakoise, au beurre blanc, à l'Africaine, à la sauce aurore* – to name a few. There is an aspect to the *capitaine* which never fails to enthuse a Malian chef.

Apart from the incessant call of, '*Donne-moi un cadeau!*', Ségou was a pretty laid-back town. Its main businesses are cloth, milk, sugarcane and tourism. At one time Ségou was the centre of a robust empire and oral traditions promote the rule of Da Monzon (1808-27) as being the high point of the Bambara Empire. The regime drew its strength from close adherence to the spirits of the water and, in later years, a more intimate adherence with the spirits of gunpowder. In due course, it was the unstoppable march of Islam, against which it had no antidote, spiritual or explosive, that caused the kingdom's terminal decline. Soon it was knocking on the door to a jurisdictional equivalent of Accident and Emergency. After that, what was left of the Bambara Empire was strapped on a gurney and wheeled into the deepest waters of the Niger.

Kalabougou village, renowned for its pottery, was a forty-five-minute pirogue ride from Ségou. Beneath the mango tree, sitting amongst a gathering of elders, was the chief. We paid our respects, and a small tax allowing us entry to his village.

In the cool shade of their huts women kneaded clay and shaped the pots. Girls fetched buckets of water. Regiments of pots stood to attention in the baking sun. Remnants of pottery lay everywhere, constantly crunching under my boots.

There was a pond in the centre of Kalabougou village, the water a humming, viscous green. Piles of rubbish were strewn everywhere. Sewage leached from holes in the back of the huts to stagnate in open drains. As we trod warily through the connecting passages our guide told us a Japanese aid agency had recently sunk a well in the village. The inhabitants at last had a source of clean water, he said. And then he'd rubbed his chin in deep thought, admitting to us how he found it puzzling why so many of them still took their water from the river. 'It's just not clean, this river,' he lamented, turning up his nose.

It was somewhere close to Kalabougou where Mungo Park first clapped eyes on the Niger River. Park notes in his book *Travels in the Interior of Africa* how Ségou consisted of four distinct towns; Ségou Korro and Ségou Boo on the northern bank and, on the southern bank, Ségou Soo Korro and Segou See Korro. He writes of each town being surrounded by high mud walls, the houses built of clay and painted white. Moorish mosques were to be seen in every quarter and he estimated the population as a whole to be about thirty thousand inhabitants. King Mansong, who resided at Ségou Koo Korro, on the southern bank, was highly suspicious of this white man arriving on his doorstep. He refused Park permission to cross the river to visit him. Continuing to negotiate access to the king through an intermediary, the explorer was forced to wait some days. Initially he was regarded with astonishment and fear by the local population. No one seemed willing to offer him shelter or victuals. At sunset, perched in the branches of a tree, for fear of prowling lions, Park was approached by a lady returning from the fields. She took him to her home, cooked a fine fish and offered him a mat for the night.

Following lunch in a café we continued east and after half an hours' driving we pulled off the road. Our wild camp was perfect; at last, back in the peace and calm of the bush, with the fire crackling, supper bubbling on the *fourneau*, nobody to trouble us. Dusk's moist air lifted the coppery smell of the earth. It was splendid. We cracked the top of a bottle of Bombay Sapphire gin to celebrate. *Quel Bonheur!* Unravelling the tent and side awnings in a hue of darkness and an overindulgence of gin caused the efforts of JP and myself to descend into a pitiful display of incompetence.

This pole goes where?

WE ARRIVED at the *bac* (a small ferry) for Djenné by mid-afternoon the following day. Ahead of us a huge truck bursting with goods for the local market ventured tentatively into the axle deep waters of the Bani River. It gurgled and growled, sinking deeper in the water before hauling itself up the ferry's ramp like an obdurate beast. Several calabashes and a couple of tyres broke free from the back of the truck, tumbling into the river. Children splashed after them. When the truck had settled its bulk, and the ferry submerged that bit lower in the river, there was no further space on the deck for us. We hung back on the riverbank, awaiting the next one.

A story lost in the mists of time attributes Djenné's existence to a young Bozo girl by the name of Pama Kayamtao. It is said that the site of the proposed town was occupied by malevolent spirits and when the first buildings were erected, soon after, the spirits caused them to collapse. The marabouts (holy men considered to have wondrous insight) were consulted, who in turn sought counsel with the good spirits. The good spirits devised a plan: sacrifice a young Bozo virgin and intern the body in the city walls. And then all would be well. The marabouts reported what they'd been told. The deed was done; the buildings no longer collapsed. As a consequence, the tomb of Tapama Djenepo

– "Our mother Pama, corpse of Djenné" – lies near the banks of the river.

I'd read how Djenné had enjoyed a glorious past. Now it was finished, unseated by Mopti, a town further east along the river. Mopti was the new centre of trade, the Niger River's new powerhouse. Structurally Djenné has not changed since the days of the Mali and Songhay empires. It's said the days of the old empires were probably the town's best for stability and trade, after which its fortunes became victim to later regimes' lack of effective government. Now it is tourists that fill the narrow streets, swelling the population of 10,000, as well as the visiting traders, who wheel their goods back and forth for the regular Monday market. Certainly, all the hotels were full when we arrived on the Sunday night. We had to pitch our camp outside the walls of Djenné Djenno, a hotel on the approach to the town. We camped within ten metres of that great African nightmare, the generator. There was nowhere else to go. It rumbled for the whole night, rising up and down in crescendo. It was a long night and little need for an alarm to get us up in time for the market.

At just over eighteen metres high the Djenné Mosque is the tallest mud structure in the world. After so many years of seeing this building in the pages of *National Geographic* et al, it felt slightly odd to be stood in front of it. It looked very ordinary in fact, and yet was far from it. There was no surprise. I think that was the problem. Like some believe the camera steals the human spirit, perhaps all those photos in the magazines had robbed an element of its wonder. Many of the buildings in Djenné are extraordinary in their design, and well-preserved, considering the materials they are constructed from. The builders of Djenné are revered as artists and magicians.

The sun had barely risen beyond the outline of the roofs when we entered the town and yet, in the square beside the mosque, the traders were already congregating. A blue truck came loaded with white hessian sacks bursting with produce. *Bonne Chance* was painted across the rear of the trailer. On another was inscribed: "It is only in times of trouble that we know our friends". The wagon that made it to the ferry before us the previous day lurched into the square in a fog of black exhaust. It bore no homilies, at least none we could read.

In the square, poles were erected, awnings draped, benches arranged, plastic sheeting placed on the ground. Barrow-boys put their backs to the job. Mammas, babies strapped about them, lugged sacks on their shoulders. The more people who arrived the more the volume rose – hands were shaken, shoulders gripped, words exchanged, laughter shared, orders barked. Woven baskets of produce appeared – fruit, vegetables, slabs of salt, dried fish, chilli, meat – until the dusty, hard-packed earth of the square vanished. As if that wasn't enough, lines of string sagged under the weight of bags and garments and sandals.

Quickly the stalls swelled, filling the square from wall to wall. It was raw, smelly, dusty and so incredibly vibrant. What an insight into Malian life. As we left, traders from miles around were still piling in, driving their mule carts through the crowds. At the edge of the town women washed their pots and pans in a pool of brackish water, clothes already drying in the rising sun.

We had a cool drink back at the hotel, packed up the car and hit the road.

Out on the N16, halfway between the Djenné junction and Sévaré, we turned off the road, weaving our way through scrubland, searching for a place to camp. As we unfurled the awnings to create some shade a couple of hunters plonked themselves on the rocks to watch us. In their spare clothes and matted hair, they looked wild and a shade crazy. Did we need any fresh meat? One of them held a dead squirrel by the tail. The other had a hedgehog dangling from between thumb and forefinger. Did we want squirrel and hedgehog couscous? No thanks. They watched us a while before sloping off beyond the trees.

The next morning, we rose at first light. As ever when wild camping, the first task of the day was to stoke life into the previous evening's fire and put the coffee pot to boil. Ablutions, by necessity, were crude – find a bush to strip off behind, take a bucket, and a cup to ladle the water over the head, torso – and the rest. A quick scrub and a brisk rub with the towel and all was done. The toilet was a deep hole dug in the ground with a trenching shovel. It might have been basic but it beat any hotel we'd stayed in so far. Breakfast was fruit or cereal, or both. And maybe a second pot of coffee if we had time. We usually did.

We got away from our camp by quarter to nine. Even at that time of the morning, packing the car caused a sweat to break out.

Mopti, our next stop, began its transition from quiet Bozo fishing village to commercial hub in the early nineteenth century, achieved by the hand of the Peul emperor, Sékou Amadou. Its development was furthered by the French after 1893. With a population in the region of 100,000, it is now the most significant urban centre in the Niger Inland Delta. The port is its beating heart, the sale of dried fish one of its principal trades. The other major trading commodity is salt. Salt comes from the mines in Taoudenni, deep in the Sahara. From Taoudenni the salt is carried south, seven hundred kilometres by camel, to

Timbuktu, and then transhipped up river to Mopti by *pinasse,* a larger version of the pirogue and supposedly capable of carrying cargoes of up to 150 tonnes. The town was a hive of activity; along the riverbank, in the narrow streets, doorways, warehouses and main roads. The people were from a mixture of communities; Bozo, Peul, Tuareg, Dogon, Bambara, Songhay. The old town of Mopti was being renovated, new pipes laid in the street, so the sewage could finally go underground; out of sight, out of mind and definitely out of the nostrils.

We wandered the cobbled streets, admiring the handsome houses. Mopti could really be something special if they stuck to this program of regeneration. The mosque had already been newly renovated and an equal to its counterpart in Djenné.

We returned the twelve kilometres down the road to Sévaré, a small re-supply town brimming with non-governmental organisations (NGO). Here, the hawkers' sales methods were intense and you had to bore through the facade to uncover the fine, friendly souls they are. Their eyes were deep pools of desperation. We bought rugs from them, visited the museum and stocked up with fresh supplies before retiring to our lodgings on the edge of town. A representative of Save the Elephants, an NGO based in Kenya, was staying at the lodge. He was there to assess the state of the waterholes in the Gourma region.

'The rains have failed,' he told us, 'and all the lakes are drying up.'

We were too early in the year to spot the main herd. His finger circled an area on the map where we might find an old bull elephant and two females. He'd spotted them a couple of days ago. The herds, whose total number ranges from anywhere between four hundred and six hundred animals, were still further south, in Burkina Faso. Each year the herds follow the water, a journey that can mean distances of eight hundred kilometres.

That evening our New Year's Eve kicked off with a pastis, followed by chicken couscous, a couple of cartons of red wine and early to bed. 2009 arrived with a hiss rather than a bang.

We were on the road the next day by ten thirty, not a hangover in sight. By lunchtime we'd arrived in Douentza, a dusty little place, and the junction for the road leading north to Timbuktu. The moment we stopped two men rushed to secure our business in one of the cafés lining the roadside. It was dark inside and we padded over the earth floor to our table. The place was empty save for two men hunched over their plates of omelette and chips. We followed their example – the only food on the menu, as it turned out – and sat back in plastic chairs with our beakers of coke.

We'd done pretty well up to then from our choice of roadside eateries. That day we were out of luck. One after the other it took us down, save JP, whose innards, I suspect, have long since been replaced with the sump from a Perkins diesel engine, and re-plumbed with a series of copper piping. Was it the eggs or the oil for the chips that did us in? An African egg can be hours in the full sun. Goodness knows how many times the oil had been recycled.

By early evening Susie's stomach was doing handstands. Mine had more gas in it than a helium balloon.

'A strong pastis, that'll cure it,' JP declared with his usual enthusiasm for its restorative qualities. He pushed back his chair and stretched his legs. 'Get plenty inside you...it'll be like an anaesthetic.'

I poured a hefty slug, dribbled water over the top and

put the glass to my lips. When I swallowed, it plummeted like a gob of mercury, gurgling somewhere beneath my windpipe and refusing to descend any further. I felt like a blocked sink. It wasn't pastis I needed. A plunger might have done a better job.

I watched Susie take a similar mouthful. She instantly turned green and bolted from sight.

The next morning Sidi Mohamed, a local guide, took us to visit a Dogon village. Leaving Douentza behind, after twenty minutes following a track beside cultivated fields, we abandoned the car in the shade of a tree and began our climb to the village, two hundred metres up the escarpment.

There are said to be some three hundred and fifty thousand Dogon living in a series of villages located along the plateau and cliffs of the Bandiagara Escarpment. The views from there were magical, what I think of as a true African landscape; endless golden grasses, umbrella trees, ochre-coloured earth, the dramatic Gandamia Mountain in the foreground. I was waiting for a steam train to sweep Meryl Streep on to the set. I could hear her voice on the warm breeze... 'I had a farm in Africa...'

Even though the village we visited on the escarpment was on the tourist map, the people accommodating, inquisitive and content to show us round, I felt our presence to be intrusive. The chief, to whom we paid our respects, sat with us for a period of time politely answering our questions.

After our audience with the chief, when Sidi Mohamed went off to buy our host a gift in the form of a live chicken, we wandered freely round the buildings. For a while we sat at the edge of the escarpment, overlooking the plain. Christine entertained the children with songs. A youth sat with JP and together they smoked their cigarettes. On the rocky plateau below, two women alternately pounded corn in a wooden pestle. Ask someone for an image of Africa and I guess this would be one of the most common given. You see it everywhere, the women pounding corn. This reassuring beat pulses through the earth, connecting the people – 'all is well,' it says. Africa's heart is beating.

The layout of a Dogon village is influenced by spiritual beliefs and symbolism, the buildings usually divided into family groupings, or *ginna*. The arrangement of each *ginna* allows for the house of the headman, followed by dwellings for his wives and children, and then a series of outbuildings, storerooms or stables. The layout of the buildings is regarded as representative of a man lying on his side in the act of procreation. The granaries, mud pillboxes with thatched roofs, were the most distinctive structures. They contained food supplies and the family's possessions. The walls of the circular hovels displayed carvings of men and women with exaggerated genitals. The women are forced to take up residence in these *maison des femmes* during their period of menstruation, as they are considered impure.

When I asked about what animals lived along the escarpment, we were led through a series of narrow passages between stone-built dwellings. We came to a hut. 'This is a hunter's house,' the youth informed us. On the top of a wall the hollow eye sockets of several monkey skulls stared back at us.

'*Nous avons des singe sur la falaise*,' the youth said.

I gazed at the monkey skulls. I was quite sure I'd asked the youth what animals *lived* on the *falaise*? Perhaps it was my accent.

Many Dogon have converted to Islam and Christianity, though a considerable number remain animist, attributing a living soul to all objects – even monkey skulls. To a large extent, whether Christian or Muslim, the lives of the Dogon are still influenced by their ancient and complex mythical beliefs; virtually everything is imbued with significance, and sacrifice, sorcery, sacred ground and totems still exist. Scores of their carvings and sculptures relate to the Nommo, the mythological ancestors sent by the supreme god, Amma. Myths tell of the seventh Nommo, the blacksmith, who stole blistering hot iron and a piece of the sun. He slithered down a rainbow, and during his descent to earth, the other Nommo pelted him with lightning bolts. He repelled them with his bellows, but when he hit the earth the blacksmith was going too fast and his body shattered, the breaks becoming the human joints, which allowed them to work and dance.

Theories abound as to why the Dogon colonised the escarpment. They were fleeing something, of that the historians are in agreement. A legend in the fourteenth or fifteenth century tells of the Dogon following a dog, in order to discover a secure place for them to live away from persecution. In due course, the dog led them to the Bandiagara Escarpment, only to find the cliff faces already populated by the Tellem, a tribe of hunter/gatherers, pygmies imbued with magical powers, and whose name supposedly means, "We found them". It is to the Tellem that some of the earliest cloth and wooden objects of the region are attributed. The Dogon, however, held the Tellem in contempt, and perhaps a little fear, believing these little men could transform themselves into giants and had the ability to fly.

It is difficult to gauge what took place next. All that is left of the Tellem are a series of caves dotted over the escarpment. The caves are full of skulls and bones and strips of old cloth. Was it disease that wiped them out, or something more sinister? If anybody knows what really happened, they're not saying.

'They died and went away,' Sidi Mohamed murmurs when we ask. *C'est la vie.*

Many of the children trailing us through the village were pot-bellied, a sign that they were suffering from malnutrition. The standard of peoples' health generally seemed to have declined the further east we travelled. Certainly, the choice of foods in the markets, and along the roadsides, had radically reduced. The *poulet bicyclette*, if you could find one, had become almost inedible.

TWO DAYS later we drove north, up the gravel *piste* towards Timbuktu. The road was horribly corrugated. We encountered virtually no other traffic and for a good part of the way it was more comfortable to labour in the deep sand bordering the *piste*. With ten psi bled out of the tyres the car pulled much more cleanly through the deeper sand. The arid terrain undulated, through hollows and over humps. We were like a boat ploughing through waves. The suspension took a heavy pounding and at each break in the journey I wriggled beneath the car, making fine adjustments to the collection of flip flops and chunks of tyre I'd tie-wrapped to the chassis. By then they were getting rather shredded. A piece of tyre had gone missing from the left side. I made a mental note to stop at the next discarded tyre we found and collect it for later use. I convinced myself my modifications helped cushion the worst of the blows between the chassis and the suspension clamp. With the flip flops and strips of tyre, all would be well. Or so I hoped.

Campement Tenéré is the property of a Tuareg called Abdou Salam. Abdou's campsite was run as a cooperative.

The inhabitants of the local village contributed either labour or money and the profits were distributed to local projects. In the village, they'd built a maize mill and established a clean water supply. One of the inhabitants had been funded to go through medical school, so he could look after his neighbours in the future. Their ambitions even extended to building a hospital, but only when they'd accumulated sufficient funds to achieve such a project.

Accommodation in Abdou's campsite was in traditional tents. There was a kitchen garden, pumps for distributing water, and windmills for generating power. All manner of vegetables sprouted from the sand. It was quite incredible. We had fresh salad and couscous for lunch, and an equally good dinner.

As we lounged under a tree reading books, replete with Abdou's home-grown produce, a Land Rover belonging to a tour company slew to a stop in the compound. The two Asian tourists climbed from the back, pacing to a table in the shade. Their guide ordered them lunch and while his clients ate, the young man slipped into conversation with JP. He was from Kidal, in eastern Mali and, as it turned out, the nephew of some of JP's Tuareg friends. JP had sold Land Rovers to his uncle more than twenty years ago. The guide was taking the Asians to Timbuktu, and thereafter to the festival at Essakane. We told him we were going to Gao after the festival, taking the tracks north of the Niger River. JP told him he wanted to catch up with his old friends in Gao.

'You won't get there in that car,' the young guide said.

When we asked why he shrugged and grinned. 'You just won't. I came that way a week ago. That car is too heavy for the sand.'

What he said made no sense. I had the distinct feeling this exchange wasn't like the usual Toyota versus Land

Rover rivalry, a topic that invariably sparked fifteen minutes of good humoured banter between overlanders. Bearing in mind what Mohammed Ali, the guy at Parc d'Arguin in Mauritania, had told us about banditry and the growing presence of al-Qaida in West Africa, we were all beginning to wonder if there was a message hidden in these words. If there was, there was no teasing it from him.

'See you at the festival,' he said the moment his clients pushed aside their empty plates.

With that the Asians gathered their hats, shoulder bags and cameras and clambered back in the car. They sped off up the *piste* in a hail of dust and crunching gears.

During the night we heard the pitter-patter of rain on the tent. Rain in the Sahara Desert? Whatever next?

The following day, after an hour's drive, the sand gave way to wetlands at the edge of the Niger. We followed a finger of land extending into the river, at the end of which lay an expanse of packed earth, where the ferry dropped its ramp. A small settlement of domed, woven dwellings had taken root beside the landing point. To our left a group of men occupied themselves with loading zebu into a pirogue, a feat which initiated much beating and shoving. While the humans cursed loud and often, the beasts lowed with indignation. Despite the herders' aggression there was a surprising serenity to the zebu as the pirogue eased into the central channel of the river. They stood with heads held high and proud, as if bovine monarchs surveying their kingdom.

Beside the road, in a domed, mud oven, a woman cooked bread. Her half-clothed child tottered by a plastic bowl of freshly washed clothes. The woman hooked out two fresh loaves, tossing them in a wire basket.

After loading eight vehicles on the ferry the passage

took forty minutes to cross the gun-metal grey waters of the Niger. JP didn't miss an opportunity to photograph the ferry's engine during our crossing. He snapped it from two different angles; as an artistic study of neglect the engine made for a first-class subject.

It was very green on the other side of the river, much more so than I had ever imagined. A new plantation of trees lined the north bank. During the crossing, we saw little river traffic; for a while four boys paddled a pirogue alongside us. The centre of the pirogue was loaded with a silvery, fine-mesh net in which they'd caught extremely small fish.

The ten kilometres of road from the port to Timbuktu was tarmac. Along the way, we passed donkeys loaded with enormous sheaves of cut grass. As we approached them from behind, all that was visible were tails, hooves and ears. After the donkeys came a large red Coca Cola sign depicting a Tuareg popping like a genie from a bottle. The sign announced: *BIENVENUE A TIMBOUCTOU*. A smaller message beside the bottle advised readers to: *Prend la vie du bon côté* (take life on the bright side). It definitely had a ring of Monty Python.

The Route de Kabara leads directly to Timbuktu. Along each side of it are banks, a stadium, a patisserie, travel offices, shops, a café, and a fuel station. Groups of tourists wandered the edge of the road and clustered by the entrance to the banks and the roadside stalls. The influx of festival-goers filled the hotels. The Festival in the Desert was Timbuktu's big moment, the time to maximise turnover. Accommodation in town had been difficult for us to source.

At the end of Route de Kabara we made a full circle at the Place de l'Indépendance, and came back on ourselves. Turning off the main road we followed a series of left and right turns down sandy tracks to our *hôtel du charme*. After checking in I parked in the compound at the back and set out our stall before repairing to the bar, where we found an Austrian couple, Peter and Sabina. In their MAN truck they had driven from Europe, following the east coast of Africa, all the way down to Cape Town. After two years on the road they were on their way north and home.

The owners of the hotel joined us at the bar, a large glass of milky pastis in hand. They looked rugged and windswept, and exchanged a few pleasantries before retiring to a table with friends, a litre bottle of Ricard and a small jug of water within easy reach.

In the early evening, we walked towards town in search of a restaurant. Strolling Boulevard Askia Mohamed I experienced the worst attack of vertigo and nausea that had been plaguing me on and off since leaving Mauritania. I stopped in the street, reeling, shoulders knotted, the muscles in my jaw tingling. I flexed my hands, taking slow, deep breaths to try and ease the weird sense of anxiety creeping over me. It didn't help that the night air was thick with dust and loathsome smells. I felt as if I'd come under the grip of a hostile spirit and harboured an overwhelming urge to be out of Timbuktu. To get out of Africa. To be as far from this place as I could. The last street on earth in which I wanted to collapse was Boulevard Askia Mohamed. At that very moment, it felt inevitable.

Up ahead the others turned. 'What are you doing?' Christine called.

I babbled something incoherent. A car hooted its horn for me to clear off the road. I shuffled to the side. 'It's this bloody vertigo,' I mumbled as they approached.

'It's the anti-malaria tablets you're taking,' Susie said. 'I'm sure of it.'

I'd taken my weekly dose that morning. Even though I'd

never experienced problems with them on previous trips, it is a prophylactic known to pack some heavy-hitting side effects. When you read the note inside the packet you are almost left toying with the thought that contracting malaria might not be a preferable option.

'I'll be alright,' I said.

I just wanted to shut myself in a darkened room, to hide from everything. I took a few more deep breaths and plodded on. A few metres further on we found a restaurant up some grimy steps. Inside, the lighting produced a vivid blue hue. The smell of cooking turned my guts. With rubbery legs, I waded after the others to the last remaining free seats. There were too many people in there – too much noise. We ordered ragout and when it arrived my stomach churned at the most unappetising sludge I'd ever set eyes on.

Back at the *hotel du charme* a band entertained the animated crowd of westerners filling the bar and terrace. They were getting into the spirit for the festival. That aggravated me even more because I couldn't bring myself to join in. I retired to the tent irritated and exhausted, though sleep eluded me.

Over coffee the next morning, from our camp chairs we watched the wild-haired owners of the hotel scramble inelegantly from nothing more than a box propped up on crates. The box was against the far wall of the compound, where various vehicle parts, bonnets and bumpers and wheels, were stacked side by side. They didn't acknowledge us because I think, at that very moment, we were beyond their scope of vision. Their eyes glistened above miniature sacks of coal. It had obviously been a good party. They stood for a moment, gathering their faculties, like a couple of defunct computers rebooting themselves.

After all the years of hearing about Timbuktu, the myths and its legends, it seemed very strange to finally be there. This was a place men had given their lives to discover. Here was the fabled city of gold.

"A mass of ill-looking houses built of earth", is how the French explorer René Caillié described the place in 1829. He must have experienced the mother of all comedowns as he crested the last dune of his journey. Of course, the English and the French argued for years. Had it been René Caillié or Gordon Laing who reached Timbuktu first? In any case, after 1829, the cat was finally out of the bag. Timbuktu was a folly in the sand.

By 1817 a number of geographical missionaries had plodded in Mungo Park's wake. And yet, despite the enormous effort and sacrifice, not a single person was known to have navigated the length of the Niger River; absolutely nobody could give account as to the number of women residing in the sultan of Timbuktu's harem. Sir Joseph Banks himself, by then knocking on the door of seventy-five, was akin to the flowers he so loved to study: shedding his petals and slowly wilting. Age, and his old enemy gout, had left him unable to walk and with failing eyesight. The African Association's driving force had most definitely entered his autumnal years.

In its heyday, the African Association had enjoyed a free hand in the field of exploration; all that was set to change. By 1817 a new boy was on the block: the British government.

Following the cessation of hostilities between France and England countless decommissioned servicemen joined the ranks of the unemployed; the British had no shortage of potential explorers. Both the Colonial Office and the Admiralty were tasked with kick-starting a new era of exploration. Lord Bathurst and Sir John Barrow were to head the initiative, though they would find the going in Africa no easier than Sir Joseph Banks and his colleagues.

In 1816 two expeditions tasked with locating the Niger River were mounted, both of them suffering an equally disastrous outcome. James Tuckey headed up the Congo River with fifty-four soldiers (they believed the Congo River may have been the mouth of the Niger River). Almost fifty per cent of them, including Tuckey himself, succumbed to fever and died. At the same time a Major Peddie was despatched to West Africa. Supported by one hundred soldiers armed to the teeth, he staged an expedition from Sierra Leone. Their weaponry was to be no match against disease, far and away the biggest enemy for the European in Africa. Peddie had barely stepped ashore when he dropped dead. By the time the stragglers returned from a tentative thrust inland, most of his company were strumming their harps alongside the good major. The conspiracy theorist would have had a field day in the face of such carnage. If Britain worried about what to do with an over-supply of her soldiers and sailors, it had found the perfect remedy. Africa killed in great numbers.

Undeterred, Barrow and the Colonial Office continued lavishing princely sums on gaining a foothold in West Africa. More explorers were dispatched, more government money expended, more men perished. The parsimonious folk at the African Association would have baulked at such numbers. Timbuktu, the city paved in gold, remained an enigma. It was getting embarrassing. Radical measures were required.

One such radical measure was introduced in 1824 by the Société Géographique, a Paris-based geographical society. It took a leaf from a Texas lawman's book. In effect, they unrolled a poster, nailing it to the doors of the Elysée Palace:

WANTED DEAD OR ALIVE – TIMBUKTU
REWARD: TEN THOUSAND FRENCH FRANCS

A bounty of ten thousand francs had been placed on the head of an elusive African city. The first man returning with a credible account took home the loot.

If nothing else the French initiative spurred on British efforts. With such an agreeable sum in the offing, surely any adventurer sporting a musket, a compass and a stout pair of boots would now be heading to the hinterlands of Africa. Or so they believed. "Damn such French impertinence," echoed in the corridors of Whitehall. They'd whipped Napoleon good and proper; no way would the frogs beat them to Timbuktu.

On the 9th May 1825 a self-assured young officer stepped ashore in Tripoli harbour. It was the turn of Major Alexander Gordon Laing to have a go at uncovering the City of Gold. Laing was met at the quayside by the British Consul, the effusive Hanmar Warrington, who whisked his visitor across the bay to his residence on the far shore. That very first evening, nursing a pre-dinner glass of gin, the salt water crust freshly washed from his hair and the scent of jasmine drifting on the breeze, Laing fell head over heels for Emma, one of the consul's three daughters.

Warrington was not best pleased at such a turn of events. Though, the consul had a keen eye for the main chance; should his new son-in-law succeed in finding Timbuktu, the advantage of such an association to a man of Warrington's ambition was obvious. He allowed his daughter's marriage with Laing to proceed, though there was one thing he did hold the major to: the marriage was not to be consummated until his return from the desert.

Laing left Tripoli on the 18th July accompanying a caravan of merchantmen making their long journey to Timbuktu. If Laing ever kept a journal during his journey it has never been found. The stream of letters he dispatched from the desert remains the principal source of information for historians. The major's retinue at the start of the long trek south included Jack Le Bore, a long-time associate of Laing's from his days in Sierra Leone; a pair of carpenters tasked with building the vessel on which the explorer would navigate the Niger River; a freed slave and an interpreter. In such company, Laing's confidence soared on the hot, Saharan breeze. He had little doubt that Timbuktu was as good as in the bag.

For seemingly a lifetime the caravan plodded over vast, featureless plains, in and out of dry riverbeds and up and down bleak plateaus. Their trek was punctuated by meagre rations and the constant search to replenish water. The further south they trudged the more they rested during the hottest part of the day, travelling increasingly in the pre-dawn and evening. After almost two months the caravan entered Ghadames, an ancient city of six thousand people, an oasis for exhausted desert travellers.

In Ghadames Laing received by messenger various letters from Tripoli, including a miniature portrait from his dearest Emma. The portrait threw him into despair. By morning he'd convinced himself the pallor of her skin revealed a wife at the onset of death. He fired a letter off to Warrington, advising of his immediate return to the coast. With his clothes and instruments hastily roped to a camel the explorer had a sudden change of heart. Having opened more of his mail he learnt how Hugh Clapperton, his arch rival in the race to discover the fabled city, had landed in the Bight of Benin, far to the south, and was heading northwards with undue haste. No way was Clapperton going to rob the major of his destiny. With his back stiffened, Laing dispatched a second letter with the same messenger: after further consideration he would continue south, he feverishly scribbled to Warrington. After all, didn't vanity rank higher than matrimonial duty?

After fifty-one days in Ghadames the caravan moved onwards to In Salah. The long night's ride reawakened all Laing's old saddle sores. His eyes prickled, a pain like that of a spear blade lanced his lower back, his stomach rumbled like a hookah in the souk and the fur on his tongue rasped the top of his mouth. For most of the night the caravan glided soundlessly across an interminable land, a recurring pattern quickly emerging as each man remained hostage to his own thoughts, suffering the earth's heat, followed later in the night by a cold that penetrated the bones. As the teeth began to chatter in the dark of the night, finally the rising sun banished the bitter chill, causing the layers of clothing to be discarded.

They rested through the worst of the heat, and by late afternoon, after a mouthful of dates, a slurp of camel's milk, a rub under the armpits with a handful of sand and a wander behind the dunes, the lovelorn Laing and his colleagues were back on the trail. They skirted the edge of the Great Western Sand Sea, a vast wilderness of dunes into which the explorer stared aghast, imagining it to be a place where only halfwits and the suicidal ventured. He took a swig of sulphurous water from his *guerba* and counted the skulls along the *piste* – cow, goat, camel, human – creatures abandoned by their gods, the bones pared down by scavengers and the glare of the sun.

It was as the sun's rays displayed their bloody finale that the explorer first caught sight of them: camels ridden by blue-robed men, the riders' heads swathed in a black *shesh*. In the dying day, the baleful shapes loped along the crest of the dunes. Laing recognised them as Tuareg tribesmen, pirates of the desert, the very people to send a shiver of fear to the core of an Arab merchant. They vanished and reappeared with an unsettling regularity, making no effort to conceal their presence. From then on Laing was a marked man.

The merchantmen delayed their departure from In Salah; reports of bandits roaming the Tanezrouft, the wilderness over which they must travel next, filled the souk. Laing paced the narrow alleys, increasingly disturbed: for every day wasted in In Salah, his rival Clapperton moved closer to Timbuktu. He could bear it no longer. The major called the merchants' bluff by loading his camels and heading into the scorching winds of the Tanezrouft. The merchants could not allow the white man to proceed without them. They readied their own camels, wrapped the *shesh* tightly round their faces and stooped before the wind.

Within a couple of days of leaving In Salah Tuareg tribesman barred their route. For a while Laing held back, allowing the sheik leading the caravan to negotiate their passage. When it seemed nothing more than hot air materialised from their discourse, the major lost patience, urged on his horse and stood it before their interlopers. The Tuaregs believed Laing to be Mungo Park and an exchange ensued that might have gone something like this:

'This man says you are Mungo Park,' the sheik leading the caravan announced to the explorer.

'Tell him Mungo Park is dead,' Laing retorted.

The sheik nudged his horse to the side, putting distance

between himself and the explorer. 'They say you shot many people...out in the river...from a boat.'

'Don't be ridiculous. Park sailed past Timbuktu twenty-one years ago. I was ten years old.'

One of the Tuareg kicked his horse forward, tugging the head-cloth from his face to reveal a brutal scar on his cheek.

'This man swears you shot him in the face with a musket.'

'I've never seen this man before.'

'Even if you are not him...what right did this Park have to come here and fire at these people?'

'I cannot answer for his conduct any more than I can justify it,' Laing replied.

'So, you are not who they claim?'

'I am not.'

'Still, they are demanding a heavy fee to allow our passage. And each day, the merchants in the caravan fear the ill omens journeying beside you.'

'Oh, come, come, sheik. It is only my shadow journeying beside me.'

'So you say, Major Laing.'

After their encounter with the Tuareg, the explorer's state of mind contracted and expanded in tune with the desert's tempo. By midday the depths of his depression flowed: should he have left In Salah in such haste, endangering the caravan? Was Emma's health holding up? Was there truth in the story Park had killed so many Africans? Would anyone care if Laing himself ever reached Timbuktu?

At the setting of the sun Laing's mood transformed, his spirits soaring with the retreating haze; in the cool and clarity of dawn, everything and anything seemed possible to him. When the wind howled and the sand filled even the pockets of his robe, Laing must have rocked at the very stairway to hell.

Twenty days after leaving In Salah and the forlorn plains of the Tanezrouft still seemed unending. In a land devoid of distraction, save the sun's sparkle on a shard of rock, or a banished acacia tree, he'd played all the mind games he could to alleviate the emptiness, until his mind was numb, even to the familiar torment: those bands of roaming Tuareg.

That evening Major Laing turned in early to brood over his growing obsession: had Clapperton and his party already reached the gates of the Golden City?

Laing needn't have worried. The Clapperton expedition had problems of its own. Deep in the jungles to the south, Dr Thomas Dickson had been killed in an altercation with the locals; Captain Pearce took to rambling conversations with his mother and later died; Richard Lander had been "bled" and gone temporarily insane; Dr Morison had died of fever on the way back to the coast, and George Dawson poisoned himself with a slug of ether. Aside from such drama in the jungle, back in the desert Laing was about to experience a setback of his own.

The band of Tuareg shadowing them for so long eventually struck Laing's encampment in the early hours. Musket balls tore through the explorer's canvas tent, followed by the blades of scimitars and daggers. The Tuareg slashed and hacked until Laing no longer moved. They rummaged his goods, killed two of his companions and rode off into the night.

Laing was severely injured in the attack, suffering a partially severed hand, several broken and fractured bones, a number of deep cuts and a musket ball lodged perilously close to his spine.

Jack le Bore extracted his boss from the shredded canvas, patched him as best he could and settled him on the back of a camel. Under the direction of the sheik they rode more than six hundred kilometres, stopping to rest at a tiny desert camp. With the help of Le Bore Laing steadily recovered from his injuries, though if he thought his run of bad luck had ended, he was to be sorely disappointed: plague now ravaged the camp they were staying in. All save one of his assistants had been wiped out. If Laing still fretted over the whereabouts of Clapperton, he needn't have bothered. Hugh Clapperton had been dead one month already.

In the company of a guide, Major Laing reached Timbuktu one year after he'd set out from Tripoli. At the gates to the city he shed his robes in preference for European clothes, held his head high and ventured among the crumbling streets. If Laing had then broken down and wept, he could be forgiven. The alleys were paved with dung, not gold, the walls made of mud, not encrusted with jewels. Instead of a rich and vibrant culture there was an air of siege and fear. The majesty he imagined awaiting him had long ago evaporated like the proverbial mirage.

The major remained for five weeks in the city, until news came to his ears that Fula warriors had been sent to kill him. It was time to move on.

Laing joined a caravan heading westwards along the north bank of the Niger River; his appetite for navigating the Niger to its termination could wait for another day. Instead, he would head for Sierra Leone, a country he was at least familiar with from his earlier expeditions, and from there he proposed catching a boat back to England.

If in finding the Golden City Laing had supped from his equivalent of the Holy Grail, the memory of it was to be short-lived. He no longer had to worry about how he might embellish a story based on a decaying Saharan city; he would not be thanked by the King of England, feted by politicians, or adored by the public. Neither, if he hadn't already, would he get to consummate his marriage to Emma. Not long after leaving Timbuktu the *slattee* (slave trader) leading the caravan set about the major with some of his men. They drove a sword through his torso, lopped off his head and left him to the vultures.

EVEN AFTER THE rose-tinted spectacles had been lifted, covetous European eyes were not prepared to lose sight of Timbuktu. After the second Berlin Congo Conference in early 1885, and the so-called "Scramble for Africa" had led to colonial jurisdiction establishing itself in the bulk of North and West Africa, a French proposal to construct a trans-Saharan railway persisted. In the carve-up of borders, France had been the greatest beneficiary of the lands to the north and south of the Sahara.

"We have given the Gallic cockerel an enormous amount of sand," was how the British Prime Minister, Lord Salisbury, pompously described the concessions made to France. "Let him scratch in it as he pleases."

Britain, having gained global supremacy over France during a series of wars between 1689 and 1815, and remaining France's greatest rival, had itself made inroads into the richer countries to the south, notably Nigeria. The French were convinced they could redress this imbalance with a railroad from Paris to Timbuktu. They were determined to create an African trade route leading, effectively, to the heart of Europe.

By the late 1800's the commercial rewards to be had from the western Sudan were more and more questionable, while the opposition from desert tribes to Europe's intrusion had become increasingly bloody.

'Build a railway over the Sahara?' the French people cried. *C'est de la pure folie* – this is pure madness.

'Commercial acumen be damned!' replied the government in Paris, on hearing such negative sentiment to their plans. Their reasons for building a railway had nothing to do with making money. The very idea of a railway slicing through the desert had come to be described as "an instrument of domination", and for which purpose alone was considered a worthwhile venture. The Gallic cockerel would subdue those savages in the desert, come what may.

Colonel Paul Flatters was sent to scout the proposed route. He was attacked and crushed by the desert tribes. Those of Flatter's men who survived the attack were forced to subsist by eating their dead comrades. Others were sent after them, falling at the hands of the desert dwelling tribes. The French persisted. Tracks were laid from the Mediterranean coast to the northern Sahara. More men died. By 1916 a Tuareg uprising in the south of the Sahara threatened France's grip on the region. Authority had to be restored immediately if French plans were not to be thwarted. Critical French reinforcements were sent in, though they came from the south, via a railway in Nigeria that had been built by the British. It was the final insult.

Build a railway over the Sahara? '*Oui, c'est de la pure folie!*'

A window in the Elysée Palace was flung open. The plan for a railroad linking Paris to Timbuktu fluttered over the garden to the bark of a resounding, '*NON!*'

AT THE HEIGHT of its powers, in the days of the Songhay Empire, Timbuktu had been the centre of caravan and river transport in the western Sudan. It had been connected to merchants in all the towns of North Africa. Trade had not been restricted to gold. Timbuktu oversaw a brisk business in tin and copper, kola nuts and salt, ostrich feathers, cowhide, ivory and slaves. Due to the abundance of cotton throughout the Western Sudan the people of Timbuktu began producing textiles, though the colours were restricted to white and blue. The only dye available came from the indigo plant. The Tuareg populations – the Blue Men of the desert – came to be identified by their distinctive blue garments.

From the twelfth century Timbuktu grew as one of the great centres of learning in the Islamic world. Over the centuries, accompanying the camel caravans from the north came scholars of Islamic learning, bringing with them bound texts of the great teachings of Islam during the Middle Ages. During a period of intellectual stagnation in the rest of Europe Islamic study in the Muslim world was breaking new ground in subjects ranging from science and mathematics, to astronomy and law. In turn, students from as far afield as Persia made the great trek to Timbuktu to learn from this accumulation of knowledge.

The revered scholars who taught at the University of Timbuktu were known as Ambassadors of Peace throughout North and West Africa. By the 1300's, and for the next three hundred years, the message of peace and the teachings of the ambassadors extended beyond Timbuktu and along the Niger River, to Djénné and Gao. However, the Moroccan invasions saw the scholars drift away to pastures new, and with their absence, the sacred manuscripts deteriorated and became dispersed.

In recent years, there has been a major endeavour by the state and private individuals to uncover the whereabouts of the missing manuscripts. The Institut des Hautes Études et de Recherches Islamiques Ahmed Baba, established in 1973, set about gathering and restoring the 20,000 to 30,000 rare and valued manuscripts thought to be at large in northern Mali. The efforts of the institute and such families as the Kati family of Timbuktu, have met with considerable success. Despite a flourishing black market, increasingly the ancient documents are becoming available for renewed study. Though, as Tuareg rebels and Islamist insurgents muster their forces, we were led to understand that many of the documents were once again hidden in secret locations.

From having been a powerhouse of commerce, it was evident during our visit how Timbuktu survives more on the income from tourism than commercial trade, and even that is now increasingly under threat. Wandering the streets, I was surprised how well the buildings had been preserved after the stories of decay that I'd heard. There was an ongoing program of renovation. Workers in yellow safety hats balanced on wooden ladders and others crouched on rooftops. Their tools tapped at the crumbling mortar, cleaning spaces for replacement bricks to be slotted. Slowly but surely, they were putting shape back in the buildings, for the mud structures of many had all the appearance of melting into the sand.

During our street tour we stopped to gaze at the exterior of Djingareiber Mosque, which was all we could do. As infidel, we were unable to enter. The mosque had been built in 1325 by an Andalusian architect. Opposite, toddlers in uniform played in the street beside the Bibliothéque Essayouti. After our stroll, we queued for twenty minutes in the library to get internet access, and then, just as Christine sat at the desk, her fingers hovering over the keyboard, TEMPORARILY DISCONNECTED flickered on the screen.

'Please come back later,' the youth told us.

Back outside we ambled some more through the narrow, earth streets, passing houses with plaques indicating where the explorers Gordon Laing, René Caillé and Heinrich Barth (a German explorer who visited Timbuktu in 1853) had all stayed. I could imagine them closing the doors behind themselves, breathing a sigh of relief, thankful to have survived another day in what had been such a hostile environment for the European. The brick buildings had intricately carved wooden doors and shutters. They were inlaid with metal designs, and carried elaborate metal hinges and door-knockers. Along the alleyways rubbish collected in every nook and cranny. Nobody seemed to care. Inexplicably, dead cats hung from the telegraph wires.

At the Grand Marché we bought supplies and walked back via the Maison des Artisans. At the entrance to the Maison des Artisans there was a gathering of westerners anxious to secure transport out to the festival. The cost of a seat in a Land Cruiser was rising by the hour. Two French motorcyclists had ditched their bikes at a hotel and were negotiating to complete their trip by camel, a journey requiring a couple of nights in the desert. As the festival started the following day they were eager to get going.

The GPS position for the Festival in the Desert had always been a well-guarded secret. There was no leaflet being handed out telling you which way to go. If you hadn't come with a tour operator you were very much left to your own devices. Before leaving England, and after some hours' research on the internet, Christine had found a website with coordinates purporting to be those of the festival. It was all we had to go on. To ask the direction from a driver of one of the Land cruisers was to be met with a cunning smile and a vague wave of the hand. No doubt it could have been had for a price. We were determined to find it for ourselves.

We left Timbuktu on the dirt road to Goundam, heading in a south-westerly direction. After thirty-five kilometres, a small sign on the roadside indicated we should follow a series of wheel marks leading north. Our GPS coordinates corresponded with the sign. The tracks we followed weaved between acacias, at various points splitting, only to re-join again some kilometres further. At one moment, the sand was hard packed and the Hilux ran smoothly, then the next moment the engine began labouring as the sump and chassis and diff sank deeper in the sand. We passed a truck lugging stage equipment for the concert. It was stuck solid in the sand, the half-dozen assistants digging a rut ahead of the rear wheels for the steel mats to be positioned.

After thirty kilometres, and with the GPS coordinates bang on our nose, the sand became whiter and the umbrella trees more dispersed. Through the trees, we spotted 4x4's, various camping paraphernalia pitched around them, and then Peter and Sabina's truck, for which we made a beeline. We had arrived at the 2009 Festival in the Desert.

TINARIWEN, who have a significant involvement in the Festival in the Desert, are a blues band – put more precisely, they are a desert blues band.

The members of Tinariwen are *Kel Taguelmous*, (meaning "People of the Veil") the collective name for the original Berber tribes who drifted south across the Sahara Desert. The *Kel Taguelmous* are more commonly known as Tuareg, a word arising from an Arabic phrase "The abandoned of God", for their apparent unwillingness to embrace

Islam. It is a culture that is neither Arabic nor black African and has taken root over millennia.

Ranged across the Sahel (in Mali the Tuareg population is estimated at some five hundred thousand), the Tuareg respect the new frontiers established after French colonial rule with as much contempt as they do the new laws. The wind and stars, and the politics of tribe, trade and water has always governed their lives. Consequently, they have taken up arms on a number of occasions against foreign oppressors, be it French imperialism, or, more latterly, the governments of those countries located in the Sahel region. After hundreds of years of tormenting the black African the tables have finally turned on the Tuareg.

Traditionally a highly organised society run on feudal lines, the prolonged drought of the early 1970's had a devastating effect on the Tuareg. The Malian government's lack of intervention forced the young to seek alternative work in the North African cities. They were soon to learn, just as the water had evaporated in the desert, so too the notion of securing jobs in the big cities of Algeria and Libya was no more than a mirage. They joined the sullen queues of the redundant. In the language of their tongue, Tamashek, they became *ishumar*, the unemployed. Among the Tuareg youth, far away from home, *ishumar* bred discontent, rebellion and the old hunger for self-determination. The former Libyan leader Colonel Muammar Gaddafi welcomed such young men to his training camps in the desert, to teach them revolution and armed insurrection.

In 1982, a group of young men in Gaddafi's camps came together to form the band Tinariwen. They created a style called *tishoumaren*, music of the *ishumar*, songs emphasizing exile, resistance and an endeavour for recognition. Played on battered cassettes their music galvanised the Tuareg youth of the southern Sahara. Collectively they dreamed of Azawad, an independent and sovereign state in northern Mali that would include the towns of Timbuktu, Gao and Kidal.

By 1990 tensions once again detonated across the desert regions of Mali and Niger. The young Tuareg men returned from Libya with their military training and their weapons, presenting a ferocious opponent for the armed forces of Mali. Tinariwen's music came to be regarded as a unifying force by many Tuareg, a rallying cry to battle. The fighting escalated as other ethnic groups in northern Mali formed militias and sought to protect their own interests. A full-blown civil war was narrowly avoided and by 1995, following prolonged negotiations, a process of disarmament commenced. The Tuareg did not realise their dream of an independent state, though they won certain concessions, such as the creation of the autonomous region of Kidal, and certain positions within the government and the military were made available to them.

The end of the revolt was celebrated in 1996 by the symbolic burning of weapons in the "Flame of Peace". And while age and experience caused the band members of Tinariwen to shrug off some of their youthful exuberance, they keep their hopes alive that someday their people will gain a land they can call their own. Recognition of the Tuareg is what Tinariwen's music, and the Festival in the Desert, is all about.

Created in January 2001 by Manny Ansar, the manager of Tinariwen, and with its origins in the big, traditional Tuareg festivals, known as *Temakannit* in the Timbuktu region, the organisers decided to open their doors to the international community.

Since the 1980s, West African Blues came to the fore

when Stevie Wonder teamed with Amadou and Miriam, a musical duo from Bamako, Mali. In 1994 Ry Cooder recorded *Talking Timbuktu* with Malian guitarist Ali Farka Touré and, following his journey to Mali in 2002, Justin Adams produced his afro-beat album *Desert Roads*. By 2003, it was therefore a natural progression for the festival's organisers to welcome performances not only by West Africa's leading music artists, but also to include musicians from around the world, such as Led Zeppelin's Robert Plant, Justin Adams, Marcus James, Leni Stern, and the Sway Machines. In that same year, British broadcaster Andy Kershaw won the Sony Gold Award for his programme, The Festival in the Desert.

During recent years, in the order of eight thousand visitors from various points across the globe converge on the dunes at Essakane. Since its inception, the festival has promoted the values of tolerance and hospitality, and continued celebrating the "Flame of Peace", in spite of rebel Tuareg groups renewing their attacks on military installations. However, the 2012 Festival in the Desert, when Bono, lead singer of U2, sang alongside Bassekou Konyate and Tinariwen, was to be the last music heard before war. The words '*Vive le Mali, vive la paix, vive la musique*' were no defence against the turmoil about to commence.

Following this latest rebel uprising the government of Mali negotiated a fresh ceasefire, though the problems were far from over. By late 2011 Tuaregs who'd been fighting to preserve the regime of their old mentor Colonel Gaddafi drifted back to Mali, following the former Libyan leader's demise. No doubt inspired by the Arab Spring, and bristling with fresh armaments, they formed a rebellion movement, the Azawad National Liberation Movement (MLNA). It's difficult to assess how representative of the Tuareg people in

Mali this movement was. Notwithstanding what support they might enjoy, in January 2012 the MLNA made their move, seizing a number of northern towns and unleashing a descent into chaos.

We established camp on the perimeter of the festival, between the Austrian's truck and a cluster of thorn-bush. Behind us a troop of soldiers languished in the shade of a tree, a row of assault rifles propped against the trunk of a felled acacia. The soldiers were surrounded by cardboard boxes, no doubt their supplies to see them through the coming days.

A matt-green pickup swept through the trees, a soldier clinging to an enormous machine gun mounted in the back. Some distance away he pulled up beside three similarly equipped vehicles. The Malian army was prepared for trouble, though amongst the people we spoke to there was considerable confusion as to the true nature of the threat. A group of Americans we met in Timbuktu said the US government had recently issued a warning for its citizens not to visit Essakane, due to the heightened chance of attack by al-Qaida in the Islamic Maghreb (AQIM). Others said the worry was the gang belonging to the Tuareg rebel Ibrahim Ag Bahanga. We'd already learnt of his assault on an army outpost in Nampala just before Christmas. Perhaps the two groups were one and the same. Nobody seemed to know. I began to wonder if anybody knew what was really going on out here.

Convinced that those al-Qaida terrorists flushed from the caves in Afghanistan were intent on re-establishing their training camps in remote areas of the Sahara, the United States announced the Pan-Sahel Initiative in late 2003. It involved flying five hundred US troops into Nouakchott and placing four hundred US Rangers throughout Mali, Chad and Niger. According to social anthropologist Jeremy Keenen, a recognised authority on the Sahara, the US initiative was predicated on intelligence supplied by the Algerian secret service. In early 2003 seven separate groups of overlanders were kidnapped by a mysterious character named El Para. But was El Para an agent of the Algerian state, and the entire incident orchestrated in order to bolster Algeria's security apparatus, a country with a history of violence perpetrated by Islamist militants? And was the US government complicit in the hostage taking, in order to extend its influence in the region? In his book *The Dark Sahara* Keenen suggests they were. Moving the thirty-two hostages from Algeria to northern Mali, as it seems El Para was ordered to do by his shadowy masters, had the effect of elevating the incident's political status – terrorism was spreading across the Sahara. The United States could no longer ignore it.

In the event, the hostages were released physically unharmed, except an unfortunate German woman, who died from heatstroke during the move from Algeria to Mali.

With such alarming theories as Keenen's doing the rounds, our confusion, as we unfurled our tent and set out our tables and chairs, was hardly surprising. Whether the US and Algeria had a hidden agenda or not, it was fast becoming apparent that AQIM actively existed in the Sahara, and no government of any sort appeared to be doing very much to stop it spreading.

Al-Qaida in the Islamic Maghreb is a Salafi-jihadist group whose roots go back to the brutal civil war in Algeria of the early 90's. AQIM started life as the Salafist Group for Preaching and Combat (GSPC), itself an offshoot of the Armed Islamic Group. From 2000, the GSPC's operations were seriously curbed by a successful counter-terrorism program waged by the Algerian government. By 2007 the GSPC had re-thought its strategy, aligned itself with al-Qaida and changed its name to Al-Qaida in the Islamic Maghreb. A new wave of savage attacks immediately commenced in Algeria, and from a base in the deserts of northern Mali AQIM sought to spread its fundamentalist ideology to the broader region. In the Sahel AQIM successfully merged criminality with terrorism and was thought to be one of the wealthiest of the al-Qaida franchises. It generated income by kidnapping foreign diplomats, tourists and humanitarian aid workers, securing sizable ransoms for their release (the Geneva Centre for Security Policy reports how the majority of the fifty-four abductions between 2003 and 2011 are attributable to AQIM). It was also believed that AQIM controlled a number of the lucrative smuggling routes across the Sahara, reaping rewards from the movement of South American drugs landed in West Africa and transhipped overland to the markets in Europe.

In 2012, AQIM snatched the chance to consolidate their hold on the Sahel region by forming an alliance with the Tuareg-led Azawad National Liberation Movement. The joint forces moved swiftly into the Kidal region. Routed, and thoroughly despondent with the government's handling of the campaign against the rebels, the army staged a coup, ousting President Amadou Toumani Touré. The Tuareg rebels and Islamist militants took advantage of the political diversion in Bamako to seize the towns of Kidal, Gao, Timbuktu, and Douentza. By early April the insurgents had effectively split the country in two. On reaching Douentza the MNLA declared northern Mali the new Independent State of Azawad, though their euphoria was to be short-lived.

As the dust from the initial surge settled, the Islamist factions, by then numbering five different groups, began to assert their influence – the black flags of the Islamists cracked in the Saharan winds. Tuareg interests were sidelined as a fundamentalist regime based on sharia law transformed the lives of those who had not already fled. Dancing, music and smoking were banned. Women had to cover their heads and faces. Iconic shrines were destroyed. Amputation, stoning and flogging were the new punishments. Stories of rape carried back to Bamako. Before the year was out Tuareg rebels and the Islamist insurgents were at each other's throats.

Tens of thousands fled the fighting into neighbouring countries. By November of 2012 the United Nations High Commissioner for Refugees estimated that both refugees and internally displaced people numbered more than four hundred thousand. The shortage of food, water, shelter and medical assistance was soon apparent. And while the interim government and armed forces scrabbled to overcome their own in-fighting, the international community grew more impatient. Not only was a dire humanitarian crisis unfolding, but many saw Mali degenerating into a failed state. Terrorist groups could flourish there with impunity and comparisons were starting to be drawn with Afghanistan.

In her January 2013 Congressional testimony, US Secretary of State Hilary Clinton compared the security risks in Mali to that of Afghanistan. When the Islamists commenced a new advance on Bamako, something had to be done. Early in the New Year, and with United Nations backing, French President François Hollande responded positively to Mali's urgent appeal for military aid, launching Operation Serval. By mid-January 2013 French airstrikes and a contingency of French and Malian troops unseated the Islamist insurgents from the northern towns, pushing them back to the desert. In the summer of the same year a tentative peace deal between the government and the Tuareg rebels was also agreed. Though the peace was to be short-lived.

By the summer of 2014 the French military had launched Operation Barkhane, with the country taking a leading role in a counter-terrorism objective in the hope of securing peace. By then, Mali had three problems to contend with: weak governance prone to military coups; a Tuareg rebellion and, thirdly, a rapidly developing Islamist insurgency. By the early 2020s the Islamist problem had begun to take root regionally, spreading to Burkina Faso, Niger and the Central African Republic. Among such misrule, corruption and subsequent poverty, it has been relatively easy for the Islamists to recruit from the discontented populations. Increasingly viewing France's military assistance as a throwback to its former colonial days, and with their own governments unable to tackle the increasing violence, a series of military coups have introduced a further layer of instability, providing fertile ground for foreign mercenary organisations such as the Russian Wagner Group to profit from the chaos.

In 2023, Mali had around 400,000 internally displaced people, 40% of the population in need of humanitarian assistance, and 200,000 children at risk of starvation. As the country shambles into the future, the immediate question to be answered is: will there be sufficient food to nourish the people?

. . .

Back in 2009 we were blind to the crisis set to unfold in Mali in the not-too-distant future. We settled into our chairs at Essakane, put the kettle to boil and got out the tea. We were camped in a landscape of beautiful country: umbrella trees, white dunes, escarpments to the east and west, to the north the Great Desert.

In the late afternoon, after we'd checked in with the organisers of the festival, and received our wrist bands, we ambled towards the sounds of music, voices and laughter. A surreal scene unfolded in front of us.

A huge bowl of white sand contained a concrete stage, black speakers as tall as a man and, enclosing it all, a structure of tubular metal poles supporting the lighting system. Here and there were clusters of tents, all sizes and shapes, from the traditional to the modern. There was a bar with karaoke, tented restaurants, artisan stalls, rugs laid in the sand, cooking pots on open fires, people eating in groups, and others sat at tables and chairs drinking beer and coke and tea. In and around all this were blue-robed men, their heads swathed in the traditional black *shesh*, rocking back and forth on camels. The beat of different music clashed. The sound check – *'Un, deux, trois'* – echoed over the dunes as the technicians tweaked their equipment.

The 4x4's that had ferried in the tourists were parked door to door, bumper to bumper.

JP and I bought a couple of tins of warm beer and gazed at the scene. Ten thousand people had congregated in the middle of nowhere – the home of the Tuareg.

When we rose for breakfast the next day a Tuareg was crouched opposite our car, a collection of jewellery and knives displayed on the sand.

'*Bonjour*,' the Tuareg chimed, introducing himself as Abdallah.

Abdallah never left our side all morning. In the nicest possible way, he was not leaving us until we'd submitted to his charm and dug deep in our pockets. For the next few hours he was going to be our best and only friend.

Along with a salesman's patter Abdallah was quite the dandy – a Tuareg dandy – draped in shiny turquoise robe and pantaloons. The Tuareg have a tendency for vibrant colours and Abdallah had most certainly raised the stakes. A fulsome, purple *shesh* covered all but his eyes, with a second, pure-white head-cloth perched atop of that; he was a double helping of whipped cream on a fruit parfait. Only the sword hanging from his belt arrested any temptation to ridicule.

Abdallah was aged thirty and he came from a settlement somewhere beyond the dunes. He'd already been married twice, he explained. His first wife, chosen by his family, was a distant relation from Marrakech. No sooner had she made the long trek south than she started missing the bright medina lights. She couldn't give two figs for her husband's goat-skin tent and his spitting camels; by the time the henna had worn off her hands she wanted out. She lasted a few moons, Abdallah told us, describing an extravagant arc with his hand. There was no drawn-out divorce settlement, no arguing over the contents of the tent. After a few cows had changed hands she was loaded on a caravan heading north.

'And then I married again,' Abdallah cooed, drawing his sword and slashing the air above his head. 'Take a photo of me,' he insisted. 'You must take a photo.'

He whirled a figure of eight with the sword, his dark eyes flashing. The sudden movement caused the whipped cream head-cloth to cant sideways and his sunglasses fell in the sand.

Didn't we agree he was the meanest Tuareg around?

'Oh, yes,' we assured him. 'The meanest of the mean.'

Christine and Susie bought some of his jewellery. I partially disarmed him by purchasing the knife tucked in his belt. There was a loud slap of handshakes when the deal was done, and we never saw Abdallah again.

A pattern to our lives soon established itself at the festival in Essakane. In the mornings, after coffee and a trip to the baker's tent, a procession of visitors came to our encampment. They emptied their bags of jewellery, carvings, semi-precious stones, cloth, and leather sandals, carefully placing them in the sand. Each one had a story to tell. Occasionally we traded. Often, they were out of luck – too much of the same thing.

Tuareg's brought camels: Where would we like to go? For how long? 'Seen from the back of a camel the sunset is at its most beautiful,' they promised. They ran their hands over wooden saddles overlaid with thick, vibrantly coloured rugs. Christine and Susie patted the camels' necks. The beasts rumbled, holding their heads with an imperial grace.

On the second morning, a Fulani man from Niger brought woollen rugs. Traditionally nomadic cattle herders, the Fulani people (also called Peul) are scattered widely throughout West Africa. His rugs were very welcome. The nights were freezing; a dry, penetrating cold that no amount of clothing held at bay. We bought four rugs. The Fulani left a very happy man.

Kids hung around us too, an eye on our bag of rubbish. They wanted empty plastic bottles, as many as they could lay their hands on.

One morning two of JP's Tuareg friends called at our camp. They were brought over by the young guide we'd met at Campement Tenéré. It was a cheery reunion. JP had last seen them more than twenty-five years ago. He'd sold them

Land Rovers that he'd driven down from Europe. They were still running tours in the east of Mali with the same vehicles, they told him. Tea was poured and, to experience the full cultural exchange, what was left of my aunt Janet's Christmas cake cut into slices and offered round. Sipping tea and nibbling chunks of fruit cake and icing, JP and his pals caught up on their news. There was growing unrest in the desert, they told us. Bad things were happening.

'You should not travel north of the river,' they said, when we told them it was our plan to visit Gao.

When asked why not, we were left with the same vague answers as before. The sand was too deep...our car was not up to the job...there might be bandits who would steal our things.

We couldn't get our heads round such nebulous talk. There's banditry of one form or another just about anywhere one chooses to travel. As for the sand being too deep for the car, the Hilux had already proved itself perfectly capable. If you are to accept that many Africans shroud the meaning of their words in fables and fanciful talk, then there was something behind what they were saying. For whatever reason, they weren't prepared to say it outright. Whatever was on their minds, why couldn't they just spit it out?

The afternoons were the time to promenade.

The main event of the afternoon was usually camel racing. The Tuareg, in their robes of blues, violets, yellows and browns, their heads swathed in a black *shesh*, cajoled, kicked and lashed their beasts into a ragged line-up. A shout went up and – YEEHA! – thirty to forty camels and their riders thundered toward a distant point. Groups sitting on the dunes cheered and punched the air. A line of Muslim women, covered head to toe in black, ululated. Tourists gazed, their senses trying to play catch-up with their eyes. Over an address system, the winner was announced, banter exchanged, the next race called. 'Would Princess Stephanie of Monaco come to the organiser's box,' the voice reverberated from the address system one afternoon. For no specified reason, she had won a camel to take back to the Principality.

To kick the sand between your toes, to wander amongst the makeshift bars, the artisans' stalls, the cooking pots; to rub shoulders with Asians, Arabs, Africans and Europeans; to hear American, French, German, Japanese, Arabic, Tamashek, Mande; to catch West African beat competing with British rock-and-roll, hip-hop and a French brass band; to see robes striding beside T-shirts and shorts, traditional head-cloths beside baseball caps, straw boaters beside carnival masks, daggers and swords besides switches and a Leatherman – it was a truly bizarre experience. A melting pot, a *folie du monde*, a Mad Hatter's tea party.

One day, returning to our encampment we noticed a Swiss owned Land Rover had drawn a crowd around its open bonnet – a Land Rover requiring a touch of maintenance, now that was a rare sight! We couldn't resist a closer look. What could possibly be the matter?

I sensed JP already rising to the challenge. He had his camera at the ready.

While preparing to leave Timbuktu for the festival, the owner of the Land Rover had jumped aboard his vehicle and started the engine. Emanating from under the bonnet, the disconcerting screech and repetitive thwacking sound had him snatching for the ignition key to quickly turn it off. The cause of the racket was down to an alley cat having chosen to pass the night in a warm engine bay. The cat had been enjoying a lazy lie-in when the cooling fan unceremoniously flicked him into the radiator. The resulting damage had rendered the radiator about as much use as a garden sprinkler. The cat himself, like his mates hanging from Timbuktu's telegraph wires, had gone the way of all fleshy things. And, perhaps, therein lies the answer to the mystery of why cats hang from telegraph wires in the first place: after a good night's sleep in a warm engine bay, a flick of the ignition key ejects them skywards into the chilly morning air.

With the Swiss man's spanners two locals were already slackening the nuts and bolts holding the radiator. 'No problem,' they assured him. We were witnessing the marvel of an African bush repair. Within half an hour the radiator was free of the vehicle and in the back of a pickup. A minute later and the pickup had transformed into a trail of dust heading east. Before lunch the following day the Land Rover was recovered to full working order.

The evenings were the time for music.

By eight o'clock the action moved to the stage. Crowds gathered in the sandy arena. Braziers were filled with charcoal and set alight. The stage lighting threw forests of shadow, their sparkle competing with the night stars. The crowd hummed in expectation. The first band gathered on the stage. For a fleeting moment absolute silence reigned, after which the first notes pricked the hush.

AFTER THE FESTIVAL, we returned to Timbuktu. To the north of the town, set among thatched dwellings, we found Hotel Sahara Passion. It was situated at the very edge of the desert, wind-blown sand heaped against its walls. Inside the compound beds lay side by side beneath awnings of hide. There were bedrooms to be had in the building at the back, except we were too late, they were already taken, and so we settled for the alfresco arrangement, lugged in our bags and picked our beds. In one corner, behind a rickety wooden door was the open-air shower and toilet. The hotel was run by Miranda, a Canadian who'd come to Timbuktu as a tourist some years before. She'd taken to the Bedouin lifestyle, married a Tuareg and had recently had a baby.

As a consequence of our four nights spent in the desert we were dreaming the impossible: a steaming shower, soft bed, a steak, a bottle of Chateauneuf du Pape ...

After a tepid shower, we went in search of the Poulet d'Or, said to have the crispiest chips in town. The dinner was a welcome change and the bottle of grotty red wine the waiter foraged from somewhere in the grid of narrow streets, worryingly, tasted rather good.

In the morning, I was awoken by the occasional waft of wood-smoke. I opened my eyes to a gnarled old man squatting on his haunches beside the wall, barely a couple of metres from me. He was wafting the fire with a fan, a kettle perched precariously on the coals. It is quite extraordinary how much time is spent wafting the coals in Africa, a pastime I can personally attest to. It was a matter of getting yourself in the right mind-set, and then wafting became marginally meditative – Zen and the art of wafting coals. The old man was a picture of contentment.

An hour later, washed and dressed, we gathered on a long table for a cup of coffee and bread and jam. The guy serving had a *shesh* hanging loosely either side of his head. He wore a padded coat to ward off the morning chill.

'Are you Jean-Pierre?' he rasped, placing a jug of steaming water on the table.

JP looked up, for a moment studying the man's face. 'Yes,' he replied.

'I thought it was you. I am Shindouk. You sold me a Land Rover many years ago.'

Shindouk was another of JP's old contacts from the past. The two men shook hands. The Land Rover had done very well, Shindouk said. Except now it was quite old, and he needed another one.

Shindouk's face softened when he explained he was the owner of the hotel, husband to Miranda, proud father of the child playing on a rug in the corner of the yard. He'd just returned from the salt mines at Taoudenni, he said, a seven-hundred-kilometres journey with a camel caravan. Even though he is now a hotelier, he liked to keep his hand in in the salt trade. Shindouk might have been a man of property, yet he couldn't let go of one of the last of the old trans-Saharan trades. We could go with him, he explained. He organised tours in the desert.

Shindouk lamented how the old ways of the desert had changed. Many of the traditional trade routes had been taken over by gun runners, drug traffickers and people smugglers.

'They carry assault rifles as if they are a toothbrush,' he said, scowling. 'There are bad men out there.'

The bad men, Shindouk explained, wanted the desert to themselves. Then they could continue their nefarious pursuits completely out of sight (except, perhaps, for the occasional American satellite drifting overhead). As such, they were hostile and disruptive to the traditional merchants such as himself. And very bad for tourism.

'I went to see those Arabs in the north,' he growled. 'I told them, if they wanted to make trouble, then the Tuareg would give them plenty of trouble in return.'

It wasn't clear who these particular "Arabs in the north" were, or who the "bad men" were, for that matter. Whatever had been said by Shindouk and his people seemed to have done the trick for now. As we took the last of the steps up to the roof of Shindouk's tower, he confirmed they didn't have any more problems with the bad men.

From the tower, we enjoyed a panoramic view of Timbuktu. Far to the north, where acacia trees submitted to the march of the dunes, camels were being driven toward the town. In the history of trans-Sahara trade, not many goods would have made it over the Great Desert without the trusty camel. While the outside world flirted with yo-yos, gunpowder, eyeglasses, double-armed catapults, electricity, steam engines and telephones, during one thousand years of trans-Saharan caravan trade, the technology and methodology for transporting goods had not progressed beyond the camel. The new-fangled inventions, the wheel and the compass, held no attraction for the caravan leader; such contraptions could do nothing towards improving his life. Recruited from desert Bedouins, the caravan leader had his own set of skills. He often led up to five thousand camels (including hundreds of people) safely back and forth. Good navigation and a constant pace were a prerequisite; to maximise profit only a small percentage of the caravan was reserved for the carriage of food. An intimate knowledge of the landscape and climate were critical; shifting dunes could radically reshape the route. Finding sources of potable water spelt life or death; wells could dry up or become contaminated. For the caravan to walk headlong into a prolonged sandstorm could foment a range of vital issues. And then there were the hostile chiefdoms with whom safe passage had to be negotiated. It can easily be imagined how a caravan leader's worst nightmare would be to arrive at an empty well during a sandstorm, with only a day's supply of food remaining, and then find his group surrounded by bandits bristling with weapons.

I took one last look from the roof of Shindouk's tower. It appeared to me that the only connection to gold remaining in Timbuktu these days was the colour of the dunes on the old salt route to Taoudenni.

In the Place de la Flamme de Paix we paused at the monument commemorating the end of the Tuareg rebellion in 1996. During the ceremony marking the return to peace three thousand weapons belonging to the Tuareg rebels and the Malian army were set alight – hence the Flame of Peace. An ornate, marble-tiled structure towered over a concrete mound, from which the barrels of the burnt weapons protruded. There was something prophetic in the fact that the monument had already begun to crumble. Children were playing tag round it. When we got out our cameras they struck various poses beside the corroded relics of war; these kids were the new hope for Mali.

While the girls replenished the food-stocks I went with JP to a tiny office above the covered market to renew the vehicle's insurance. An hour later, with our crispy-clean insurance certificate, boxes of fresh produce and a full tank of fuel we headed out of town in an easterly direction.

The rather grandly named R32, a sandy *piste*, followed the north bank of the Niger River to Bourem, and thereafter it joined the N18 to Gao. On leaving Timbuktu, the track had been difficult to find and even trickier to follow. It was a mishmash of tyre tracks, splitting in various places, leaving us in the thorny situation of almost licking a finger to feel which way the wind was blowing; finding the correct route was entirely guesswork.

In a very short time we left behind any sign of habitation and were soon into dry savannah. After sixty kilometres, we reached the settlement of Ber. Here we asked a group of soldiers which of the many tracks leading out into the desert would take us in the direction of Bourem.

For a road that was no more than parallel wheel marks weaving through the arid landscape it was incongruous to come across the occasional road sign sprouting from the sand. They were your everyday metal post with a triangle outlined in faded red paint. They warned of bends and bumps, of stray cattle, and of lanes narrowing to single file. The only vehicle we saw all day was a truck towing a loaded flatbed to Timbuktu.

Occasionally we passed tiny settlements of domed tents made from woven material, clothes stretched out on the roof to dry, multi-coloured water containers stacked together by the entrance. Women pounded cereal and chickens pecked the earth. Stacks of mud bricks dried in the sun and wheelbarrows stood close by. Thorn-bush had been hacked down and waited in clumps for the cooking fire.

The midday sun bleached the panorama of all colour and by late afternoon, we made camp at the foot of a dune, suitably hidden from the track by trees and tussock grass. To reach the crest of the dune was a climb of some one hundred metres; even higher when you allowed for the depth your feet sank in the sand with each step. I laboured up it as the descending sun turned the dune into a rich golden colour. To the south, beyond the vast plain of sand and trees, a slither of the Niger reflected the orange sun. Beneath the southern flank of the dune stood a huge rock formation, surrounded by clusters of palm trees. The light breeze caused the silvering fronds to shimmer and crackle. I scanned the horizon. The land went on forever, no matter in which direction I looked. Occasionally the breeze carried voices from a distant settlement. It was extraordinarily peaceful after the bustle of Timbuktu. In that moment, there was something magical about being a part of that scene, to rest in the sand, gathering the thoughts and images of the past month and turning them over in my head. There were no distractions. Only the raw beauty of a land stripped to the quick.

I've heard often enough how a long journey is undertaken on two levels: the physical and the spiritual. On a purely physical level, I could never claim that travelling through West Africa is a breeze; though in our circumstances, with a capable vehicle transporting us and our creature comforts, neither could I complain. But it wasn't just the manner in which we travelled that came so starkly into focus. We were privileged in that we could move on whenever we chose to. It might have been tomorrow...the next day...the next week. How many times on that journey had I looked into the eyes of people who would have given their all for such freedom? And imagine, in a curious fusion of time and space, had I bumped into Mungo Park who, during his return from the Niger River to the Atlantic coast, was robbed, stripped of his clothes and forced to walk one thousand miles on rotten shoes. I'm quite sure the intrepid Scotsman would have harangued me with, 'You've got it lucky, friend. When I was a wee laddie...' And quite rightly so.

I'm humbled by what those early explorers achieved, their unwavering spirit and their bravery. Often their tale is one of survival rather than discovery, and it is just as remarkable. I asked myself often enough on the trip: could I have done what they did? I like to think I would have been up for the challenge. Don't we all? Of course, there was one way to find out; I could always return to Banjul, buy myself a couple of donkeys, a compass and ... no, maybe not.

On a spiritual level, I felt I was no more tolerant, or patient, or sociable than when I set out on the journey. Neither had cooking in the Great Outdoors enthused me to do more than the usual man pursuit of chucking a slab of meat on a grill and blackening both sides. As for learning new languages there was little hope; with my flow of French vocabulary remaining fused and unresponsive, there was not much point moving on to Mandinka or Wolof. Nor, it seemed, had a blinding flash of light stimulated me to acquire new skills, other than learning to tie-wrap a pair of flip-flops to the chassis of a Toyota Hilux. Worryingly, I thought myself more unhinged than when Christine and I boarded the ferry from Spain to Morocco. My nerves had become frayed due to insomnia and the bouts of vertigo, though I was quite sure it was all due to the weird cocktail of chemicals I'd ingested, namely in the form of the anti-malarial pills, and that soon all would be well.

As I stretched on the dune, my head resting on my clasped hands, there was an aspect to my character I could definitely put my finger on. The notebook of lists I'd left Europe with had not seen the light of day since before Christmas. I'd unburdened myself of the need for a schedule. When in Africa, sticking to the strictures of time and expectation is futile.

Despite all, I'd rather taken to the life of an overlander. I felt a certain sense of achievement. We'd got as far as Timbuktu; such a journey has killed many who tried. I couldn't resist the sense of smug satisfaction as I closed my eyes to enjoy the moment. Up there on the dune, the peace and quiet after Essakane and Timbuktu was complete.

In the dying light, I loped down the dune and joined the others. At the end of our boots the breeze agitated the flames of our fire; the branches cracked and sparked. The smell of cooking mingled with the wood smoke. Soon the sky was awash with stars. In the firelight, the darkness ebbed and flowed about us.

Around the campfire, we made the final decision concerning our route: we would not continue to Gao. Instead, we'd try to locate the embarkation point for the ferry crossing the river to Gourma-Rharous. The old Tuareg friends of JP had been trying to send us a message. Even if a little oblique, the warning not to travel the north bank of the Niger had come on sound authority. I had no doubt JP's friends were full of good intention when they told us to retrace our steps to Douentza. It was just that none of us had wanted to heed it. When you travel like this you must accept a level of risk. You accept destiny and chance, and you try not to be in the wrong place at the wrong time. Sometimes it is difficult to gauge how far to push the boundary between adventure and foolhardiness. The warning bells were ringing.

Ten days after we'd made our decision that night by the campfire, a group of three vehicles heading to a festival in Anderamboukane were held up by armed bandits in the region of Gao. One of the vehicles containing three tourists managed a rapid U-turn, escaping with bullet holes in the vehicle's bodywork. They were lucky. The other two vehicles, transporting four tourists, slithered to a halt, their tyres shredded by gunfire. The two Swiss, one German and a British man were carted off into the bush. For a month, nothing more was heard of the kidnapped tourists or their abductors. Then AQIM declared their hand. They wanted a radical cleric releasing from a British prison and the payment of an eight-million-pound ransom. The cogs within the British Foreign office ground inexorably. Various third parties entered negotiations with the kidnappers.

Finally, the Swiss and the German citizens were released. The Foreign Office deliberated some more. Despite threats to execute the British hostage unless AQIM's demands were met, the FO continued to stand by its dictum not to negotiate with terrorists. As a consequence, by early June the British hostage had been murdered.

From this sad tale, all of us could only conclude that JP's friends knew something was in the air. Your run-of-the-mill bandit can make good money selling westerners to terrorists. The temptation is great. The word spreads. If you're in the wrong place at the wrong time, you're in trouble.

We made the embarkation point for the ferry to Gourma-Rharous by mid-morning the following day. Finding it was not without its complications, raising a great deal of questions along the way, and not a little self-doubt. For instance: why would a ferry come to a place where there is no infrastructure? How long do you follow the false track? Does the nomad staring blankly from his camel really understand what you're asking of him? Why are there no ferry signposts on the desert *piste* to Gao?

Eventually, we happened across a row of woven huts beside the river. Crowds of children broke from their games and came howling towards us. A man looked up from the pirogue he was whacking with an axe. A couple of youths stopped chopping wood.

JP climbed from the car, ushered the children aside, and went to the man crouching in the pirogue. The man straightened, listened for a moment and then pointed to the mud-flat ahead. It seemed we were in the right place, after all. A couple of youths, joined by a few women, ambled towards the car, frowning, chattering between themselves. We were quite the oddity, the event of the day...or the week, perhaps. Did nobody ever come out here? It certainly felt that way.

We drove down the sandy bank and out on to the mud-flat. For a while a noisy swarm of children followed us. One by one they fizzled out.

Ahead of us the mud-flat covered a vast area, a thick margin of reeds marking the edge of the river. We drove across the mud-flat to the edge of the river, following the bank until reaching a clearing where the mud had been churned by the passage of vehicles. It was as if the vehicles had entered the water and simply vanished beneath the surface. Other than the wheel-marks there was nothing to suggest it might have been the embarkation point for a ferry; no sign, no ticket kiosk, no timetable, no passengers – no nothing. I wound down the window. The strong wind carried the distant TAP! TAP! TAP! of axe on wood, and the screech of the children absorbed by a new game.

Two hours passed and we wondered, after all, if we might have to drive to Gao. A motorbike arrived with rider and pillion, parking beside us.

'Yes,' they replied, in answer to our question. 'The ferry comes here.'

'When?'

'When it arrives.'

The pillion looked up at the sky. 'It's very windy today,' he said. 'The wind is not good for the ferry.'

The driver lifted his sunglasses and wiped his red, streaming eyes with the blue scarf wrapped around his neck. He was a teacher working for an aid agency, he said. He was going home to Gourma-Rharous.

'I cannot ride my motorbike in these cold winds,' the teacher moaned, admiring the goggles attached to the back of the headrest in the Hilux. '*C'est un grand problème pour moi.*'

Christine unhooked the goggles and handed them over. We had another three pairs. They were ski goggles; purple, with tinted lenses. I'd brought them with us for that perfect sandstorm, or if the windscreen ever got smashed and we had to drive the car many kilometres with no windscreen. I was trying to be a good boy scout, though felt certain the teacher could put them to better use. He fixed the goggles over his head and beamed; purple ski goggles were the height of desert-chic, an accessory every red-blooded Saharan biker aspired to wear.

'*Merci beaucoup*,' he gushed. He raised the goggles to his forehead, testing the amount of flex in the strap before setting them back over his eyes. He looked down, concentrating on his feet. He lifted one foot and studied the sole of his shoe, and then he lifted the other. He raised his hand, turning it back and forth and wiggling his fingers. Finally, he craned his head skyward.

'D'you have a telephone?' he asked.

'*Non!*' I snapped, guessing what might come next.

'If you had a telephone, I could call the ferry and ask them where they are.'

'What a good idea.'

We might have been in the middle of nowhere but we had a couple of signal bars on the phone. That was one of the extraordinary things in West Africa. Everybody had a mobile telephone – except teachers like the one stood before us – and the network was extensive. In the more remote regions the mobile phone network had negated the need to install landlines. The biggest problem for the African in the bush, however, was recharging the battery. We had many a nomad disturb our lunch with a request to recharge his telephone's battery. In the villages and towns, I'd noticed how a lot of people made money recharging the mobile phones of others.

'The ferryman says it's very windy,' the teacher informed us, disconnecting the call. He returned the phone to Christine. 'But he's coming.'

Finally, beyond the reeds and the distant trees the steel superstructure of the ferry eventually poked into view. For long moments, when the wind blew hard, the ferry made no forward progress whatsoever, as if it might have been roosting in those far treetops, like an enormous African ferry-bird. Ever so slowly it came that little bit closer.

The vessel that entered the narrow inlet between the reeds was roughly twenty metres in length and constructed entirely in steel. A pirogue, powered by a forty-horsepower outboard engine, was lashed to the side of it. The outboard was the only means of propulsion, because the ferry's main engine was temporarily out of order. This is what I love about Africa. They will always find a way to carry on. We jumped back in the Hilux and prepared to board.

As the vessel nudged into the shallows, the ramp slapping in the mud, a deep roar penetrated our cocoon. We gazed over the mud-flat, searching for the source of the noise.

'What on earth is that?' Susie asked.

An orange-coloured truck, a caravan bolted to its back, raced towards us. Twin, vertical exhaust pipes belched tubes of black smoke, the cab dipping and rearing with each upward change of gear. The growling engine and pounding rock music sent a seismic shock quivering through the earth.

'Who's in control?' I murmured after witnessing the muzzle of a German shepherd poking from a bush of dreadlocks. A second dog barked from the open passenger window, its tongue and ears flapping in the rush of wind. More dreadlocks filled the passenger seat. It was the oddest sight, a crazy melange of Mad Max and a Battersea Dogs Home breakout.

The deck-hand on the ramp of the ferry threw up his hand to stop us boarding, his eyes widening as he watched this devil-truck bearing down on his boat. The captain thrust his head out of his box-like bridge to bellow instructions. The deck-hand skittered across the deck, flapping his hands. Air brakes on the truck hissed and a rear wheel locked, gouging chunks of earth.

'At that speed, he'll go straight out the other side,' JP uttered.

The thump and clash of AC/DC competed with the crash of gears and blipping throttle. The truck slowed. Rumbling and barking it submerged into the river, sinking deeper in the mud, its all-terrain tyres mangling a passage through the ooze. With a howl from the exhausts it crashed up the ramp, settling on the cargo deck like a malevolent steel monster.

The six metres of marshland between us and the ramp had been churned into a quagmire. Mud and river water slopped in the holes. For a second or two JP and I argued over which gear best suited the occasion. I set the Hilux in four-wheel-drive High and stamped on the accelerator. We bucked and splattered through the mud, bounced up the ramp and slithered to a halt centimetres from the pink bicycles strapped to Mad Max's spare wheels.

Reaching the other side of the river, we cruised the few sandy streets of Gourma-Rharous, calling on the butcher and buying bread from a stall. With nothing to detain us in this sleepy place we joined the *piste* heading south. A few kilometres from the town I pulled aside to allow a car full of youths and thumping music to overtake us. It was lunch time, and there was a gap in the bush up ahead, and so after the youths had gone I drove fifty metres into the bush and we opened up the back of the car. No sooner had we got our lunch spread over the tailgate than the car with the youths was back, this time rocking to a new beat. The car followed our tracks into the bush, coming to a stop behind us.

The driver cut the engine, followed by the music, returning the bush to its previous silence. Five of them climbed out. They strolled towards us, fanning out. It was difficult to gauge from their expressions if their interest in us was purely curiosity. A couple of them were smiling. The others were not.

What were we doing here, they wanted to know? As if it wasn't obvious, we held up our sandwiches of tinned sardine and raw onion; our customary lunch-time nourishment. We invited the youths to join us. They gazed at our sandwiches and shook their heads. Fair enough. Tinned sardines aren't to everyone's taste. I'd become a little weary of them myself.

So, what were they after, these boys, if it wasn't food?

For a couple of bites of the sandwich JP joked with them.

Then one of them blurted, 'What have you for us?' And the smiles slipped.

'Nothing at all,' we replied, and I pondered with the idea of grabbing the pepper spray, though, if I breathed on them, it may have had a more lethal effect.

It was as if the youths were undecided what to do next. A slightly uncomfortable minute of silence passed. They exchanged glances with each other and rocked from one foot to the other. Was it a try on, or did they believe they held the upper hand? We continued chomping through our lunch. If things turned nasty our choice of immediate weapons was limited. I could have slapped them with the butter knife, or even pummelled them with a half-eaten onion. I really hadn't a clue where the pepper spray was. In time the youths arrived at a silent conclusion to whatever it was they'd been deliberating. They nodded their heads, muttered something unintelligible and slunk back to their car.

They roared off on a wave of hip hop, dark looks and rhythmic tapping.

Not long after the youths left us we got back on the road ourselves. The *piste* meandered, the torrid conditions and the motion of the car leaving us quiet and sleepy. The tyres hummed on the patches of *feche feche*, an ultra-fine powdery dust which cast us in a shroud and seeped through the doors. The dust irritated our noses and crunched in our teeth. In places, the last heavy rains made stretches of the track impassable. We were forced to pick our way over the deep ruts left behind by the trucks. From time to time we crossed paths with herdsmen and their beasts. They were heading back and forth to the infrequent lakes.

We made camp that evening tucked far enough from the track to remain undisturbed.

THE TRACK SOUTH from Gourma-Rharous brought us out at Gossi and any thoughts of visiting it were instantly dismissed when we stopped for coffee at the shacks alongside the junction. Even the very idea of drinking a coffee had to be abandoned when we were set upon by the aggressive bands of children living there. They tore at our clothes and thrust their hands in our pockets. They demanded this and they wanted that. What a nightmare.

We jumped back in the car and made for Hombori, the Réserve de Douentza and a session of zealous elephant hunting.

The combination of the Hombori Mountains and the falling sun cast a pattern of grotesque shadows, shot through by shafts of sparkling light. Hombori Tondo, a sandstone mesa, rose eleven hundred metres from the plain, as if it were a cork plugging an immense hole in the earth. The Hombori Mountains are the highest range in Mali, attracting a number of European climbers to their vertical faces. The most famous of them is Le Main de Fatima (Fatima's hand). From a distance this rock formation appears to be a hand laid on the plain, the vertical rock columns the fingers rising skyward.

On entering the settlement of Hombori, one of the first mud buildings we came to displayed the sign:

ANTIQUAIRE – Vente d'Objet d'Art (chez Kailouta)

Beside carvings and traditional wood chairs, a number of pairs of snow skis leaned against the wall, their attendant boots attached to the bindings. And for those who liked to add a little spice to their dune skiing, there was a choice of two snowboards. We slowed down beside this surreal sight and were instantly mobbed by the local touts. The most insistent of them, the grandly named Ibrahim le Magnifique, trotted the last kilometre beside the open window of the car, intent on directing us to the best hotel in Hombori. He warbled the whole distance, barely drawing breath, cheering us with a full account of his worth. Sweat beaded his forehead when we parked in front of the small hotel. For tenacity alone, he won hands down.

Inside the hotel, we dumped our bags on the rock-solid

beds and slumped in chairs in the restaurant overlooking the road. A round of beers was ordered and Le Magnifique continued where he left off: if we wished to see the elephants of Gourma, we were left in no doubt that he was our man.

'Alors, mes amis,' our guide announced with a flourish. *'Demain sera un journée magnifique.'*

Halfway down the second bottle of beer we'd agreed a price. With a deal cut Le Magnifique sprung to his feet and the night swallowed him up.

We left at the crack of dawn, five of us squashed in the Hilux, and tracked north-west from Hombori. Travelling through stunning country, we crested gentle hills and crossed vast plains of pink sand and grasslands, dotted with acacia and green, wispy shrubs. In other circumstances, this country could provide the backdrop to a most spectacular game reserve. I could see a guest lodge perched here on the crest of the hill in front of us, amongst trees, overlooking the savannah and herds of wildebeest, zebra, gazelle and giraffe. It was perfect cheetah country. I imagined the land we were gazing at to be exactly what Mungo Park and Gordon Laing found at the time of their travels. Except now the reserve is heavily grazed by large herds of cattle and there are numerous settlements dotted about. The social disorder of attempting to repopulate the reserve with game, and the poaching that would undoubtedly follow ... it didn't bear considering. Mali's wildlife had already been hunted mercilessly.

After four hours' searching for tell-tale signs of elephant, we descended a hill to an area of dense woodland. We were beginning to wonder if Ibrahim was so Magnifique after all. Except, our hopes had never been high in the beginning. The further we went the less assured he became.

Our questions hung unanswered and our guide retreated into an air of moodiness.

Under Le Magnifique's guidance I drove to the edge of the woodland and we set off on foot. A boldness seemed to have returned to our guide's step. We were at In-Adiattafene, located more or less at the centre of the reserve, where a waterhole allegedly ensured the elephants presence.

'Now we will see them,' he cried, plunging us among the tangled woodland.

When we found it, all that was left of the waterhole was sloppy mud and pockets of stagnant water. We edged our way around it, not needing Ibrahim to tell us that these footprints the size of a very large cooking pan were those of an elephant. He put a finger to his lips, commanding silence, his hand swatting us onward.

As quietly as we were able we pushed aside branches, placing our boots carefully on the uneven ground. For half an hour, we crept along like this, deeper into the woods, communicating in hushed voices, our senses increasingly lulled by the heat.

When the bushes ahead rustled, all of us were brought rudely awake.

Ibrahim crouched, pointing. There is an elephant up ahead, he mouthed. He flicked his hand, so that we should follow him in single-file.

We moved on, cat-like, scanning the tangle of foliage with total concentration. My heart was thumping; perhaps Le Magnifique had come good, after all. Completely hemmed in by woodland, goodness knows where we were supposed to seek cover if the elephant charged us.

It was then the branches to our left cracked and shook.

I spun round, crouching, the breath hissing through my teeth.

And there it was...not an elephant at all. We'd come face to face with a camel nonchalantly chewing leaves.

'I thought it was an elephant,' our guide declared, standing upright.

We ambled from the woods and resumed our search by car, returning to higher ground. From there we were sure to see the elephants, Ibrahim told us. We settled in our chairs while Ibrahim insisted on making us all a cup of tea.

We waited the rest of the afternoon, spotting nothing more than a few goats. Still, it was a very pleasant place to while away what was left of the day. And, if nothing else, he made a good cup of tea. Before sunset we descended the slope and crossed the open plain to the far side of the woods. There we made camp beside umbrella trees and Le Magnifique, much to his credit, prepared the leg of goat we'd purchased in Hombori, roasting it over the open fire.

In the early hours of the morning, while still dozing in the tent, the sound of branches being torn apart filled the air, just as the guide had predicted. The elephants were feeding in the woods.

At breakfast, through the steam rising from a cup of coffee, I watched the bull elephant cross the open ground before us, making his way back to the cover of the trees. He seemed a bit stiff, as if one of his legs was giving him trouble. He moved at a leisurely pace, proud and commanding, like a grand old gentleman strolling to the shops.

Gourma means "place of the well" and for several months of the year this northern section of the range is home to the estimated 500-strong herd. Following an anti-clockwise circuit, these "desert-adapted" elephants are said to have the longest migratory route of any elephant in the world, ranging over an area of some 32,000 square kilometres. Depending on how the rains fall, around November they begin their journey north from Burkina Faso, hang around the waterholes and lakes of the Gourma region during the dry season, and commence their southerly route back to Burkina Faso in June, when the feeding is better.

At the time of our visit, the elephants existed relatively harmoniously beside man. They trampled the vegetation and grassland, creating paths, and thereby aided the local herders and their cattle. The moment the elephants raided the smallholders' plots was when things turned ugly. Studies by conservation groups have determined how the local populations as a whole recognise the importance of preserving the herd; what is good for the elephant is good for them. This attitude has been key to galvanising them into better managing the biodiversity of the region, not only towards protecting their own environment, but also with the aim of reducing human-elephant conflict. This has had the added benefit of improving the condition and value of their livestock.

However, events since the Tuareg uprising in 2012 have ensured the future of both the human and elephant populations have become that much more precarious. Despite France's counter-terrorism initiative, Operation Barkhane, by 2015 security in the Gourma region worsened considerably, and the jihadist activity, in conjunction with international trafficking networks, led to a rapid escalation in poaching. During that year, 83 elephants were lost, and in 2016 a further 51. Predictions at that time estimated the herd could be wiped out by 2021, if poaching continued at the same rate.

Building on the existing community spirit and conservation structure, further initiatives have been developed with such organisations as Chengeta Wildlife, who have assisted in forming and training anti-poaching units. Such work has provided the youth with employment, and a good deal of pride in the work they do, at the same time diverting them from the jihadists who were recruiting fighters with the promise of a daily payment of as much as between USD30 and USD50. There has been a degree of success in preserving the herd and there is the hope, despite the considerable headwinds, that this may be carried forward into the future.

We dropped Ibrahim le Magnifique by the settlement of Boni, so he could catch a bus the short journey back to his home in Hombori. Back in Douentza, we called in at Campement Hogan for a beer and a chat with Hogan, and to ask about the best directions for the next section of our route. We had learnt in the last couple of weeks how the maps in certain areas we travelled through bore little resemblance to reality. What appeared on the map to be a clearly defined road between villages was often nothing more than a series of confusing tracks.

By early afternoon, on Hogan's instructions, we followed the track via Frombori, along the base of the Bandiagara Escarpment, to the heart of Dogon country. Heading west, the sheer, ochre-coloured walls of the cliff rose to our right, crumbling in places, in other places nestled the square, mud-brick dwellings of the various villages. Thatched, conical-shaped roofs poked from the fallen rocks like witches' hats. To our left the low dunes undulated, dotted with thorn-bush and swathes of grassland, all the way to the distant sky. The track leading through the villages at the foot of the escarpment, was barely wide enough for a donkey and cart. We crawled slowly on, attempting to minimise the disturbance on village life. And there we came across the same old problem, the aggressive, demanding children roaming in feral packs. Not far behind them, though slightly more restrained, were the self-professed guides. Even those who are not *faux* guides need to be chosen with care, for the Dogon are a diverse, socially complex people and a knowledgeable, sympathetic guide is needed in order to lift the lid even a little.

Here, along the base of the escarpment, it had not even been possible to keep our visits to the villages on a superficial level. We'd have enjoyed wandering the narrow streets, absorbing the atmosphere, stopping to exchange greetings with the inhabitants, to perhaps learn something of their lives – to just simply communicate. It didn't take long before you began to wonder who was intruding on who. Tourists spent multi-day itineraries hiking Dogon country. I could only assume their guides kept the rabble in some form of order, or else it must be unbearable.

Latterly, and in the wake of the rising Islamist violence and breakdown of state oversight, old rivalries between the Dogon and the Fulani pastoralists have re-emerged. In recent times the Fulani herdsmen have come to dominate the pastures of the Seeno Plains, to the south-east of the plateau, an area where the Dogon farmers also grow their crops. With the Fulani having been accused of collaborating with the jihadis, in response the Malian army are said to have trained and armed Dogon militias. In 2019, a Dogon militia force massacred 160 Fulani at Ogossagou (close to Bankass), after which the communal violence gradually expanded beyond the Bandiagara Plateau, to the regions of Mopti and Ségou, and northern Burkina Faso. In many cases it is the Fulani, an ethnic group of around 30 million people widely dispersed across West Africa, who have borne the brunt of the spreading violence. In Mali, they represent 14% of the population. During a spring 2022, Wagner-backed military offensive, some 300 of them were killed at

Moura. Such ethnic cleansing can only facilitate the Jihadi expansion. The fear is that this combination of the security force's heavy-handedness, ethnic clashes and Islamist insurgency, will ensure this conflict becomes more entrenched in the coming years.

At the village of Banani we took the steep road leading to the plateau. High up in the sheer rock face were the caves where the Dogon, and the Tellem before them, buried their dead. From the top, we looked south over the vast plains, all the way to Burkina Faso, the next country on our route.

6

BURKINA FASO

THE LAND OF HONEST MEN

There was something immediately apparent about Burkina Faso. Not long after we'd crossed the border at Tiou, on the Bankass to Ouahigouya road, it was clear we'd entered a country with an entirely different atmosphere, as if passing from one room to another. The country is extremely poor and yet it was orderly. The discarded rubbish we'd often seen in Mali was missing. And the people, especially the children, after what we'd experienced in the last month, were positively Zen-like. That's not to say we were ignored. The West African is curious by nature. They were polite and calm and jovial. They were altogether different.

On the approach to Ouahigouya we stopped opposite an ATM. I drew out some money while JP visited the shop next door to buy a SIM card for his phone. It was walking back to the car I spotted a pool of liquid collecting in the shadow beneath it. It came from the vicinity of the fuel tank. I dropped to my hands and knees and peered beneath the vehicle, silently cursing. I stuck a finger in the liquid and smelt it.

JP squatted beside me. 'What's the problem?' he asked.

'I think the fuel tank's ruptured.'

I didn't want to believe what I was looking at. I stuck my head further underneath. A streak of diesel seeped along the edge of the protective steel plate beneath the fuel tank, forming a rhythmic drip at the front section.

'Yeah, it's definitely leaking.'

I got up from my hands and knees and sighed. It was a bespoke, 110 litre fuel tank specially fitted to extend the range of the vehicle and I could only assume all the dragging and pounding in the deep sand had stressed a weld. We had to fix it. But where could we go for such a repair?

Our plans of heading out to Bobo Dioulasso, a town down in the south-west of the country, had to be shelved. And it was too late in the day to press on to Ouagadougou. I really didn't want to be driving round the capital city in darkness, searching for a hotel. We cruised round town looking for local accommodation, checking in at the Hotel l'Amitie, instantly repairing to the bar for a round of thought-inducing beer. How might we find someone capable of welding an aluminium fuel tank in Burkina Faso? Surely there would be someone in Ouagadougou capable of such a task.

'The trouble is,' JP started, 'if they don't know exactly what they're doing, they could destroy the tank. They need to be very precise with their welding technique.'

But how could we ever know if the welder we engaged

had a precise welding technique...until he'd set about the job...when it might be too late. I didn't fancy the idea of trying to get a replacement fuel tank in Burkina if it all went wrong. We could have been stuck there for months.

Our conversation went in circles discussing what we should do. Even through the bottom of a beer bottle our predicament didn't lighten any.

'We'll get it fixed in Ouagadougou,' I announced with greater determination than I felt.

I think all the hassles of West African travel, the fatigue and all those little things that add an extra twist to the knot in the shoulders were beginning to weigh on us. Perhaps it was just me they weighed on. We ordered another round of beer. And then a few brain cells clicked into place.

'I may have something that could do it,' I muttered.

I scuttled outside to the Hilux. At the roadside, I unpacked my store of spares under the watchful gaze of a group of art students who'd earlier, very helpfully, sourced us a bowl to catch the diesel drips. I dug through fuel filters, brake pads, inner tubes, wiper blades, bags of nuts and bolts, bulbs, until...yes, there it is. I finally uncovered what I was looking for. I retrieved a collection of glues I'd thought to buy only at the last minute. I repacked everything and went back inside the hotel.

'What do you think of these?' I said to JP.

He put on his glasses and read the back of the packaging. 'This would do it,' he said, finally.

I smiled. I had in front of me one of the best engineers I knew. We'd fix this damn thing ourselves. The beer immediately tasted sweeter.

The first thing I did in the morning was check the bowl catching the drops of diesel. It held about half a litre – not that critical.

We paid the hotel and called in at an orphanage on the outskirts of Ouahigouya. The orphanage cares for children whose parents have been the victims of HIV/Aids. And there are many of them. According to the World Health Organisation Burkina Faso faces a generalised HIV/AIDS epidemic. About 75% of cases are between the ages of 15-40. The orphanage in Ouahigouya survived on the generosity of a dedicated French couple and the funding they raised. We dropped off a box of food and the five footballs and the hand pump we'd brought all the way from England. For a while we chatted to the staff, two ladies who corralled a group of boisterous kids. After inflating a couple of footballs for the kids to have a kick about, we headed south for Ouagadougou.

The access to Ouagadougou, a city with a population estimated at 1.5 million, was chaotic. Its northern artery was chocked with mopeds, taxis and heavily loaded bicycles. I never knew so many live chickens could hang upside down from the handlebars of a bicycle. The cyclists' heads poked above a hillock of rust-coloured feathers. As we chugged along in the line of traffic a motorcyclist breezed down our right-hand side. He had a sheep tied round his waist, the legs trussed together before him. It was a heart-rending sight; even in the face of such humiliation the sheep continued to hold up its head with a degree of dignity.

Eventually we found our hotel, the Pavillon Vert, run by a genial Frenchman called Gillaume. As well as overseeing the management of the hotel Gillaume organised 4x4 and off-road motorcycle tours in Burkina Faso and the surrounding countries. In fact, he'd just returned that very minute with a group of French motorcyclists from a tour of the north-west of the country. The bikes were lined up against the wall, the riders' faces caked in a layer of ochre-coloured dust. They looked like owls when they lifted their goggles and removed their helmets. They wore more body armour than a gladiator.

After we'd settled in our rooms we spied a corner of the property, out of harm's way, where I supposed we might establish our temporary workshop. We asked Gillaume's permission, who expressed a calm resignation that overlanders must do what overlanders must do, even if it included stripping bits and pieces from their vehicles in the hotel's gardens. We squeezed the car between several obstacles, parking it on an area of flat concrete. From the open window of the reception we heard Barak Obama being inaugurated as the 44th President of the United States.

The following morning JP and I removed the fuel tank and set it beside the car. Our problem was immediately apparent: a section of weld had split. We gathered our jerry cans and tipped out the remaining fuel into the cans.

During the removal of the tank I'd discovered the nut missing from the bolt holding one of the leaf springs in place. It was most probably one of those things Tim at Trek Overland had told me to check with a spanner every once in a while. In any case, it had worked itself loose and dropped off. I undid the nut at the other end of the leaf spring, to give me a match, and put it in my pocket. While JP set about the tank, Christine and I went foraging in the city.

'We need one of these,' we said to the taxi driver outside the hotel, showing him the nut. He knew the exact place for such a thing.

Ten minutes later our driver deposited us in the centre of Ouagadougou, in a street lined either side with traders selling every conceivable item for a motor car, van or truck. I had every hope for a fair outcome. After all, the name Burkina Faso means "The land of honest men".

The moment we piled out of the taxi we became a magnet for the middlemen patrolling the street. They collectively decided it wasn't a nut we needed but a car radio, floor mats, a lock for the steering wheel, a windscreen blind with Manchester United across it, a perfumed pine tree to hang from the rear-view mirror ...or how about a gear stick knob – in polished wood.

'Stop, my friends. We're searching for a nut exactly like this one.' Christine held the nut aloft between finger and thumb, as if it might have been one of old Mansa Musa's golden nuggets.

A serious-looking youth stepped forward. '*Suivez moi*,' he said.

The youth led us to the far end of the street, where the less glamorous end of the motor accessories trade resided. The hand cart was loaded with wooden boxes. The boxes were full of what appeared to be every conceivable nut and bolt known to mankind.

'This man sells nuts,' the youth announced rather redundantly.

The man took the nut from Christine and he held it to his right eye, turning it back and forth. He hummed, as if summoning mystical forces. Sufficiently empowered, he let his hand drop into a box. 'It's not a problem,' he declared.

After ten minutes rummaging the nut seller came up with nothing. I couldn't accept that he didn't have a match somewhere in that lot. I felt we'd been lucky the leaf spring hadn't already worked itself loose. I didn't want to test our good fortune further. If I didn't find a replacement, the possibility that the leaf spring might drop off was just another one of those things to niggle away, much like the flip-flops and strips of tyre that had become an integral part of the Hilux, and without which we should surely founder.

'Keep looking,' I said.

Encouraged, the nut seller joined forces with his colleague at the adjacent hand cart. Forty minutes later we had the exact replica.

'Wonderful!' I declared. '*C'est combien?*'

'*Trente-cinq Euros*,' the man announced.

Yeeks!

We countered with a considerably reduced number. The nut seller glared, poker-faced. These guys knew all about the distressed purchase. Perhaps they'd even invented the phrase. I reached out, recovering my own nut, marginally reducing his negotiating power. And then we haggled, interjecting each counter with a suitable exclamation: '*Mon ami!*'...'*Mon dieu!*'...'*Quel bandit!*'

We settled on an excruciating fifteen Euros. I weighed the two objects in my hand, clicking them together. I can confirm that, in a continent awash with peanuts, the most expensive nuts in all of Africa are not even edible.

'Would you like another one?' the trader asked, his features softening to a sly grin.

'Cheeky blighter!'

We hailed a taxi and headed back to the hotel.

On our return, JP had thoroughly cleaned the grime and diesel from the top of the tank with a tin of turpentine, sealing the crack with several coats of glue. When he'd finished, the repair was the most robust part of the tank – quite possibly the whole car. Nothing short of a howitzer shell was going to undo his work. By the late afternoon, the tank was back in place and re-plumbed.

For JP, repairing the fuel tank had been a rudimentary job, a mere afternoon's distraction. The complete relief of conquering what had seemed an insurmountable hurdle twenty-four hours earlier was mine alone. It was quite ridiculous; all I'd done was help get the thing out and back in, undid a few bolts, disconnected the odd pipe, worked a jack handle, and yet, for all of that, I walked just a little bit taller.

That evening we traipsed through the darkness shrouding the open-air market. It seemed, by night, that some market stalls doubled as the traders' residences. Small braziers had been lit. Cooking pots bubbled on open fires. Blankets were stacked to one side. Three or four Burkinabes huddled round each of the fires, the voices of their dodging shadows no more than a murmur.

On the far side of the market we found Baratapas, a restaurant owned by a corpulent and jolly Frenchman. The courtyard was full of ingenious metal sculptures and vibrantly-coloured paintings; the toilet was spectacular. The food they served was of varying quality: the *poulet bicyclette* was small and brawny – a sparrow on steroids. The curried pork was excellent.

The next day, with only three days left before JP and Susie were due to fly out of Ouagadougou, we reloaded the car and headed out of town. From Ouagadougou we followed the N1, a good road leading all the way to Bobo Dioulaso, a distance of three hundred and seventy-five kilometres. On the way, we passed field after field of cotton plantations. Harvested cotton as white as pure snow stood heaped in bags at the roadside.

Burkina Faso has considerable resources of gold. Nonetheless, in a country of few natural resources, it is cotton that is the economic mainstay for the Burkinabes. The country is Africa's biggest producer of cotton. In a productive year, it accounts for over half the value of the country's principal exports of gold, peanuts, karité nuts and sesame. The cotton industry provides work for seventeen per cent of the population. In West Africa cotton employs four million farmers and production has grown from 100,000 tonnes in the sixties, to 900,000 tonnes by the end of the century. But selling it overseas is an uphill struggle. According to Martin Meredith's *The State of Africa*, by the end of the 20th century, production costs in the United States were almost twice as high as those in West Africa, and yet twenty-five thousand US farmers enjoyed a subsidy of four billion dollars – a number greater than the value of the entire crop. The subsidy enabled the US to gain nearly one third of the world cotton market. Oxfam claim the trade losses suffered by West Africa's eight major producers, on account of the US subsidy, outweighed the benefits they received in US aid. It really is a crazy world!

Similar to Mali, Burkina Faso suffered a jihadist insurgency in 2015, which has since continued to expand throughout the country. According to a report by Human Rights Watch, attacks by these armed groups have resulted in over 237,000 people fleeing their homes in 2021, raising the total number of internally displaced people since 2016 to over 1.4 million. Civilians from all walks of life have been abducted and many of them killed. In the government's response to the insurgency, military forces and militia groups have also become implicated in numerous civilian massacres. In 2022, two military coups occurred and to date the country continues to be governed by a military junta.

To the south of Bobo lies Banfora. This is the last town of any significance that migrating Burkinabes pass through in their traditional search for work in the neighbouring country of Ivory Coast, sixty kilometres further along the road. Since independence political troubles have held back the development of the country and much of the industry is dominated by unprofitable, government controlled corporations. As a consequence of this, many workers must seek employment in Ivory Coast and Ghana.

In Banfora we treated ourselves to the newly opened Calypso Hotel, a series of smart rondavels set in a walled garden. It was our base from which to take in the various local sights. Few of Burkina Faso's attractions are indicated, and if they are, it's usually a rotten signpost lost to the foliage of a deep ditch. To find the domes of Fabedougou, striking rock formations said to have evolved over a period of 1.8 billion years, we travelled several kilometres back and forth in a sugar plantation. Our quest meant we passed a lot of wild-looking men wielding machetes.

None of us were too keen to get out of the car and ask them directions and so we continued following the labyrinthine tracks, our silent perseverance finally reimbursing us. Needless to say, the business of sugar cane in the south west of Burkina Faso is an expansive affair.

Later that morning, on foot, we followed the course of the Karfiguéla Falls, up into the hills. We laid out our lunch in the shade of the trees and sat on gnarled roots to eat it. The river was in full flow, though bathing in the idyllic pools was discouraged due to the problem of bilharziasis (an infection caused by a parasitic fluke boring through the flesh). In Africa, beauty so often comes with an edge.

Despite the harmattan winds bringing the dust from the Sahara, a reminder of where we had come from, the views to the south were distinctly green, lush and tropical. The desert and the savannah were now firmly behind us.

Replete from our lunch and a short snooze, on the way back down the falls we came across four girls struggling to lift bundles of bound wood. JP and I took an end each, hoisting them on to each of the girls' heads. It was remarkable how they carried such heavy loads. For a while we walked with them down the steep slopes and carved steps, the girls measuring each step, struggling to balance their loads. They were making for the village at the foot of the hill – still a long way to go.

Soon we had left them behind. At the very bottom of the hill, close to where we'd parked the car, a young, fit-looking youth sat beside the mango trees with his hand held out, asking us what we had for him. We couldn't help but berate him for sitting on his backside. We told him to go and help his sisters. He muttered something in return and looked the other way.

In the failing light, we drove along the edge of Lake Tengrela, searching for a recently opened campsite we'd read of. After some time, we arrived at a cluster of tall trees stretching inland from the lakeshore. In the cover of the trees was a hut. Tables, chairs and furled sunshades stood outside. A young woman came out of the hut, followed shortly by a man. For a moment, they simply stared at us. Finally, the man beckoned with his hand.

'Do you think this is the camp?' JP asked.

'I think it is,' I said, letting the car roll forward.

They were about three hundred metres from us, on the other side of a ploughed field. The only way to get to them was to drive across it. I set off, stopping beside the tables and chairs outside the hut.

'Is this Campement Le Rancart ?'

'No,' replied the young man. 'This is restaurant Le Rancart. Our camp is over there.'

We followed his pointing finger. In the same field, a further two hundred metres distant, stood a picket fence, the round thatched roofs of two huts poking above it. It was located in a sea of furrows.

'You are welcome to stay,' he said.

'We would like that.'

'My name is Drissa. And this is my sister.'

Drissa's sister smiled at us coyly.

'She can cook you dinner. We have chicken and chips. And salad.'

'That sounds even better,' we told him.

I followed Drissa with the Hilux, the suspension creaking as the vehicle dipped in and out of the furrows, and parked inside the picket fence. Drissa showed us inside the two mud huts, of which he was very proud. The huts were tiny, with room for little more than the bed itself. The frame of the bed was made from recovered wood, the mattress an enormous sack stuffed with chopped maize stalks.

'We have our own beds,' we said. 'And a tent on the roof of the car.'

Drissa nodded, dragging the door of the hut closed behind him. 'We've only just opened. We have a little more work to do. I am a student still and so my sister helps when she can. I will make this place bigger, when I have the money.'

An hour after nightfall the call to dinner drifted to us. We trudged across the ploughed field in the direction of the single oil lamp. Our chicken and chips awaited us. The sister was a good cook.

The next day we witnessed sunrise from the lake, huddled together in a pirogue. Distant woodland crept from the darkness. The outline of a fisherman crouching in his pirogue emerged from the far end of the lake. It was cold. A thin mist held a watery sun at bay. The breeze, accompanied by the water lapping against the wooden hull, were the only sounds. Drissa picked flowers of vivid orange and lilac from a patch of water lilies. He gave one to both Christine and

Susie, placing them behind the right ear. He was quite the romantic.

Every now and again, the hippos broke the surface with a hiss, chuckling at our passage. Goodness only knows what the hippos found so amusing. Is it what they see under the water that causes such mirth, or above it? We didn't much care for being too close to them. After mosquitoes, civil wars and ethnic cleansing, the hippo is one of Africa's biggest killers. He could have bitten clean through our pirogue, had he a mind to.

I could have stayed longer at Drissa's camp but we had to move on. It had been JP and Susie's last night under canvas. They donated their double mattress to Campement Le Rancart and we wished Drissa good luck with his plans. It was heartening to see him striving to achieve something, not slumped with his hand out under a mango tree.

It was fitting that our last evening together coincided with my forty-sixth birthday, not that we'd ever been short of a reason to crack open a bottle. We dusted off our Sunday best and took a taxi to Le Forêt, a swanky restaurant in downtown Ouagadougou, where the maître-d'hôtel showed us to a table beside the swimming pool. Soft lighting illuminated the lush vegetation surrounding us. It was a far cry from the nights spent in the desert, and a remarkable contrast to the stormy evening in a Bornholm restaurant, where we'd first cooked up the idea for this adventure. We'd come a long way since then. I ordered a couple of bottles of Côtes du Rhone to go with the couscous Royale. It was a splendid farewell. And a memorable birthday.

Before leaving the capital of Burkina Faso to continue our journey south, Christine and I visited the Ghanaian Embassy to secure our entry visas. We found the embassy down a busy, tree-lined street, behind a high concrete wall.

The security guard slid back the solid door, guiding us to a waiting room. 'Someone will arrive soon,' he said with conviction. I think he genuinely believed they would. Even if we didn't. Time...it's all relative. I'd come a long way since that mad dash to catch the ferry in Tarifa. I'd learnt to sway to Africa's rhythm.

Twenty minutes later we were joined in the waiting room by a smartly dressed lady. No, she didn't work for the embassy, she said. She wanted a visa, too. It was very calm in that small Ghanaian outpost. I've been to some corkers. On the embassy website, the official opening time for the office processing visas was stated to be 08:00 hours. The real opening time was 09:15 hours. We gave the completed form, our passports and the fee for the visas to the official. She gave the forms a cursory glance.

'Come back tomorrow,' she said.

After leaving the embassy we checked in at the OK Inn, an establishment in the southern suburbs of the city, using the rest of the morning to spruce up the car, check emails and reduce our load of dirty washing. The equivalent of a faded motel in England, to us the OK Inn was the height of luxury. The bedroom had a small sitting room, air conditioning, a TV, a telephone, WiFi connection, and a bath. There was a swimming pool in the garden. The kitchen fulfilled the menu's promise. The beer was cold.

After lunch, we dozed and watched a trashy movie. Two days later and we were back on the road.

There had been warnings of banditry on the road to Pô, in southern Burkina Faso. The narrow bridge crossing the River Nazinon had become notorious for holdups. Desperate men from the Ivory Coast were said to roam the jungle. "If you are confronted by armed bandits, do not resist", had been the inspired advice. Could my pepper spray match a Kalashnikov? The odds were appalling. On the road to Pô the law of the jungle prevailed.

On the way to Pô Christine wanted to stop for a picnic by a river she'd identified on the map. In the circumstances, I was prepared to forgo a picturesque lunch by the river. A Yorkshireman is not good at being parted from his money at the best of times. If there were bandits about, I preferred to just keep moving. Despite our rumbling stomachs the decision to keep moving carried the motion.

For several reasons, I could see why the last two hundred metres of road before the infamous bridge over the River Nazinon made an ideal place for an ambush. The tarmac surface had disintegrated into a series of craters. There was a sharp kink in the road, and the old iron bridge was not wide enough for more than one vehicle at a time. It was also very remote.

I covered the ground as quickly as the road permitted, aware of every twitching leaf in our immediate surroundings. At the very last minute, men in fatigues cradling assault weapons appeared from the shadows of the undergrowth. Already slightly spooked, my heart leapt into my throat. One of the men waved to us casually. We waved in return.

It was OK, we assumed. Bandits never wave casually before opening fire. Neither do they lounge in chairs beside a guardhouse when two prized *toubabs* rock up in a car normally reserved for government ministers.

From Pô a dirt track leads in a south easterly direction to the village of Tiébélé. We were in Nahouri Province, land of the Gourounsi people. Our accommodation for the night was the Auberge Kunkulo, a property owned by a Frenchman. I drove into the compound and we got out of the car. The only evidence of the proprietor was his off-road motorcycle leaning against the wall. The property had seen better days. Even the motorbike had two flat tyres. The Rasta in charge mumbled that the Frenchman had gone, though where he'd gone and for how long, remained a mystery. When we asked he simply gazed back at us with crimson eyes.

After we'd unpacked our bags from the car the Rasta showed us to a circular hut. A bucket shower and a beer did wonders to sluice away the fatigue of the road.

Our reason for choosing Tiébélé as an overnight stop was to visit the old village, a living museum affording a glimpse of domestic life for the Gourounsi going back the last few hundred years. As everyone in Tiébélé claims to be a guide, we enlisted the assistance of the Rasta in finding one. After a couple of calls on his mobile he produced a fellow by the name of Herman, one of eight official guides in Tiébélé. With that task completed, the Rasta wobbled off on his bicycle in search of something to cook for dinner.

Herman shook our hands warmly and gave a loud yawn. 'I was playing football at six o'clock this morning,' he announced. 'I play for the local team.'

Herman wanted to be a PE teacher in France and play professional football. His dream was to play for Paris Saint-Germain.

'Follow me,' he called and we set off on foot down the road.

The old village of Tiébélé was a higgledy-piggledy collection of dwellings. Painted in a background of white or reddish-brown, the walls were covered in frescoes of black diamonds, triangles, squiggles, snakes, humans and salamanders. The square-shaped buildings, Herman explained, were for a couple, and the circular ones for bachelors. We kicked off our shoes and dropped to our hands and knees, squeezing through the low opening of a hut.

'This is my grandma's house,' he said.

Grandma's house consisted of three circular huts interconnected by a small access. The walls were thick and windowless and the interior pleasingly cool. The shelves and floors were packed with his grandma's terracotta pots, wooden bowls and woven baskets. The last hut contained her wooden-framed bed.

'I think we should go now,' Herman said. 'I think my grandma would like her house back.'

Outside a shrivelled lady crouched on a wooden stool eyeing us curiously.

'You should give her something,' Herman said.

I fished some coins from my pocket and placed them in the folds of her palm.

During dinner two little boys edged toward us from the darkness. They wanted to put on a play for our benefit. Why not? we thought. With broad smiles they scurried off, returning ten minutes later, half the village in tow. Our two chairs were positioned before a makeshift stage and everyone gathered round. A group of half a dozen children danced and sang a series of performances, renditions of African village life. The finale was a play about circumcision, provoking bouts of tittering from the crowd. In a way such openness surprised me. I wasn't sure if the play presented a silent protest, or simply the drama of cultural rituals being enacted for all to share.

Over breakfast the following morning it turned out the Rasta was a prince. He was a descendent of the Tiébélé royal bloodline. We were honoured to spend our last night in Burkina Faso in the company of royalty.

7

GHANA

‘...OF AFRICA AND GOLDEN JOYS.’

(William Shakespeare)

‘Good morning,’ I said to the customs officer.

He was a giant of a man, even slumped in his chair. He didn’t bother looking up from his papers when he replied.

‘How are you today?’ I pursued.

The giant glanced at me. ‘Fine, fine,’ he rumbled.

It seemed odd to be speaking English again. And something of a relief. Officialdom is less daunting in the mother tongue.

‘Please can I buy a temporary import for a car?’

The giant looked down at the papers he was working on, sighed, raised his left hand languorously and studied his watch. It was approaching lunch time. He had a big stomach to fill. I already knew his reply.

'Come back later,' he growled.

Later. Sure. That had been the exasperating thing about Africa: forever trying to define what later really meant. It certainly had nothing to do with the passage of time as measured by a clock. A bus does not leave the station according to a schedule; it leaves at the moment when the requisite number of passengers are judged to have boarded. That's the first thing to understand. If you don't get the concept, it'll send you crazy. And even when you do get the concept, it still sends you crazy. In the context of a frontier crossing *later* can be as simple as when the queue is sufficiently long enough to warrant opening the office. It can be determined by the heat of the day, the length of an afternoon nap, an errand to be run, the size of a dash, the need to parade authority. *Later* takes as long as it takes. There's not much point trying to shorten it.

'Haven't you a carnet?' the customs officer snapped.

'A carnet de passage? Of course.'

'Why didn't you say so?'

I'd given up on the carnet de passage, dismissed it as just another one of those useless things you think indispensable on a trip to Africa. Fairly soon into the journey and you haven't a clue which grubby corner of the car to stuff all these redundant things, not daring to dispose of them, lest their purpose is only evident a few thousand kilometres later. By contrast, the carnet de passage had a large monetary bond attached to it, and so I looked after it rather well.

I unzipped the document holder with a flourish, leaned over the counter and slipped the crisp carnet into the officer's hand. I wanted to gush how he held the honour of being the first to write in it, and then thought better of it.

What did he care? He was probably sick of the sight of them.

Following a squiggle, a stamp and a grunt, I was back outside in the steamy, forty-degree heat. It had taken less than five minutes to complete the paperwork. I liked Ghana already. There was a spring in my step as I returned to the car, jumped in and fired up the engine. A soldier, a jolly-looking fellow, lifted the striped wooden pole blocking the road and waved us through.

Leaving Navrongo, a settlement not more than a few kilometres from the border, we were casually waved aside by two soldiers, assault rifles like fashion accessories dangling from their shoulders. We studied them more closely. Did they want us to pull over, or were they just being friendly? We erred on the side of caution. The country might have exuded a more disciplined air during the sixty minutes we'd been there, but men with guns...well...they are still men with guns. I stopped at the roadside and walked over to meet them. I had a fair idea what they were after.

'Eh! Where are you going?' They barely suppressed their grinning faces, the pair of them appearing about as menacing as a couple of Action Man dolls loitering at the entrance to a toy shop.

'To Accra,' I told them.

'To Accra.' They traded quick glances, clicking their tongues. 'And what have you for us?'

I smiled and shook my head. The Action Man doll of my childhood would never have behaved like these two slackers, with their scuffed boots and crumpled fatigues. Action Man was an honourable fellow, far too busy saving the world. When you pulled the string on his back he always obliged with – 'Ready for action!' Even if you pulled the string until it bust, never would he have come out with –

'And what have you for us?' The question simply wasn't in his vocabulary.

'Listen, my friends.' I held my arms out wide. 'I have come all the way from England...what do you think after such a long journey? I have nothing left.'

'Eh!' They clicked their tongues in unison and giggled. 'All the way from England. That is far, far.'

'Far, far,' I repeated.

'How long?'

'Many days.'

'Then you go give us sum'ting.'

'I have nothing left.'

'Eh! Okay. Welcome to Ghana.'

'You're very kind.'

It didn't take long before we felt the vibrancy of Ghana. People moved with a sense of purpose, preoccupied with their own business. We were no more than a curiosity moving through the landscape, not the focus of sly observation, catcalls and aggressive mobs of children. Our earlier encounters in the Gambia, Senegal and then Mali had already been watered down in Burkina Faso. Sure, like everywhere, they had their scoundrels in Burkina Faso, though they were a gentle people, and polite, of a different nature. Here in Ghana they were even more willing to let you be.

In Kumasi, we had a rendezvous with friends who run a business importing wines and spirits from Europe into Ghana. They were due to fly in from Europe in five days' time. One of the events they'd organised was a promotional evening for a champagne house they represented. We were on the guest list. The company of friends, and a glass of fine champagne to mark the end of our trip – things were really looking up.

In the meantime, it was a matter of deciding how to fill the intervening days, which wasn't too difficult. In Timbuktu the Austrian couple, Peter and Sabine, had spoken glowingly of the Green Turtle Lodge, a guesthouse down on the coast. They'd spent a few weeks there after a tough journey up the west coast, chilling out, parked on the palm-lined beach, sipping cocktails and fattening up on the restaurant's excellent food. In the heat and the dust of Timbuktu it had sounded like paradise. Any time our spirits had ebbed the Green Turtle Lodge was held up as a beacon of hope – 'Soon we'll be there,' we promised ourselves. As we approached the hot and steamy suburbs of Kumasi, the promise sounded as good as ever. A few days on the coast were exactly what we needed.

For three centuries Kumasi served as the royal capital of the Ashanti state. From being the crossroads of a substantial eighteenth century slave trade it is today a modern, frenetic city with a population fast approaching one and a half million people. If we thought Bamako and Ouagadougou were busy, this place was off the scale.

Coming from the north we joined the city's western bypass and the slow-moving lines of traffic. That afternoon it seemed the whole of Kumasi was on the road. Trying to understand the signs, as well as manoeuvre to the correct lane, proved tricky after the last few days of quieter roads. Somehow, on our first effort, we thankfully found our way to the Old Bekwai Road. At the Ahodwo Circle we turned right, heading south. A short distance further on brought us to the Four Villages Inn, a small, homely lodge owned by Chris and Charity, a Canadian/Ghanaian couple. Not only can you stay at the Inn, for lovers of sausages, you can indulge yourself in the range of Four Villages Inn Sausages made by Charity, who apparently learnt the art of sausage-making from the Cree First Nations people in Mistissini, Canada.

With eating at the forefront of our minds, in the evening we ventured back into the chaos of Kumasi, not to find sausages, but to seek out the Moti Mahal restaurant. The Moti Mahal was cited as the best Indian restaurant in Ghana, if not the western world. This was always going to give rise to lofty expectations, though I didn't care; after a long drive from England, who can ever deny themselves the opportunity of a pint of lager and curry? Even in such an unlikely place as Kumasi. It was well worth the trek. What the restaurant lacked in decor was thoroughly compensated for by their chicken tikka masala.

The next day, fortified by some of Charity's fine sausages, our route to the coast headed deeper into the jungle. We passed through Obuasi, the centre of Ghana's gold mining industry and home to the AngloGold Ashanti mining company. For a region containing such natural wealth it was surprising to witness the shambling town of Obuasi.

Ghana is Africa's second biggest exporter of gold, with the precious metal accounting for the country's third largest export revenue earnings, after cocoa and tourism. Nonetheless, we learnt how the AngloGold Ashanti mine had been suffering some problems and the town was mourning the death of two of its workers. Despite an initiative to improve health and safety one miner had been killed in a land subsidence incident, and another crushed by a dump truck. In addition to this, the company had had to make a large capital expenditure on neglected infrastructure, and power costs, as they were everywhere, were going through the roof. Operations were also affected by the age-old problem of pilfering. Trespassers sneaking on to the site and stealing gold-bearing material had become a grave concern to the management, not only from the point of view of safety, but also for the impact on lost income. In 2008, the company reported a loss of twenty-five million US dollars.

The journey to the Cape Coast took us four hours and it wasn't until we wound down the windows on the coastal road, letting the sea breeze cool the worst of the heat and humidity, that we found some relief. It was also a significant milestone in our journey. We had made it from the Barbary Coast to the Gulf of Guinea. We parked at the side of the track to catch the moment, enjoying the cool, sticky salt-air coating our faces, watching the artisanal fishing boats beyond a thinly veiled sea mist, and the emerald-coloured ocean turning white and thundering on the beach.

The Green Turtle Lodge is located on Akwidaa beach, ten kilometres along a jungle track to the west of Dixcove, and met our expectations entirely – we'd struck gold. For the next three days, to the sound of the crashing surf, we lazed in our chairs, read books, drank coconut milk straight from the fruit, slept, played Scrabble, drank sundowners at the bar and ambled to the restaurant. For three days, we didn't drive anywhere.

Akwidaa beach is a nesting site for marine turtles during September and March. Leatherbacks, the green turtle and the olive ridley are the three species to be found nesting on Ghana's beaches. Along with the Wildlife Division of Ghana, Tom and his wife Jo, owners of the Green Turtle Lodge, have various conservation projects on the go. Marine turtles have been around since the time of the dinosaurs, though their numbers are now dwindling fast. The biggest threat is getting caught in the nets of the commercial fishing vessels when, during the nesting season, thousands can be killed in only a few weeks. Hunted for their meat and eggs, current projects in Ghana are attempting to educate the locals concerning the importance of protecting them, promoting their value to tourism alive, rather than on the plate. It's a story prevalent throughout Africa, from poaching in the Kruger Park, to the slaughter of primates in the Congo; the trading of bush-meat, rhino horn and elephant tusk is as rampant as ever. Not until the African in the street benefits more from the influx of tourism in the game reserves will there be a collective effort to preserve the wonderful wildlife resource they have. The Green Turtle Lodge was making its own efforts towards this initiative. The staff organised small groups to observe the turtles coming ashore at night. Using locals as guides, the income generated from these excursions goes towards benefiting the local community.

When we arrived at the lodge we pulled up beside Sarah and Paul, whom we'd met in Senegal with their Unimog truck. They were reclining on hammocks slung between the trees. Sarah had found the place on the road to Bamako where her friend had been killed on his motorcycle. She'd completed her pilgrimage and seemed to have other adventures in mind that had little to do with her Unimog – it was already up for sale. Paul had dropped the idea of climbing the Hand of Fatima in the Hombori Mountains. Having witnessed its vertical walls for myself I couldn't blame him.

Sarah and Paul had been joined by Andrew. In a 110 Land Rover Andrew and a friend were making that once-in-a-lifetime trans-African trip. Only it had all gone wrong. On the long road between Morocco and Ghana differences between the two characters had been too great to patch up. They could go no further together. Andrew's friend had packed his bag and cadged a lift with an English couple heading south. For Andrew, his heart had gone out of the dream. Later, after a couple of beers in the bar, his demeanour began to crack. It was a shame to see it, particularly after so much spirit had been invested in the preparation of their trip. Despite all, he was not prepared to go on alone. He'd agreed with Sarah to share the cost of shipping their two vehicles back to the UK. He too was heading back to Britain and an uncertain world, given what snippets of news we'd heard concerning the unfolding global financial calamity.

According to Tom, it was what many overlanders had been doing that year. Getting as far as Ghana, they'd spend a few days relaxing at Tom's lodge and then ship their vehicles back home. We also had to start thinking of our own arrangements. Our plan was to ship the car south, to Durban in South Africa, where we'd recommence our trip, a seven-country loop of southern Africa. While the Hilux floated south we would head back to Europe for a couple of months. Somewhere in my list of lists I had the name of a shipping agent in Tema, though I could hardly bear the thought of all the hassle and kept delaying the moment.

At sunset, I sauntered to the beach, a mere one hundred metres away from where we camped. Rollers crashed along the shoreline. Out to sea a fisherman's pirogue rocked back and forth through a saline mist. A little further beyond the pirogue I fancied I could see the vessel bringing Richard Lemon Lander back to Africa, on his second mission to plot the route of the Niger River. He'd landed here on the Cape Coast in 1830, to collect Pasco, a trusted participant of the 1825 expedition, before continuing to Badagari, in today's Nigeria. A man who had spent so much of his life as a butler was about to become a famous explorer. It was a remarkable transition.

. . .

After Captain Hugh Clapperton, Gordon Laing's arch-rival in the race for Timbuktu, had expired at Jungavie from his fevers, his then manservant, Richard Lander, laid him to rest in the jungle. At that point, Lander was the sole survivor of the 1825 expedition and he needed to rely entirely on his own ingenuity to get himself home. Deep in hostile bush it was a tall order for a man who had been "in service" since the age of eleven, had previously never set foot in the hinterland of Africa, and had pitifully little experience as an explorer. Lander knew all there was to know about pressing a dress-shirt, polishing boots, exactly the amount of tonic to go with the master's gin, ringing the dinner gong and when to make himself scarce. In the bush, he was at a distinct disadvantage. A compass and a bearing meant as much to Lander as a clothes iron might have done to Clapperton.

After burying Clapperton, and racked with malaria himself, Lander collapsed, physically and mentally exhausted, in his hut at Sokoto. Sultan Bello, the local chieftain, couldn't give a damn that it was possible to fry an egg on the *nasrani's* forehead, or that the Cornishman was a class act as a gibbering dunderhead. He wanted Lander out of Sokoto at the earliest opportunity. He didn't need any more lectures from a white man as to why he should quit selling slaves on the coast. If the intruder didn't push off soon, the sultan would have him dealt with.

In spite of Lander's dire situation, after a couple of weeks' rest his spirit revived appreciably. His mind turned to getting back to the coast, a journey he estimated taking some one hundred and fifteen days. On the way, he rather fancied completing what Clapperton had failed to do. Why couldn't Lander himself plot the route of the Niger? Why not, indeed. It was a bold idea. Not only had he been thoroughly bitten by the exploration bug, such an achievement as navigating the Niger to its end would raise his stock immeasurably in England. With a smidgen of luck, perhaps the Cornishman could make the splendid transition from a loyal batman to an intrepid discoverer.

Lander had a gift for charm and diplomacy. He appealed to members of Sultan Bello's court, persuading them to provide him with an escort out of Sokoto. However, when he broached the subject of canoeing down the Niger they gawped at him as if he might have been stark-raving mad – which, by then, he most probably was. Tribal warfare to the south, they jabbered, would more than likely result in him being nailed to a tree upside down, until the water in the pot was sufficiently warmed to cook him. No, there was to be no paddling down a river, they declared. The *nasrani* must walk to the beach.

After a tedious journey, Lander eventually broke free of the jungle at Badagari, though his joy at reaching the coast was soon shattered by what he found there. In Badagari he beheld a scene of apocalyptic proportions. The streets teemed with lines of slaves chained together by the neck, a fleet of Portuguese ships anchored in the bay awaiting them. Lander witnessed brutal gang-masters prodding the lines forward, weeding out the undesirable. The infirm or old were affixed to weights and slung in the sea. Others were led away to be ritually sacrificed. Under the approving gaze of the local chief, King Adooley, the unwanted slaves were bludgeoned to death, their heads severed with axes and the blood sucked from their hearts. Everywhere Lander turned he faced equal horror; birds of prey feasted on the innumerable corpses hanging from the fetish trees, and from out of the brooding jungle, decapitated heads stared back from eyeless sockets.

Among such horror, Lander hurried to the docks,

hoping to secure passage to England as quickly as possible. He was not to be so lucky. On the way there he was seized, marched directly to King Adooley's hut and slung through the door. Once his eyes adjusted to the gloom he saw, against the far wall, Adooley himself crouched on a stool, surrounded by his elders and the skulls of the butchered.

'You are a spy, white man,' Adooley pronounced, banging the floor with the shaft of his spear.

Lander became transfixed by the witchdoctor shuffling towards him, the calabash in the wizened man's hands bubbling with poison.

'If you survive,' the witchdoctor croaked, holding the calabash in front of Lander, 'you shall not be guilty.'

The poison smelt like nothing Lander had ever drunk before. Not even his old man, the publican of the Fighting Cocks Inn in Truro, could have knocked up a concoction like this one. While hundreds jostled outside, agitating for the Cornishman's blood, the would-be explorer imbibed the bitter liquid and staggered from the hut.

Outside the king's hut the crowd parted in hushed silence, stunned that the white man should still be upright, let alone walking; perhaps his spirits were good after all, they speculated. A hum of approval rose above the heads of the crowd.

Weaving the two hundred paces back to his hut Lander finally peeked over his shoulder. With the coast clear he darted behind a tree, stuck two fingers down his throat and emptied his stomach.

The following morning, to cries of 'White man, he no go die!' Lander's status assumed a mystical dimension. He had survived the deprivations of the African bush that had killed his fellow Europeans. He had shrugged off the morning dews and the fever-bearing fumes belching from the swamps. Against all odds, he'd found his way back to the coast. And now, praying that it had been the ultimate test, he'd cheated a calabash of the king's finest poison. Even Lander began to believe he was blessed with divine powers.

Richard Lander returned to Portsmouth three years after he'd left as a member of Hugh Clapperton's hurriedly assembled expedition of 1825. When he stepped ashore on British soil a Jew ran forward, embracing him warmly and asking after his Hebrew brethren. With his flowing locks, fulsome beard and ragged clothing, Lander had been mistaken by the Jew for a pilgrim returning from the Holy Lands.

From Portsmouth Lander made his way to London, handed over a trunk of papers, Clapperton's journal and the remainder of the expedition's equipment and promptly returned to Cornwall. Back in Truro he secured work in the port for the local customs and excise office, though the pay was paltry and so he turned his mind to producing his own published account of his adventures in Africa, in a hope of supplementing his income. His brother John joined him, helping to put together the manuscript. When complete, the manuscript was sent to the Admiralty, where Sir John Barrow, Second Secretary to the Admiralty, decried it as a waste of paper, promptly sending it back, though he might have known African explorers were nothing if not tenacious. Lander left it with a publisher in New Burlington Street, who produced a two-volume account of his journey in 1829.

Like the others before him, Africa had ignited a fire within Lander that no reasoning could douse. Tired of his menial job as a weighing porter on the quayside, he fixed a meeting in Whitehall, telling Sir John Barrow he was ready to finish what he'd started. Lander had been tantalisingly close to answering one of the questions that had so enthralled Sir Joseph Banks: the mystery of where the Niger ended.

Contrary to the belief of Barrow, who held that the river flowed into Lake Chad, Lander was by then convinced it was the Gulf of Guinea where the river terminated. He challenged Barrow to allow him to end the speculation once and for all. At the risk of his own embarrassment Barrow agreed to fund a further expedition; after all, the budget Lander proposed was one of the cheapest missions to Africa the Admiralty man had ever known. There was none of the engraved watches and fancy scientific equipment Clapperton had felt the need to burden his enterprise with. Added to this, the remuneration Lander proposed, a personal pension of one hundred pounds, and the same for his wife, was peanuts compared to the thousands of pounds some of the Admiralty's Arctic expeditions had run to. Lander's brother John, who was to accompany him on the forthcoming expedition, was to be paid nothing.

In March 1830, the two Landers leapt on to the beach at Badagari. Richard spurned the heavier clothes of his previous mission in favour of a straw hat with a brim wider than a sunshade, a scarlet Mohammedan tunic and ballooning Turkish trousers. He scoffed at the tittering fishermen distracted by the curious sight he and his colleagues made and marched up the beach. When the breath of the jungle, hot, wet and overripe, slapped his cheeks, Lander knew it was going to be a long while before he again appreciated this cool sea breeze.

The Lander brothers led their small party through the streets of Badagari. Richard breathed a sigh of relief; the reek of rotting flesh was less evident than on his last visit. Some things hadn't changed, though: drunks heckled from the gloom of makeshift bars; sailors gorged the local talent over barrels of rum; sinister Portuguese merchants colluded with slavers from the hinterland, and mangy dogs fought over the elbow joint of a luckless prisoner. Against such a background Richard Lander kept his party moving, marching to King Adooley's hut, where he hammered on the door. When a young warrior ushered him inside they found the chief perched on a stool. Based on the detail recorded in Lander's journal I imagine the conversation might have gone as follows:

'What adventures have you this time?' the king asks.

'We are bound for Bussa, King Adooley, to determine the fate of Mungo Park. And thence we shall paddle down the Niger. The people of Britain feverishly await news of where the Niger leads, and I intend satisfying their curiosity.'

'I can save you the trouble,' the king interjects. 'The Niger terminates on the other side of the Bight of Benin. I could have somebody row you across tomorrow.'

'I'm sure you're right, King Adooley. And your offer is most appreciated. However, we must find it for ourselves.'

The king mumbles incoherently.

'And how is Lantern?' Richard asks, taking in the strapping young lad crouched by the king's feet.

'My son is well. But great misfortune has befallen us since your departure.' The chief drops his head theatrically to his hands. His council of elders cluster round him. 'Illness becometh me...' he groans, patting the sides of his fulsome belly. '...for I am a mere shadow of my former self.'

'I think you look in splendid shape, if I may say.'

'Many of my best generals and warriors have been slaughtered in battle. And General Bombanee–' a sob punctures the king's words, 'Oh, General Bombanee, my great and trusted friend. Can you believe it when I tell you those savages across the water sliced off the general's left hand, and then they nailed the other hand to the side of his head. In such a manner, they forced poor Bombanee to parade in the streets of Lagos, ridiculed until the crowds tired of him, whereupon his head was hacked from his shoulders.'

Richard winces.

'And that's not all! Bad juju visited fire on my house. It contained our armoury and gunpowder. The whole village exploded. And musket balls felled those who came with buckets of water to quell the flames.'

'This is terrible, your highness.'

'Terrible! Terrible! Many things Captain Clapperton gave me were destroyed.'

Richard shuffles his feet. 'I'm not sure what to say.'

'There are no words.'

'I can imagine.'

'So, my dear friend. What have you for me?'

LANDER and his brother couldn't leave Badagari fast enough, an urgency placed on their departure with news that three hundred unfortunate souls were to be bludgeoned and hung from the fetish trees. That night, above the beating drums, the giggling hyenas and the drunken revelry, struck the doleful wails of the condemned.

By now Richard was acquainted with the ways of the African chiefs and the pattern of travel in the jungle. In addition to the long hikes and crippling fevers, each of the villages they visited required gifts, often followed by a period of detention. When it came to delaying the expedition's progress, the African chiefs never lacked a vivid imagination. The chief of Yauri offered them a posy of feathers torn from the backside of an ostrich. On presenting the gift to the explorer the chief all of a sudden deemed the plumage insufficiently florid for his tastes.

'The white men must wait until the bird has produced fresh growth,' the chief proclaimed.

When Richard complained bitterly at such a ruse, two thousand cowrie shells worth of butter was massaged into the tormented creature's backside, to encourage the new feathers to grow.

Further north, Richard Lander reacquainted himself with the widow Zuma, though her circumstances, if not her corpulence, were much reduced. Barely squeezing through the entrance of the brothers' hut, she slumped to the floor, whingeing of how she'd lost half her slaves to skirmishes, and a good deal of her furniture to the sultan of Wawa. Fortunately for both men her previous ardour had dissipated in step with her loss of standing, and they breathed a sigh of relief when at last she turned to leave.

'She's quite a lady,' John hissed as he witnessed the widow's hips dislodge the crumbling doorway.

Having reached the rapids at Bussa, ready to prosecute their voyage down river, the brothers experienced yet further delay. The king could not secure a canoe of sufficient size to transport the combined bulk of their retinue and stores.

As they waited at the king's pleasure their financial means dwindled to nothing. Efforts to obtain food in the market became more challenging by the day. Even the rains ensured any attempt at shooting partridge and guinea-fowl was unproductive, and buttons and needles, of which they possessed plenty, had lost their lustre for the African. Nevertheless, not all was doom and gloom. The unappetising tins of soup they'd lugged all the way from England, and were close to ditching because of their weight, were greatly prized in the jungle. The tins, and the dull labels affixed to them, had a value to the Africans if not to the Europeans. Richard noted in his journal how several individuals had been spotted going about their business with the label "Concentrated Gravy" stuck to their foreheads.

The Landers took advantage of their delays in both Yauri and Bussa to forage for information concerning Mungo Park's fate. In one village, they uncovered his book of logarithms (not the missing journal, as they had hoped). The book contained a tailor's bill, and an invitation to dine with Mr and Mrs Watson of the Strand. The invitation was dated 9th November 1804, two and a half months before Park departed on his second expedition to West Africa.

From the chief of Yauri the brothers purchased a shotgun and cutlass Park had gifted, and elsewhere they acquired the robe Park had supposedly been wearing when he drowned. In Bussa, they added an iron-sprung leather cushion to their horde of memorabilia.

When a report came to their ears of a man in Wawa having accumulated a store of papers retrieved from Park's boat, there followed a flurry of excitement, only to be quashed by news that said papers had in fact rotted long ago, and blown away. Could they have been Park's missing journals? The trail grew colder by the year.

Just as they were despairing that the journey down the Niger might never get underway, the king of Bussa came up with the goods – two undersized, though very welcome canoes, plus their attendant paddlers.

On the morning of their departure the king and queen visited the Lander's hut, seeing them off with their blessings, a bag of goora nuts and two pots of honey. On the way to the river bank with all their belongings, Richard Lander was touched to see their path lined with people on bended knee saluting them. The people of Bussa had indeed been most hospitable.

As the canoes struck out for the centre of the river it was soon apparent the royal blessings had not extended to the worthiness of their transport – the canoes leaked like a pair of sieves. The smaller of the two, carrying a cargo of six people and several sheep, was soon perilously close to sinking. Three men baled water for all they were worth, until they ran the canoes aground on an island occupied by Borgoo tribesmen. The boats were dragged from the river and overturned, and while the chief obliged the Landers to join him in an improvised beer fest, followed by a request to discharge all their muskets, the canoe builders made hasty repairs.

For the next month, their journey down river passed in a blur of verdant plant life, magnificent trees, malaria, prosperous villages, the bestowing of gifts, detentions, palm wine binges, native hospitality, more malaria, promises of better canoes and yet more detentions. In the midst of the rigours of the voyage Richard Lander, true to his roots, was still capable of laying on a little pomp and ceremony. At their meeting with the King of Dark Water, they laid an awning of white sheets over the canoe and ran the Union flag up a makeshift pole. Richard put on an old naval uniform coat and had his brother dress as "grotesquely and gaudily" as the African chief and his entourage.

On the 22nd October, a seagull flew over their heads. The journey's end must be nearing. Or so they thought.

Two weeks later, abreast of the market at Kirree, Lander spotted fifty canoes closing on them fast. A curious mix of flags cracked at their prows. Among the British Union flag there fluttered an altogether odder representation: one depicted a man's leg, another tables and chairs, and yet another decanters and glasses. Lander screwed his eyes against the brilliant reflection on the water. The occupants of the canoes wore European dress, including shirts and jackets, and were a mixture of men, women and children. The sight gladdened his heart; here, at last, was civilisation.

Lander was about to leap to his feet and offer a hearty wave when something held him in check – something to do with all those peculiar flags, and all those weapons they were waving. And what about the blunderbuss roped to the bow?

On the approaching canoes the oarsmen thrust energetically in the water. Drums began to beat. Weapons were raised.

'What the devil–' Lander snatched his own fowling piece.

But it was all too late.

The pirogues slammed together mid-river. Grunting men, mewling children, screaming women, barking dogs and bleating goats all spilled into the water. Lander's clothes, his journals, weapons, collection of Mungo Park memorabilia, nine elephant tusks given by the King of Wawa, several leopard skins and a variety of seeds all bobbed on the current. In the shallows of the river, hippos thrashed, and the crocs slid from the bank. The attack happened so quickly Richard and John barely had chance to swing a paddle in their defence. In an instant they were seized, directed to the shore and ordered to wait in their canoes while a palaver took place to agree their fate.

Left to fry in the sun, the end of the journey so close, the knowledge concerning the termination of the Niger within their grasp, the two brothers oscillated between hope and despair. All afternoon they waited, while local women supplied them with bananas and coconuts to keep up their energy. The palaver concluded with the setting sun, the council members ambling to the water's edge to give their conclusion. It was decreed the two white men should consider themselves prisoners, to be delivered down river to King Obie. The king would know what to do with them.

The canoes departed the following day at sunrise.

Within a few days paddling, dishevelled and in need of a bath, they were presented at the infamous court of King Obie. Even though some of the Landers' goods had been recovered, everything of value had gone. They had nothing left with which to barter their freedom. To their boundless relief, what they found standing before them was a kindly-looking young man in one of the most outlandish get-ups they'd yet clapped eyes on – and they'd seen a few. King Obie was adorned in coral ornaments, his head topped with a cap shaped like a sugarloaf, a red frock coat with gold epaulettes strained against his torso, and skin-tight, knee-length trousers restrained his thighs. On his wrists, the king sported a profusion of bangles. In the eyes of the Landers, right down to the little brass bells tied to King Obie's ankles, the monarch was the Ibo dude personified. Here was a man they felt sure they could do business with.

Except looks can be deceptive – as they were about to find out.

What Obie lacked in sobriety he made up for in commercial acumen. He beamed, clasping their hands. 'Welcome to the land of the Ibo,' he boomed, immediately laying out his terms for their release.

'For the sum of twenty slaves,' Obie cooed, 'you can be as free as the hippopotami wallowing in the river.'

The two brothers looked from one to the other, turning out the linings of their pockets. 'But we're skint,' they chorused.

'Tough.' Obie giggled, rubbing his hands in glee.

Luckily King Obie wasn't the only wise-guy in the delta. There was an equally wily trader by the name of King Boy, a man adept at keeping an ear to the jungle drums. He happened to be aware that an English merchant ship, the *Thomas of Liverpool*, was at anchor at the mouth of the delta, and he sniffed a deal in the offing. Realising he could turn a healthy profit King Boy made a beeline for Richard Lander, enlightening him to this cheery news. Lander couldn't believe his luck – an English ship in the port. He had to secure their passage.

'Okay. So, what's the deal, King Boy?' he asked.

The Ibo cracked his knuckles. 'You get the captain on the *Thomas of Liverpool* to pay King Boy the equivalent of thirty-five slaves, plus a barrel of rum, then we have a deal, my friend.'

Lander scratched his head. Could he persuade the captain of the *Thomas of Liverpool* to play ball? He had to. How else was he going to get them all out of there?

'Agreed,' snapped the explorer.

Had he fully appreciated this was the country to spawn the 419 Scam (a type of advance fee fraud perfected in Nigeria) one hundred and sixty years later, Lander's reply might have been a little more circumspect.

King Boy tore off a scrap of paper. Scribbling out an IOU, he tucked it in the left epaulette of King Obie's red frock coat and ushered the two Englishmen to his waiting canoe. The Landers stepped aboard, plonking themselves on a pile of yams. King Boy squatted beside his wife, Addizetta, who took snuff and simpered in equal measure. Her beautiful eyes, pretty smile and unseemly scars (the shape of arrowheads had been carved in the flesh at the corner of each eye) helped Lander alleviate the discomfort of the yams.

Down river King Boy outlined the deal to his father, King Forday, an inveterate drunk. The father immediately poured a round of rum, burped loudly, slapped his son on the back and declared: 'What an eshellent...arranshment.'

'Okay,' announced King Boy, a glass of rum in hand. 'This is what we're gonna do.'

Even if he didn't much care for it, by the time the Ibo had finished outlining his scheme Lander felt positively giddy with rum and the prospect of freedom. As insurance for the deal turning sour his brother had had to remain with King Forday. Richard, in the meantime, was paddled down river to find the captain of the *Thomas of Liverpool* anchored at the mouth of the delta. The idea of leaving his brother behind filled Richard with dread. And yet he dismissed from his mind the prospect of not pulling it off. There was nothing to be gained by questioning anything but a successful outcome. Besides, why would an English captain not delight in the company of somebody with Lander's references?

Cruising along in the canoe, fingers trailing in the cool water, Lander allowed his imagination to run riot. With sixty miles to go, to all intents and purposes, their mission was completed. The Niger was in the bag. They had answered one of the burning questions asked by the great European minds of the eighteenth century. The denouement concerning the Niger River was his and his brother's to reveal. And it was going to make them famous. Lander chuckled in quiet self-congratulation. Indeed, the captain of the *Thomas of Liverpool* would be honoured with being the first European to hear the news that Messrs Lander and Lander, men previously of no consequence in Britain, had made such a significant discovery concerning the geographical complexities in Africa. It was a glorious vision in which the explorer basked. Back in Britain, Lander planned on personally delivering a copy of his printed journal to the King of England.

As the canoe entered open water, up ahead they cast their eyes on two ships tugging at their anchors, one a Spaniard, the other the *Thomas of Liverpool*. Lander could not hold back the smile. 'There she is,' he voiced above the plunging paddles.

King Boy turned on his seat and punched the air. 'Whooha!' he cried.

As the canoe cut through the water Lander grew increasingly agitated. Not a single sailor could be spotted on the decks of the brig. He found that very odd. If nothing else he'd imagined there would be a twenty-four-hour anchor watch to guard against all these bandits and pirates. They heaved-to, clunking against the solid hull of the boat.

'The *capitano's* name is Lake,' King Boy hissed, settling back on his elbows, the sun warm on his shoulders.

Lander nodded at the Ibo, turned his gaze upward and cupped his mouth. 'Ahoy!' he called, and immediately set about heaving his way up the ladder.

What Lander found on board sent a chill along his spine.

'What's up, bro'?' King Boy shouted from down in the canoe.

Lander dared not answer. Four of them out of the eight-man crew were dead, the other half confined to their hammocks in a rage of fever. With the crew incapacitated, how would they ever get the ship to sea? Worse still, how would he negotiate a deal to free himself and his brother?

A figure, pale and corpse-like, appeared on the poop

deck, bony fingers gripping the railing. The explorer paced forward expectantly.

'I'm looking for Captain Lake,' Lander called.

'That'll be me.' The man's murmur was barely audible above the wind in the rigging.

'I've got a bit of a favour to ask.'

Lander explained who he was, where he'd come from, who he worked for, his difficult circumstances and the deal he'd struck with King Boy. When he felt his words could lay no further weight to his situation he took a step forward, holding up a soggy, crumpled version of Sir John Barrow's orders. He thought the story all sounded pretty magnificent. 'If the captain only wished to take a look at this paperwork...'

A flush of colour in the captain's cheeks preceded a tirade of four-letter expletives that sent the explorer reeling. Lander was devastated. He balled the piece of paper in his fist. Nowhere in Africa had he come across such a crude and brutal man. Never had he expected such an answer from a fellow Englishman. Sure, he quite appreciated Captain Lake was ill...his crew in a parlous state...and no doubt a tidy profit looking less certain by the day. Lander appreciated all of those things – he wasn't a fool. But damn it all! They were all ill, for god's sake. Diseased, exhausted, starving, and fearing for their lives.

'Captain Lake,' Lander pressed more firmly, 'I can assure you, you will be recompensed by the British government.'

'F*** off!'

'But I've given King Boy my word.'

'King...what?' The captain, brow furrowed, sauntered to the side of the ship. He had enough on his plate without all this nonsense. Gazing down at the African in the canoe, the coral necklace and the pretty crucifix made of beads, he shook his head. King Boy, indeed.

'Tell yer friend to sling 'is f*****g 'ook.'

Lander squirmed. 'We are eight people,' he said, 'two seamen among us. By the look of things, you need us to help sail this ship. We can get you back to sea, Captain Lake. But I have to free them first. My brother is there.'

A flicker of light came to the captain's eyes as he realised the bearded, dishevelled waif in front of him had a point.

'You get 'em 'ere,' he growled, 'an' we'll 'ave a look at 'em.'

Lander clasped his hands together. 'Thank you,' he breathed.

Turning from the captain, he paced to the ship's side and gazed across the bay. Now what was he supposed to do? The explorer felt queasy. A clammy sweat washed over him, no doubt the onset of malaria about to do its worst. He descended the ladder with rubbery limbs and slumped on the seat in the canoe. He was quite out of breath from his exertions.

King Boy, his legs stretched out before him, scrutinised the explorer. 'So?'

Lander battled against the fatigue clogging his head. What could he tell King Boy? He certainly couldn't repeat Captain Lake's response. Somehow, he had to come up with a plan to free himself, his brother, Pasco, the ladies...all of them. But how should he do it?

For a moment, the explorer shut his eyes, feeling the canoe bobbing gently on the swell, the smell of the paddlers and the salty air thick in his nostrils. 'Hold on a minute,' Lander muttered, grinding his sweaty palms. He looked King Boy full in the eye and said, 'I've got this splendid idea...'

. . .

It was during our journey back to Kumasi that we learnt how much the Ghanaians love a coffin. And I'm not referring to a few planks of fresh pine, or a chunk of shiny mahogany with brass handles. The ones in demand in Ghana (and increasingly so in Europe) are known as 'Fantasy Coffins' and the possibilities regarding their design are endless. Among the Ga tribe fantasy coffins are big business.

The story of its dawning is said to go back to the turn of the twentieth century, to a carpenter called Ata Owoo. Owoo, who lived in Teshi, a village on the coast, had a business building elaborate sedan chairs for village chiefs. Having completed a chair incorporating a particularly intricate carving of an eagle, an admiring chief from the next village asked if he could have a chair in the shape of a cocoa bean. The carpenter duly complied, only the chief died days before it was commissioned. The family, not wishing the chief's precious investment to be wasted, adapted the chair to become a coffin. On the day of his funeral, to many admiring gazes, the venerated man went to the afterlife buried in a wooden coffee bean. A new business enterprise was instantly born.

The choice of design for a fantasy coffin often reflects the deceased person's occupation, hobbies, character traits, standing in the community, or quite possibly their aspirations in the afterlife. On our drive between Cape Coast and Kumasi we saw ships, shoes, chickens, aeroplanes, beer bottles, sewing machines, various models of luxury car and a lobster.

Aside from the business of coffins, another perplexing aspect of the burial process was their funerals. The Akan are the largest of Ghana's four ethno-linguistic groupings, incorporating the Ashanti and Fante people of the central and coastal regions of the country. Akan funerals are mostly held on Saturdays and should not be mistaken for weddings, as we often did when approaching the large, festively dressed and rowdy crowds congregating in the various villages through which we passed. A funeral is an occasion to celebrate life and the passing of a loved one. Dressed in their finery, they dance, bang drums and get very drunk.

Religion plays a significant role in Ghanaian society. Sixty per cent of the population are Christian. Islam, confined mainly to the north of the country, represents in the region of twenty-five per cent, a notable reversal to the countries we had so far visited. Whereas the Muslims are more conservative, by contrast, a symbol, or the music of Christianity can be seen or heard at every turning in Ghana. In a twist of quirky humour and religious fervour, many businesses and public services display the oddest of names:

"Sweet Mother Aluminium Co. Ltd" (a steelworks)

"Glory and Riches Ventures Ltd" (financial services)

"God First Fire Ministry" (the local fire station)

"Last Shop Funeral Shop" (an undertaker)

These were just a small example to amuse us on the long and pitted road back to Kumasi.

We might still have been in Africa, but our Toyota Hilux, with its all-terrain tyres, jerry cans, bull bars, winch, stack of wood, rusty *fourneau* and roof tent couldn't have looked more out of place in the car park of the Golden Tulip Hotel, a four-star establishment in the central business district of Kumasi. Here, BMW, Mercedes, Audi and a clutch of polished 4x4s were the order of the day. Neither could we personally have appeared more unsuitable for such a swanky hotel. From the crown of our heads to the soles of our feet, including all the clothes inside the dusty bags we pulled out of the back of the car, we were stained by the ochre-coloured dust of our journey. Like the couple we met back in Morocco at Les Deux Chameaux, we had acquired the West African blush.

From the car, for a second or two, we contemplated the hotel in front of us, that model of western capitalism, the mass of glass and immaculate white paintwork, the sexy down-lighters throwing golden circles, the strips of clipped, green lawn, the colonnade supported on thick marble columns, the suited doorman, the big sliding glass door. I gazed down at my dusty sandals and baggy, soiled clothes. I must have looked like Gandhi returning from one of his virtuous outings in the suburbs of Delhi.

Much to their credit the staff at reception did not do the anticipated double-take when we presented ourselves in the soft light and polished marble. Perhaps we were not such a curiosity after all. The credit card still slid smoothly across the counter – that was all that really mattered; from Ghana to Guatemala, money blinds.

With the imprint of my card completed our bags were whisked away. We were asked to follow a porter across the reception. He would escort us to our room. Porters – now here was a new thing. I'd quite forgotten about porters.

A lift carried us to the fourth floor and we glided down a long corridor, past umpteen dark, solid-looking doors. Once in the bedroom, for the next five minutes, I pushed and prodded the various buttons, all the ones the porter had been at such pains to explain. The room was decorated in browns and creams. The bed was flat, dressed in crispy-white sheets and the size of an aircraft carrier's deck. The carpet enveloped the feet, tickling the soft skin between the toes. The window overlooked a swimming pool and an outdoor bar and the city. When we'd sufficiently recovered our wits, we rummaged in the bags for some half-decent clothes. Even then we had to send them to the laundry, hoping to see the last of the orange collars and cuffs.

By comparison with the pace of the previous three months the next forty-eight hours were a whirl of activity. The time for action had arrived; my lists could no longer be set aside. I took out my notepad, opened it to a fresh page and feverishly began recording the tasks we had to complete – we had arrived in civilisation with a bump.

By early evening our friends arrived from Accra, their guests due within the hour. The only task left was to have the hotel plonk on ice a few cases from the champagne house our friends represented, before we popped the corks and mingled with the movers and shakers of Kumasi. Cruising the room of people that evening it was up for debate as to who was the most astounded; us to be at a champagne tasting evening after having driven through West Africa, or the locals, who (almost) fell for the tale of how we'd driven all the way from England to attend a champagne tasting in Ghana.

It was with a slightly woolly head that I reversed the Hilux up to the front of the hotel the next morning. A crowd of us posed for the photograph, a bottle of champagne displayed prominently on the bonnet of the car. I'm not sure what the champagne house made of it, but the photo, and account of our adventures, appeared in the *Spectator* newspaper a couple of days later. The headline read: FROM DESERT TO WINE TASTING. I couldn't have written it better myself.

. . .

Much of Ghana's early commerce with Europe started at Elmina Castle, which is exactly where we headed for the following day. In January 1471, two captains employed by Fernão Gomez rounded Cape Three Points and dropped anchor. At the village of Sharma, on the mouth of the River Pra, Gomez made a base from where he acquired gold from the native tribes. The coastline between Cape Three Points and Cape Coast soon came to be known as the Gold Coast, for the abundance of the precious yellow metal brought there from the hinterland. The coast was so rich in gold, within a couple of years the Portuguese merchant had made his fortune.

Fernão Gomez's contract to exploit the coast terminated after three years. Thereafter, it was exploited by the Portuguese government itself. For his efforts, they granted Gomez a coat of arms and the surname Mina, in honour of the gold mine he discovered. No doubt Gomez, glowing in such recognition, and coupled with his healthy bank balance, retired a happy man.

With Gomez out of the frame, the Portuguese government decided it an opportune moment to consolidate their position, and what better way of doing so than constructing a fort. Dom Diogo de Azambuja was dispatched with several boat-loads of bricklayers and carpenters, including several cargo ships packed with the requisite materials. The captains in Azambuja's fleet included some notable Portuguese seamen, including Bartholomew Diaz, who went on to discover the Cape of Good Hope. Historians speculate whether Christopher Columbus was also among them.

When Azambuja arrived off the African coast, he and his fellow officers made their way ashore, immediately commencing negotiations with the local chief, Kwamin

Ansa. Initially, the chief didn't much appreciate the white man's idea of a fort on his doorstep. After all, their predecessor had never felt the need of such protection. Nevertheless, for the price these crazy foreigners paid for the yellow pebbles his people dug out of the rivers, not forgetting the ground rent he'd negotiated, he was of a mind to set aside grievances concerning how the appearance of this new fort would disrupt his long-enjoyed sea view.

The fort was called São Jorge da Mina (St George of the Mine) and no sooner had the paint dried on the walls than they were building more of them. Despite their flourishing strongholds, it wasn't long before the Spanish, French, Dutch and British were raiding the Portuguese gold convoys en route to Lisbon, and pummelling their forts. The Portuguese countered by deploying naval patrols, sending additional troops from home and, if they could get their hands on them, executing these "pirates" on sight. They also twisted the arms of their native traders in their quest to monopolise the Guinea trade; woe betide the African who sold goods to anyone but the Portuguese.

Such enthusiasm, in time, began to cost the exchequer back in Lisbon dearly and when Vasco da Gama finally opened up the sea route to India and East Africa, Portuguese enthusiasm for the Guinea trade waned.

During the sixteenth and seventeenth century, out of all the interlopers, it was the Dutch who gained the most significant foothold on the Gold Coast, constructing a series of fortifications and effectively surrounding St George's castle. In 1637, a Dutch force took command of St Jago hill, a militarily strategic position just to the north of the castle, and rolled in its big guns. Following a twenty-four-hour siege, they forced the Portuguese governor to unfurl the white flag and hand over the keys to the door.

By 1642 one hundred and sixty years of Portuguese dominance on the Gold Coast ended. It was now the turn of the Dutch.

At the same time as the Europeans clung to the rump of Africa, squabbling and bickering for a share of the spoils, so too the native kingdoms of the hinterland wrestled for supremacy. With the sale of gold came power.

Not only was gold enhancing the local kingdoms' wealth, the value of the slave trade was slowly gathering pace as the New World opened up, and the demand for labour to work the Caribbean plantations grew. As far as the savvy African trader was concerned there was money to be made, or at least plenty of fine cloth and horses to be acquired. And even though the Gold Coast was not the only source of gold and slaves for the Europeans, their demand steadily increased. The African kingdoms grew fat in a game of playing one European merchantman against another. They were not about to let opportunity slip them by.

During the Dutch occupation of St George's Castle, several kingdoms to whom the Dutch paid a ground rent came and went. By 1699 it was the turn of the Ashanti to spread their influence. Hitherto a landlocked kingdom, the Ashanti wasted little time in acquainting themselves with the European traders, creating in the process a magnificently wealthy empire.

Where the trade in gold, ivory and slaves had previously dominated the Portuguese occupation of the castle, it was the growing hunger for slave labour that was to be the economic driver for the Dutch. And the Ashanti were only too willing to oblige.

The Dutch set about enlarging the size of the castle and building a garrison, Fort Koenraadsburg, on St Jago hill, so they could not be as easily deposed as the Portuguese were. They converted the chapel to a trading hall and the castle became a depot for slaves, after which they were held in the dungeons awaiting shipment. At the height of the trade, thirty thousand slaves a year are said to have passed through St George's Castle, until the Dutch government outlawed the business in 1814.

As the British gradually strengthened their grip on the Gold Coast, the castle ceded to them in an Anglo-Dutch treaty in 1871.

TODAY, St George's Castle, better known as Elmina Castle, has become a tourist attraction, and a guided tour an informative, though sobering experience. Its thick, dank walls and its stark, utilitarian architecture evince a tale of deprivation and cruelty. The sound of the constant sea breeze moaning through its corridors materialised like the curse of the dead.

An element of the visitor's experience when visiting Elmina is to be temporarily locked in the Death Cells. There were two cramped cells positioned in the main courtyard, where troublesome soldiers and slaves were left to die. Released from the cells, we were next herded into a vaulted dungeon, the reek of sulphur thick in the throat. It was the place in which the women were held captive from the day they arrived, until the day they left. Then we stood in the square outside the dungeon, looking up and, to the words of our guide, imagined the governor leaning over the balustrade to pick his woman for the night. Finally, we were led down a narrow, musty stairway to the Door of No Return. Staring from it, I surveyed the bay where the slave ships would have awaited their cargo and the start of a harrowing journey across the ocean that many did not survive.

Accra became the capital of the British Gold Coast colony in 1877 and has remained the country's capital ever since. We arrived in Accra, now a sprawling, modern city of two million inhabitants, on a late Sunday afternoon, when its streets were relatively quiet. We sped across town with ease, passing Independence Square and finding our hotel for the next couple of nights on the eastern side of the city. The next day, with time running out before having to catch our flight to Europe, we visited the port of Tema and in particular our shipping agent, Ishmael.

The distance from Accra to Tema is barely twenty-five kilometres and is notable for two things: an abundance of stores selling fantasy coffins, and its mountains of shipping containers. There is barely breathing space between Teshi, the heartland of Ghana's fantasy coffin production, and the angular, steel suburbs of Tema. We could only hope there didn't exist some perverse connection between the undertaker and the shipping agent. Neither of us wanted to lose our trusty Hilux to the after-world, to end its days as the fantasy coffin of a Big Man with a passion for all things Toyota.

After visiting the agent, it was apparent we needed a wad of US dollars with which to pay our shipping costs to Durban. At each foreign exchange bureau, I hopped out of the car as Christine held the tooting traffic at bay.

My question, 'Any dollars?' was constantly met with a shake of the head. At the close of business, and beginning to despair, we happened upon the seedy-looking "Wise Men For-ex Bureau". Stuffing the packet of Euros deep in my pocket, I slipped through the loitering crowd of unsavoury-looking characters. Getting robbed was not an option.

'Yes, we have dollars,' the sour-faced man said from behind the thick, but nevertheless cracked, glass screen. He looked like a croupier from the Casino of Shattered Dreams. The walls were streaked brown. The ceiling had collapsed in the corner. Some heavies crouched on stools.

'I'm buying with Euros,' I told him.

He clacked the buttons of a calculator and turned it towards me. Some of the numbers were illegible but I got the gist of what he was offering. I slid the Euros beneath the glass screen and received my dollars in exchange. I could only hope they were the real thing. I took a second to bury various wads in different pockets and hurried back to the car.

Ishmael's face lit up at the sight of the money when we walked into his office the next morning. 'This is a good thing,' he said, relieving me of the dollars. 'My colleague will take you to the port. The container will be there.'

True to his word, in the middle of a container compound, not too distant from the entry to the port, our own container stood with its doors wide open. We parked in front of it and walked inside, stamping our feet on the wooden floor, tapping our knuckles on the metal sides. It looked quite new – worthy of our car.

'Can we put the vehicle inside?'

'We must wait for customs.'

For the next four hours, we experienced the highs and lows of life in a container compound. The grizzly bunch of stevedores who were to "stuff" (a shipping term) the Hilux in the container came and went; the portly customs lady came and went; the shipping agent came and went; curious onlookers came and went; a truck loaded with bags of nuts came, was unloaded, and went. And still the Hilux waited outside in the sunlight. We grew thirsty and hungry and very familiar with the arc of the sun and the coolest shadows in which to hide. At some point, we found a bench tucked between two walls of containers and pulled it out. It had one leg shorter than the other three, and hence it wobbled when we perched on it. At least it was something to sit on.

The portly customs lady finally returned with the carnet de passage stamped. I put it carefully in my folder. Then the drug squad arrived with a dog. We had to open every nook and cranny and remove the boxes and bags containing all our possessions. The dog found it the height of amusement – a lot of conflicting and most interesting smells had his muzzle twitching this way and that. He must have had quite a tale to tell back in the kennels.

All of a sudden, a dozen men materialised from the ether. Like the dog, they took an intense interest in everything we had inside the car. They pointed and discussed, sotto voce, the bits they liked best. I couldn't believe this experience was going to end well. I was quite sure they were planning to come back later.

When the drug squad left, the stevedores drove the pickup into the container, lashed it down, slammed the double doors shut and the shipping agent snapped the seal closed on the clasp. The container would remain in the compound until the ship's arrival in two weeks' time. The question was: would the Hilux still be inside it? I gave a wad of our remaining Ghanaian Cedis to the chief stevedore in the forlorn hope they would look kindly on our car.

When we'd finished on the dock we flagged a taxi to take us back to the hotel. It was a small car and we squeezed in, telling the driver where we wanted to go. The driver set us in motion with a spin of the wheels, racing through the gears, dodging in front of a truck at the roundabout. The gear lever rattled wildly as the speedometer crept higher. I hadn't travelled that fast for months, though with my mind wrestling over the thought of whether I should have fitted a lock to the container door, I barely noticed.

I think Christine and I both felt a little melancholic as the rows of fantasy coffins passed in a blur. The feeling of post-trip blues had already set in. A momentous journey had come to an end, and we'd put our good friend, our transport and our house, inside a box and sent it to an uncertain future. Despite all, I was sure we would be reunited. New adventures in Southern Africa awaited us, of that I was certain. And I firmly believed the Hilux would be an intrinsic part of them.

I let the memories of the last few weeks flood my mind – the unpromising first night under canvas in Winnebago City; the simplicity of Vetten's eco-camp on the beach in Mauritania; the panic of losing my passport in the sand; the sense of history gleaned from wandering the streets of Timbuktu; the whimsicalness of the Festival in the Desert; the hilarity when the Bombay Sapphire got the better of JP and I and we couldn't put up the awning; the beauty of the country we crossed during the search for the elephants at Gourma; the satisfaction of repairing the fuel tank in Ouagadougou; the sheer joy of our wild camps; the pleasure (and occasional aggravation) derived from the people we'd met; the amusement of champagne tasting in Kumasi, and the horror of Elmina Castle. I raised my hat to my childhood heroes, too – to the explorers and the adventurers. I felt quite exhausted by what we'd done and we hadn't achieved one hundredth of what they had.

And last but not least: we'd covered fifteen thousand kilometres of African roads without a single accident. Not a bad achievement in itself.

It was when the Land Rover Discovery bearing down on us flashed its headlights that I realised something was amiss: our driver was speeding us the wrong way down a duel carriageway, in the fast lane.

I snatched a look to my right; a concrete barrier separated us from the carriageway we should have been in. Despite the oncoming car hurtling towards us the driver showed no sign of lifting his foot off the accelerator.

'We're in the wrong bloody lane,' I shouted at him.

It was then, when I took proper notice of the person sat next to me that I was gripped by a surge of dread: the pimply youth driving us couldn't have been more than fourteen years old.

He scowled back at me, bristling with adolescent anger. 'I always drive this side of the road,' he snarled.

It was too late to argue.

There was a greater urgency from the flashing headlights ahead of us. They grew larger by the second. The driver of the Discovery took shape...a man...sunglasses...beard...white shirt...

I balled my fists – *we're about to die.*

At the last second the Discovery swerved into the other lane. The horn blared loudly.

We rocked as he swept past.

AFTERWORD

In recounting the story of Richard Lander and his brother John, I rather left you hanging concerning their fate. Here is what happened:

Having reached the mouth of the Niger River Richard Lander had to employ all his persuasive powers to secure the release of himself, his brother, and the rest of their entourage from the grip of King Boy. They sailed on the *Thomas of Liverpool* to Fernando Po (Equatorial Guinea), where they changed vessels, arriving back in Portsmouth on the 9th June 1831. They had successfully completed a major element of what the African Association set in motion forty-three years earlier – they had determined the course and termination of the Niger River. Though certain personalities within the higher echelons of the world of science and geography dismissed the Lander brothers' observations as the work of amateurs, Richard Lander became the first winner of the Royal Geographical Society Founder's Medal "*...for important services in determining the course of the Niger*". The brothers published their account in *Journal of an Expedition to Explore the Course and Termination of the Niger* and were paid one thousand guineas. The three volumes came out in 1832. By then John Lander was financially broke. He wrote several letters to Lord Bathurst at the Colonial Office, exploring the possibility of a suitable post. Apparently, he never received a reply. Richard returned to his old job at customs and excise, until approached by Liverpool merchants, who offered him a position in their company with a view to establishing trading bases along the Niger.

Richard passed his customs job to his brother and returned to Africa. It was to be his last expedition. Like Mungo Park before him, something he encountered in Africa had changed him. Where before his even temper and diplomatic skills had stood him well, by the time of his third visit to the continent his heart had hardened. His encounters with the tribes along the river often resulted in violence. During a skirmish out on the river he was shot through the thigh, a wound from which he was not to recover. He died in February 1834, leaving a wife and daughter back in England.

One month later the Liverpool merchants pulled the plug on the expedition. Of the original forty-eight expedition members who arrived in West Africa eight months earlier, only eight survived.

EQUIPMENT LIST

To list all the equipment we took with us on this trip would be too tedious for you to wade through. Here are my top tips:

Folding trench-shovel. First class for dealing with the calls of nature and fire duty.

The *fourneau* BBQ. Acquired in a Gambian market and fabricated from reclaimed materials. Robust, efficient and wonderful to cook with. You have to go to Africa to get one.

Turboflame blowtorch lighter. (They say you can even weld with this thing. I never tried it. www.turboflame.co.uk)

Tyrepliers. The thought of having to mend a tyre with these tools initially filled me with horror. I did, however, manage to repair a tyre with them on the next leg of our trip in Tanzania. They're an excellent piece of kit. www.tyrepliers.com.au

Ladies fan. Excellent for wafting life into a campfire. Christine brought a prettily-coloured Spanish fan with her, which we often used to encourage the flames.

Flat-topped cast iron pan. For placing in the coals to cook stew and bake bread.

Cork screw. For when all else fails.

Thank you for reading *City of Myths, River of Dreams*. I really hope you enjoyed the story. For occasional news and articles, or to find out more about my books, why not join me at www.latitude14.com

Printed in Great Britain
by Amazon

41932457R00158